Greatest Moments in
NOTRE DAME
FOOTBALL HISTORY

John Heisler

TRIUMPH
BOOKS

Triumph Books and colophon are registered trademarks of Random House, Inc.

Library of Congress Cataloging-in-Publication Data

Heisler, John.
  Greatest moments in Notre Dame football history / John Heisler.
     p. cm.
  Includes bibliographical references.
  ISBN-13: 978-1-60078-102-5
  ISBN-10: 1-60078-102-0
  1. Notre Dame Fighting Irish (Football team)—History. 2. University of Notre Dame—Football—History. I. Title.
  GV958.N6H43 2008
  796.332'630977289—dc22

                                                        2008025274

This book is available in quantity at special discounts for your group or organization. For further information, contact:

Triumph Books
542 South Dearborn Street
Suite 750
Chicago, Illinois 60605
(312) 939-3330
Fax (312) 663-3557

Printed in U.S.A.
ISBN: 978-1-60078-102-5
Design by Patricia Frey
Photos courtesy of the University of Notre Dame, Getty Images, and AP Images.

To my parents, whom I finally convinced that journalism and sports could combine to create a career path.

Contents

Foreword

If you're talking about great moments in Notre Dame football, you could include my entire collegiate career on that list. Not because of anything I did on a personal basis, but because that's the way I think of what playing football at Notre Dame was all about—it was the greatest experience of my life.

When I enrolled at Notre Dame in the fall of 1987, I probably wasn't really ready to play. I'd been a linebacker in high school, and the switch to nose tackle took some time. But, during that '87 season, I had a chance to watch what Lou Holtz was doing to turn the program around. I had a chance to watch what a championship performance was all about as Tim Brown won the Heisman Trophy that season. And I learned what it would take to have an impact on Notre Dame football.

Once the 1988 season began, it became a storybook scenario for all of us. I'll never forget the Michigan game that started that year. I still get chills when I think about it. My first time coming down that tunnel in Notre Dame Stadium, knowing I was going to play. A prime-time game on CBS. Reggie Ho winning the game at the end with a field goal. It was the start of a great run.

I was so fortunate that, during the three years I played at Notre Dame, we won 33 football games and lost only four times. Of those 37 games, we came into 21 of them as the No. 1 team in the nation. That's what those games meant from one Saturday to the next.

We beat Michigan three years in a row, and those Michigan teams came into those games ranked ninth, second, and fourth in the polls in those three seasons. We beat USC three years in a row. We beat Miami twice—once when they were No. 1 and once when they were No. 2. That was probably the defining rivalry for us when we were in school. We played 17 games against ranked opponents (13 in the top 10) and won 14 of them. In a way, we were spoiled based on the success we had.

Winning the national championship in '88 was amazing. We beat USC out in the Coliseum when we were ranked No. 1 and they were No. 2. Then we beat an unbeaten West Virginia team that was ranked third in the Fiesta Bowl. The '88 Miami game still ranks as one of the greatest events I've seen or been part of. It's been 20 years and yet you run into people who remember that one game like it was played yesterday.

We had a great group of people and a great group of football players that were around when I played. My entire time in South Bend was a fantastic experience, and it's what I would hope every Notre Dame football player has a chance to taste and experience for themselves.

Now, I have a chance to return to Notre Dame within the athletic administration. It's a great opportunity for me to be a part of something I love and believe in.

With all that in mind, I hope you enjoy *Greatest Moments in Notre Dame Football History*. It brings back great memories for me—and, like all Irish fans, we all hope many more great moments in Irish football are on their way.

—Chris Zorich

Acknowledgments

To Susan McGonigal and Carol Copley, Notre Dame sports information staff assistants, for helping find the files that supplied lots of the raw material contained herein.

To Charles Lamb in the Notre Dame archives for running down many of the long-ago newspaper clippings and game summaries cited.

To Steve Boda and Bud Maloney for creating many of the historical scoring and statistical summaries that now exist for Irish games.

To Roger Valdiserri, longtime Irish publicity chief (and his predecessor, Charlie Callahan), for having the foresight to never throw anything away. They knew all those game files and clippings would come in handy for something someday.

To Tom Bast at Triumph Books for his support and guidance—and for believing that the Notre Dame football nation is an insatiable lot.

To all the newspapers, magazines, and authors whose work is cited here. From the great Grantland Rice to Dan Jenkins to Jim Murray to longtime *South Bend Tribune* sports editor Joe Doyle, they made the descriptions of Irish football exploits sing.

To all those involved with the Notre Dame *Scholastic* and its annual Football Review for helping create one of the better ongoing records of Irish football doings.

To Bill Orr of Tel Ra Productions for granting permission to use the video (actually it all was shot on 16mm film) on the accompanying DVD.

To all the Irish players and coaches mentioned on these pages (opponent counterparts, too), without whose achievements these pages would have had no reason to come to life.

To my wife, Karen, the best proofreader I know.

To my sons, Scott and Tim, for their patience during this project. They have been spending (most) Christmas and New Year's Day holidays at bowl sites since the years they were born. They've seen more than their share of Notre Dame games for their ages, but they still think my collection of Notre Dame "stuff" is way out of hand.

Introduction

We love lists, don't we? We make laundry lists and grocery lists. Our spouses and parents give us to-do lists.

Jack Nicholson, Morgan Freeman, and director Rob Reiner created the *The Bucket List*.

David Letterman's nightly Top 10 list has become such a staple of our culture that newspapers reprint the lists on a daily basis.

Former Notre Dame football coach Lou Holtz even created a list of 107 things he wanted to accomplish before he died—and then he kept track and marked them off as they were accomplished (I think he's past 100).

It's no different with Notre Dame football.

How about a list of Notre Dame's top coaches? That's not hard because five of them—Knute Rockne, Frank Leahy, Ara Parseghian, Dan Devine, and Holtz—have won national championships. That's how you separate the men from the boys in South Bend, Indiana. A sixth Irish coach, Jesse Harper, is also in the College Football Hall of Fame. Rank those five (or six) in order? We're not touching that one.

How about a list of Notre Dame's best football players of all time? Now that's a tall order. We can give you All-Americans (several hundred of those from Notre Dame). We can give you consensus All-Americans, as designated by the NCAA (almost 100, far more than any other school). We can give you Heisman Trophy winners—all seven of them. Want to rank them in order of how good they were? Good luck!

Several years ago Sports Illustrated Presents produced a commemorative edition about the history of Notre Dame football. They asked me for an all-time Notre Dame team. I'd never actually tried to create one (but I had a cop-out—I said it was too political). So I sent them to Lou Somogyi of *Blue and Gold Illustrated*, and he was happy to provide one.

Sports Illustrated Presents picked Joe Montana as the all-time Notre Dame quarterback. Hard to argue with that. On the other hand, who's going to explain that to Angelo Bertelli, John Lujack, Paul Hornung, and John Huarte (all those four did was win Heisman Trophies)—not to mention Frank Carideo, Harry Stuhldreher, Bob Williams, Ralph Guglielmi, and Joe Theismann (those last five are in the College Football Hall of Fame)? We haven't even mentioned Frank Tripucka, Daryle Lamonica, Terry Hanratty, Tom Clements, Blair Kiel, Steve Beuerlein, Tony Rice, Rick Mirer, Ron Powlus, Jarious Jackson, and Brady Quinn, and I'm going to stop now before I get myself in trouble. And that's just the debate at quarterback.

Phew!

So now we come to Notre Dame's greatest games. This becomes really complicated, as much as anything because Notre Dame has played nearly 1,150 games in its history (through 2007) and won 824 of them. Lots of potentially great moments in that mix.

Back in 1999 Notre Dame wanted to find a way to recognize the top Irish football moments of the 1900s. The university and I created a video and called it *A Century of Greatness: Celebrating Notre Dame Football in the 20ᵗʰ Century.* We built out our own list of events—mostly games—to consider. Those went on a ballot that was featured on our athletics website, www.und.com, where fans could vote online. We also created a printed ballot that we distributed to fans in attendance at the '99 season-opening game. Once the votes had been tabulated, we had our own top 20 moments. We produced a video to recognize the winners. We also produced a 24-page insert for the final home game program that same year, with feature stories on each of the Top 20 moments.

Still, how do you possibly limit the list to 20? That's where *Greatest Moments in Notre Dame Football History* comes in. Even if you're just a casual Notre Dame football fan, you have to have heard about a handful of the greatest Irish games from the past.

The landmark home victories over number-one ranked University of Miami in '88 and number-one ranked Florida State University in '93 (they finished first and third, respectively, in that '99 voting). The unforgettable 10–10 tie with Michigan State University in '66.

The green-jersey game against the University of Southern California in '77, and Harry Oliver's epic 51-yard field goal to beat the University of Michigan in '80.

The huge list of bowl wins against the likes of the University of Texas, University of Alabama, West Virginia University, University of Colorado, Texas A&M University, and Florida.

Don't forget the birth of the Four Horsemen, the "win one for the Gipper" game, plus four straight seasons under Frank Leahy without a loss.

We decided to give you the scoop on all those games and lots more.

We categorized dozens of the most memorable Irish gridiron achievements. We can tell you which games changed the face of Notre Dame football and which games framed the Fighting Irish tradition.

We give you an inside look at the great Notre Dame bowl wins and all the contests that were rated "games of the century." We've got all the details on the games that involved unbelievable endings—and the games that featured amazing individual performances.

We've got the half-dozen games that created Montana's legacy in South Bend. On top of that, we've got more than 30 games that can make their own claims to fame in Irish annals—and we've even got a list of losses that still have Notre Dame fans pulling their hair out.

For dozens of these games, we've included full-blown statistics and scoring summaries. We tell you who was ranked where coming in and what happened to the teams after the games were played. We tell you when and how the games were won, we dug up the most telling quotations from coaches and players, and we tell you how media around the country reported the events.

We've got dozens of great photos, plus an accompanying highlight DVD to show you how all these great Fighting Irish moments transpired.

The bottom line? This book documents in detail far more Irish football games than have ever been presented in any other publication.

We would be the first to suggest that you will find fault with our various lists and categorizations—and that's perfectly acceptable. You'll think this game should be in that category—and that game should be in this category.

We understand.

We like the idea that there is all kinds of room for debate. Like the polls and the Bowl Championship Series, that's what we love about college football—there is so much open to discussion. (Actually, to avoid *too* many more arguments than necessary, you should know that within each chapter we opted to list games in chronological order as opposed to ranking them.)

We wouldn't presume to suggest that *Greatest Moments in Notre Dame Football History* represents the final word on this subject. Consider it simply a comprehensive opening argument—with an attempt to give you a somewhat breezy take on all these events.

So, enjoy!

Then make your own lists and send them to us.

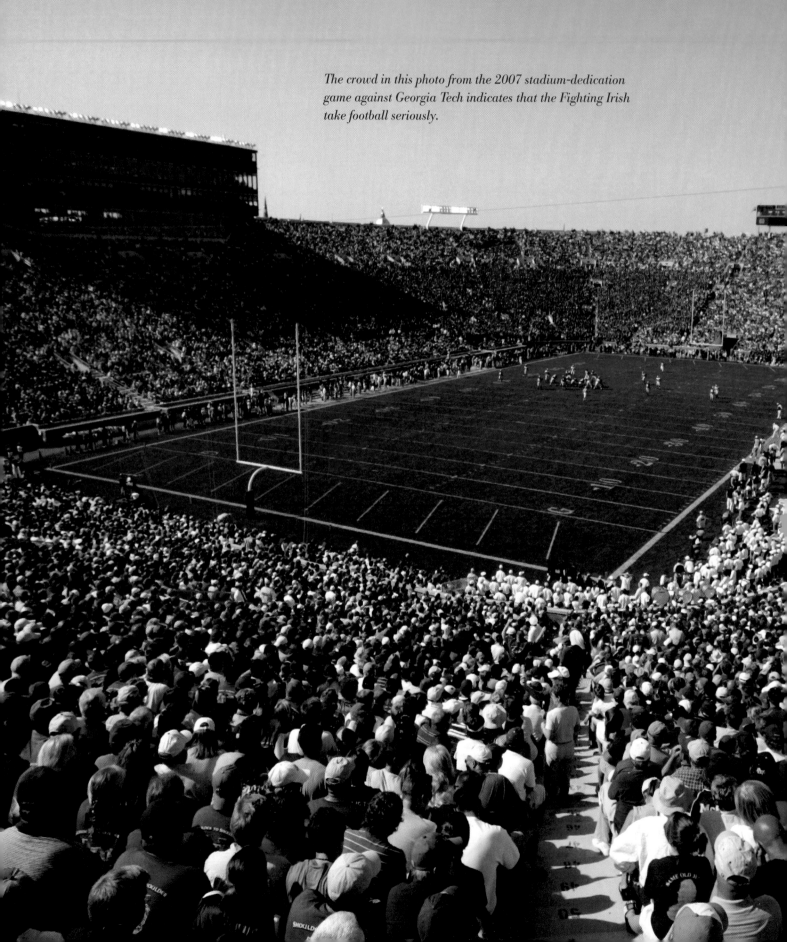

The crowd in this photo from the 2007 stadium-dedication game against Georgia Tech indicates that the Fighting Irish take football seriously.

Six Games That Changed the Face of Notre Dame Football

These aren't necessarily the biggest wins ever by Notre Dame's football teams. In fact, one of the six games actually was an Irish loss. But these half-dozen contests arguably changed everything about the Notre Dame program.

If not for the University of Michigan's team boarding that train for the trip to South Bend (actually Niles, Michigan) that November day in 1887, who knows when football on the Notre Dame campus would have blossomed?

The Notre Dame team gave up its relative Midwest anonymity in 1913, when it ventured to West Point, New York, to take on an Army unit far more established on the national college football scene. That game went a long way toward establishing Notre Dame's independent tradition of playing all over the country.

All by itself, the '64 Irish win at the University of Wisconsin didn't create great waves. But coming off the longest dry spell in Notre Dame football history (five straight seasons without a winning record), that victory sent a strong message that the Irish (under new coach Ara Parseghian) were back on a par with the big boys on the college scene.

Five years later, the University opted to change its postseason bowl policy after 45 years away from the New Year's Day games. At a time when bowl matchups were far more handmade than they are now in the Bowl Alliance and Bowl Championship Series era, Notre Dame decided that playing teams that were higher ranked in the polls was a good thing to do. That started a great tradition that saw the Irish face top-ranked opponents in bowls at the end of seasons in 1969, 1970, 1973, 1974, 1977, 1980, 1989, and 1990.

Back in the Knute Rockne era, green jerseys were no big deal. The same could be said for most of the Frank Leahy teams at Notre Dame. However, Dan Devine transformed green into a curiosity as well as a motivational ploy when he changed uniform colors for a game against the University of Southern California in '77.

Notre Dame's conquest of top-rated University of Miami in the middle of the '88 season turned heads not simply because it immediately injected the Irish into national championship conversation (again), but also because it signified such a rapid reversal of form from the '85 campaign when the Hurricanes dispatched the Irish by 51 points.

Indeed, Notre Dame had risen from the ashes.

Michigan 8 • Notre Dame 0
NOVEMBER 23, 1887, AT NOTRE DAME

There's Always a First Time

The Run-Up: This marked the first time Notre Dame played an official varsity football game.

Michigan came in 1–0, having beaten Albion College 32–0 that season. Michigan had been playing on an intercollegiate basis since 1879 and was 12–6–1, cumulatively, over eight seasons. The Wolverines were the champions of the West, not having lost a contest since 1883.

The Pertinent Details: More than a century of football at Notre Dame had to start somewhere—and this was that day and that game.

The Determining Factor: The actual game was shortened to a part of one *inning*, as quarters were known then, so the visitors from Ann Arbor had time for lunch and could take 1:00 PM carriages to Niles to

Notre Dame team photograph taken prior to the second Michigan game on April 21, 1888. The first game between these teams, and Notre Dame's first football game, was played in the fall of 1887.

A shot of the field from the Notre Dame-Michigan game in 1887.

catch their train to Chicago for another game the next day.

The Star of the Show: There was no way to know who the game's real standouts were because the two players who scored for the Wolverines were never recorded nor identified because of the casual nature of the event.

Of further note, there were no goalposts and so no conversions.

What the Headlines Said: There weren't many reports of the game because not all that much significance was attached to the event at the time. However, the Notre Dame school paper, the *Scholastic,* noted, "The game was interesting, and, notwithstanding the slippery conditions of the ground. The Ann Arbor boys gave a fine exhibition of skilful playing. This occasion has started an enthusiastic football boon, and it is hoped the coming years will witness a series of these contests."

The Rundown: This marked Notre Dame's only game of the 1887 season. Michigan followed up the win the next day with a 26–0 victory over Harvard of Chicago (a prep school) to finish 3–0.

It would be 14 more years before, in 1901, the legendary Fielding H. Yost would become the Michigan head coach, and another nine years before Knute Rockne would enroll at Notre Dame as a student.

Still, it was the beginning of a noteworthy rivalry, considering that, at that time (1887), the Army-Navy rivalry had not yet been born, and the list of institutions not yet even playing football included the University of Alabama, Auburn University, Florida State University, University of Georgia, Georgia Institute of Technology, Miami, University of Nebraska, Ohio State University, Oklahoma, Penn State University, University of Texas, Texas A&M University, University of California at Los Angeles, and USC.

Notre Dame 35 • Army 13
NOVEMBER 1, 1913, AT WEST POINT

Upset at Army Puts Notre Dame Football on National Map

The Run-Up: Notre Dame came into the game with a 3–0 record under first-year coach Jesse Harper, having outscored its first three opponents by a combined 169–7.

Army came in 4–0 under first-year coach Charles Daly, having outscored its foes 72–6.

The Pertinent Details: Army was the perennial national power, Notre Dame was the Midwest upstart. Harper had been looking for an East Coast showcase for his program; Army looked at this game as little more than prep for the big Navy game. Said the Army's mascot, Willet J. Baird: "Everyone, however, was convinced that Saturday would bring a breather, and no great amount of trouble was expected."

Notre Dame brought 18 players and 14 pairs of cleats and received a $1,000 guarantee.

Among the Cadet reserves was Dwight Eisenhower.

Thanks in great part to this attention-grabbing contest, this game set off one of college football's great rivalries, with the two teams playing every season through 1947, including 22 times at Yankee Stadium.

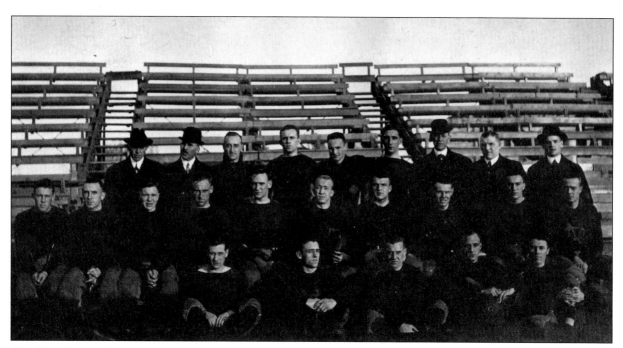

The Notre Dame football team poses on the West Point bleachers on October 31, 1913.

Knute Rockne completing the startling "Dorais to Rockne" pass that would modify the entire game of football.

Gus Dorais's first two pass attempts for Notre Dame went incomplete. After that, the Notre Dame quarterback put on a show unlike anything seen in the college game.

Harper called a near-perfect game, sending bruising runners like Joe Pliska and Ray Eichenlaub into the line anytime the Cadets lined up to stop the passing.

The Determining Factor: Notre Dame's passing attack kept the Cadets on their heels on defense all day. When Army spread out its defenders to stop the aerial efforts, Harper returned to the running game, with fullback Eichenlaub gashing the Cadets for a pair of second-half scores.

The Stars of the Show: Notre Dame's throw-and-catch combo of quarterback Dorais and end Knute Rockne stole the show. They had perfected their craft on the beach while working as lifeguards the previous summer at Cedar Point, an Ohio resort on Lake Erie. They weren't the first to use the forward pass (it had been legal since 1906), but this game marked the first time it had been used effectively to win a major game. Dorais completed 14 (some reports said 15) of 17 throws for 243 yards—unheard-of statistics in those days.

What the Headlines Said: "More than one paper sees in the Varsity's victory over the Army a great triumph of Western over Eastern football methods. It is, we think, a great triumph of the new game over the old-style of play; but it is rather a triumph of Notre Dame's style of the progressive, wide-open game over the rest of the country's conservative attack than a victory of the West over the East"—Notre Dame's *Scholastic*

"The yellow leather egg was in the air half the time, with the Notre Dame team spread out in all directions over the field waiting for it. The Army players were

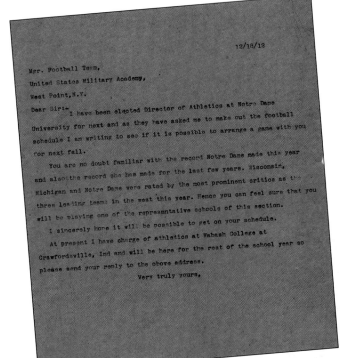

A letter from athletic director Jesse Harper to the football team manager at West Point, trying to arrange a game between Notre Dame and Army for the 1913 football season.

Scoring Summary

Notre Dame	7	7	0	21	35
Army	6	7	0	0	13

First Quarter
Notre Dame: Rockne 25 pass from Dorais (Dorais kick)
Army: Hodgson 1 run (kick failed)

Second Quarter
Army: Prichard 1 run (Hoge kick)
Notre Dame: Pliska 5 run (Dorais kick)

Fourth Quarter
Notre Dame: Eichenlaub 1 run (Dorais kick)
Notre Dame: Pliska 5 pass from Dorais (Dorais kick)
Notre Dame: Eichenlaub 8 run (Dorais kick)

hopelessly confused and chagrined before Notre Dame's great playing. The Westerners flashed the most sensational football ever seen in the East."—*The New York Times*

What the Players and Coaches Said: "After we had stood terrific pounding by the Army line, and a trio of backs that charged in like locomotives, we held them on downs. Dorais, in a huddle said, 'Let's open up.' It was amusing to see the Army boys huddle after a first, snappy, 11-yard pass had been completed for a first down. Their guards and tackles went tumbling into us to stop line bucks and plunges. Instead, Dorais stepped neatly back and flipped the ball to an uncovered end or halfback. This we did on a march up the field, gaining three first downs in almost as many minutes," said Rockne.

The Rundown: Notre Dame won its final three games of the season to finish with a perfect 7–0 record and extend its streak to 25 games without a loss (dating back to 1910).

The Cadets won their last four games by a combined 168–16 for a final 8–1 mark.

Notre Dame 31 • Wisconsin 7
SEPTEMBER 26, 1964, AT MADISON

Parseghian's First Game Sets Tone for "Era of Ara"

The Run-Up: Unranked Notre Dame was playing its first game under new head coach Ara Parseghian, coming off a 2–7 record in '63 under interim coach Hugh Devore.

The University of Wisconsin's record stood at 1–0, having beaten Kansas State University 17–7 the previous Saturday. The Badgers were in their ninth season under coach Milt Bruhn, having finished 5–4 the previous season and beaten Notre Dame each of the last two years.

The Pertinent Details: Notre Dame had gone five straight seasons without a winning record, the last season under interim coach Devore. Parseghian gave quick notice that there was a new order for the Irish.

Notre Dame's defense intercepted five Badgers passes—and no Wisconsin runner managed more than eight net yards on the ground. The Badgers ended up with minus 51 yards net rushing.

The Determining Factors: The Irish broke open a close game with three fourth-period touchdowns—and ended a dark period in which the Irish had lost nine of their last 10 games against Big Ten foes.

The Stars of the Show: Quarterback John Huarte, who had played sparingly in previous seasons and who nearly missed the '64 season after separating his throwing shoulder during spring ball (he couldn't even play in the final spring game), threw for 270 yards.

Quarterback and Heisman Trophy winner John Huarte.

Fellow senior Jack Snow caught touchdown passes of 61 and 42 yards (he caught nine overall for 217 yards).

What the Headlines Said: "A sellout crowd of 64,398 braved wind and rain today to see the unveiling of Ara Parseghian's first Notre Dame team. The Fighting Irish displayed their wares handsomely and overwhelmed the Wisconsin Badgers, 31–7."–Notre Dame *Scholastic*

"The Irish looked like a Notre Dame football team today.... It was tough and versatile football–and Notre Dame won in such a big way that Ara Parseghian was picked up and carried briefly as he went off the field at the conclusion of his effort to follow in the coaching tradition of Knute Rockne and Frank Leahy."–*Chicago Tribune*

Scoring Summary

Notre Dame	3	10	0	18	31
Wisconsin	0	0	7	0	7

First Quarter
Notre Dame: Ivan 31 field goal (0:06)

Second Quarter
Notre Dame: Snow 61 pass from Huarte (Ivan kick) (4:55)
Notre Dame: Ivan 30 field goal (0:18)

Third Quarter
Wisconsin: Jones 45 pass from Brandt (Kaye kick) (11:30)

Fourth Quarter
Notre Dame: Kantor 1 run (pass failed) (14:57)
Notre Dame: Wolski 2 run (pass failed) (8:23)
Notre Dame: Snow 42 pass from Huarte (pass failed) (3:12)
Attendance: 64,398

Coach Ara Parseghian on the field with players.

"Notre Dame students had swarmed into Madison to get a glimpse of their 1964 squad. They got that glimpse, and some returned to South Bend yelling, 'We're number one.'"—*Scholastic*

What the Players and Coaches Said: "They stopped our running attack cold. We couldn't get off the ground. What really hurt us was that we ran into one of the finest passing combinations I have ever seen with Huarte and Snow," said Bruhn.

"There has been a lot of criticism over the years about Notre Dame not being a second-half team. But our conditioning showed up, and we wore them down. This was a team which really wanted to win," said Parseghian.

The Rundown: The Irish, behind eventual Heisman Trophy–winner Huarte, won eight straight games after beating the Badgers (that win jumped the Irish to ninth in the Associated Press poll). After ranking number one in both the AP and United Press International polls four straight weeks, the Irish dropped their season finale 20–17 at USC to end up 9–1 and ranked third in both polls.

Notre Dame was declared the national champion by the National Football Foundation, via presentation of the Grantland Rice Trophy. The University of Arkansas, at 11–0, was the lone major college to finish unbeaten, while Alabama (10–1) was declared both the AP and UPI champion in the polls taken before the bowls (Texas beat the Crimson Tide in the Orange Bowl). Wisconsin lost five of its next six games and finished 3–6 overall, 2–5 in Big Ten play (tied for seventh).

Statistics

Team Statistics

Category	Notre Dame	Wisconsin
First Downs	23	15
Rushing	11	2
Passing	12	11
Penalty	0	2
Rushing Attempts	50	28
Yards Gained Rushing	176	28
Yards Lost Rushing	27	79
Net Yards Rushing	149	-51
Net Yards Passing	270	234
Passes Attempted	26	31
Passes Completed	15	13
Interceptions Thrown	0	4
Total Net Yards	419	183
Fumbles: Number Lost	1-0	2-1
Penalties: Number-Yards	8-89	5-38
Punts-Yards	2-64	5-174
Average Yards Per Punt	32.0	34.8
Punt Returns-Yards	1-13	1-0
Kickoff Returns-Yards	1-21	7-152
Interception Returns-Yards	29	0

Notre Dame's Individual Statistics
Rushing: Farrell 9-25, Wolski 17-77, Eddy 5-16, Huarte 2-(-6), Carey 1-(-9), Kantor 13-46, Andretti 2-0, Bonvechio 1-0
Passing: Huarte 24-15-0-270-2, Bonvechio 2-0-0-0-0
Receiving: Snow 9-217-2, Wolski 1-(-4), Eddy 2-24, Sheridan 2-32, Rassas 1-1

Wisconsin's Individual Statistics
Rushing: Kurek 7-7, Silvestri 8-8, Smith 2-2, Brandt 9-(-55), Kaye 2-(-13)
Passing: Brandt 26-13-3-234-1, Kaye 5-0-1-0
Receiving: Jones 5-122-1, Farmer 3-43, Smith 4-51, Neubauer 1-18

4 Texas 21 • Notre Dame 17
JANUARY 1, 1970, AT DALLAS IN THE COTTON BOWL

Notre Dame's First Bowl Game in 45 Years

The Run-Up: Notre Dame finished the regular season at 8–1–1, with a loss to Purdue University and a tie with the University of Southern California. It was ranked eighth by the AP and ninth by UPI after winning its final five regular-season games.

The University of Texas came in with a perfect 10–0 (with a 19-game overall win streak) and ranked first in both polls. The Longhorns eight times had permitted 14 points or fewer—and six times scored at least 45 points. Texas beat number-two ranked Arkansas 15–14 to end the regular season.

The Pertinent Details: Notre Dame had disdained postseason bowl games for decades (since its lone appearance in the 1925 Rose Bowl), in great part because of conflicts with the University's academic calendar. But Parseghian's presence on the Notre Dame campus put the Irish football program consistently in the national focus, and Parseghian helped convince the administration that it would be tougher to win a title without the ability to play bowl games. The University opted to use bowl revenue from this contest ($340,000) for minority scholarships and academic programs. In announcing the revision of the University policy, Reverend Edmund P. Joyce, C.S.C., executive vice president, noted that athletes in all other Notre Dame sports engaged in NCAA playoffs and that many of the football players and coaches participated individually in postseason games, largely during vacation time.

The Cotton Bowl basically would be an even game, in which both teams finished with 25 first downs. Notre Dame held leads of 10–0 and 17–14 (the latter lead after scoring with fewer than seven minutes remaining). Texas came in as an eight-point favorite, only the second time a Parseghian-coached team at Notre Dame had been an underdog.

The Irish lost out on a call late in the first half, when Texas fumbled the ball away at its own 2-yard line, but officials ruled that a Texas substitute had called for a timeout before the play began.

This One Was Determined When... Texas running back Billy Dale capped off a 76-yard, 17-play drive (15 of them runs) over 5:39 minutes with a one-yard run on third down to give the Longhorns the lead again with 1:08 left in the game. Texas converted twice on fourth down on that march, the last on a pass from James Street to Cotton Speyrer on fourth and 2 from the Irish 10.

The Longhorns had earlier rebounded from a 14–10 deficit with a similar 18-play, 77-yard excursion that included the end of the third and start of the fourth quarter. The Irish quickly rebounded with an 80-yard, eight-play drive to regain the lead on a 24-yard throw from Joe Theismann to Jim Yoder at the 6:52 slot.

The Stars of the Show: Texas's Steve Worster ran for 155 yards on 20 carries; Notre Dame's Theismann threw for 231 yards (a Cotton Bowl record) and two

Quarterback Joe Theismann was an outstanding player throughout the 1969 season, but shone in the Cotton Bowl, throwing for 231 yards.

and Street—proved to Notre Dame's three surviving Four Horsemen of 45 years ago that the youth of America hasn't lost its leg power. Fullback Steve Worster, halfbacks Jim Bertelsen and Ted Koy, and quarterback Jim Street of Texas rushed for 331 yards in the Cotton Bowl New Year's Day, with just a little help from teammates. And then the land-grabbing quartet sang the praises of the Notre Dame defense that made every yard a bloodbath in Texas's 21–17 victory over the Fighting Irish."—*Chicago Sun-Times*

"Notre Dame's bowl-game winning streak, unchallenged and uncontested for 45 years, ended here on a sun-splashed but chilly New Year's Day, but not until a batting Irish team fought Texas yard by yard to the finish in a stirring Cotton Bowl Classic."—*South Bend Tribune*

"A herd of Texas Longhorns, as quick as quarterhorses, stampeded through more muscular and much slower Notre Dame in the fourth period today to solidify their claim to the national championship with a spectacular 21 to 17 triumph in the 34th Cotton Bowl classic."—*Chicago Tribune*

"And so there lies a young man named Cotton Speyrer, all 5'11" and 169 pounds of him, ringing out the old hundred years of college football and ringing in the new, holding onto something called number one and clinging also, for whatever sentimental value it may have been worth around Austin, to the very overwrought lives of Darrell

touchdowns and also ran for another 48 yards; Notre Dame's Bob Olson was selected as the defensive Most Valuable Player.

What the Headlines Said: "Those modern Four Horsemen of college football—Worster, Bertelsen, Koy,

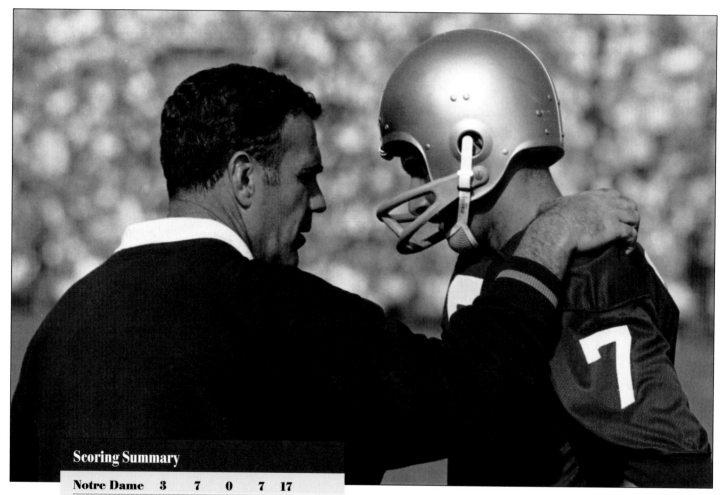

Scoring Summary

Notre Dame	3	7	0	7	**17**
Texas	0	7	0	14	**21**

First Quarter

Notre Dame: Hempel 26 field goal (8:41)

Second Quarter

Notre Dame: Gatewood 54 pass from Theismann (Hempel kick) (14:40)

Texas: Bertelsen 1 run (Feller kick) (3:22)

Fourth Quarter

Texas: Koy 3 run (Feller kick) (10:05)

Notre Dame: Yoder 24 pass from Theismann (Hempel kick) (6:52)

Texas: Dale 1 run (Feller kick) (1:08)

Attendance: 73,000

Ara Parseghian and Joe Theismann talk on the sidelines during the 1969 Army game.

Royal and his hordes of Texas Longhorn followers. Speyrer has just wheeled back, knelt, lurched, and scooped up a forward pass thrown by another obstinate elf, James Street, on a gravely executed play that will simply have to be filed away among the real treasures of the sport. For it was this gamble in those last fading moments of the Cotton Bowl—this fourth-down pass from one gutsy urchin to another—that enabled Texas to defeat a valiant Notre Dame team 21–17 in as courageous a game as any two schools played throughout the whole of the century."—Dan Jenkins in *Sports Illustrated*

What the Players and Coaches Said: "I've never been hit harder in my life. Olson, their linebacker, is the best I've ever played against," said Worster.

"It was the happiest I've ever been catching a football," said Speyrer of his late reception that set up Texas's final points.

"I thought the pass (to Speyrer) was a poor pass, too low and favorable to us. It was a great catch," said Parseghian.

"On that fourth-down play, I thought, this may be my whole football career, just coming down to this one play," said Street.

"On offense, they were the best we've met," said Theismann.

"We had you on the ropes and you won," said Notre Dame athletics director Moose Krause to Royal after the game.

The Run-Down: Texas finished as the consensus national champion following its win, out-pointing number-two Penn State (11–0) and number-three USC (10–0–1). Notre Dame moved up to fifth in the final AP poll at 8–2–1.

Statistics

Team Statistics

Category	Notre Dame	Texas
First Downs	23	15
First Downs	25	25
Rushing	13	19
Passing	12	6
Penalty	0	0
Rushing Attempts	43	67
Yards Gained Rushing	213	333
Yards Lost Rushing	24	2
Net Yards Rushing	189	331
Net Yards Passing	231	107
Passes Attempted	27	11
Passes Completed	17	6
Interceptions Thrown	2	1
Total Offensive Plays	70	78
Total Net Yards	420	448
Average Gain Per Play	6.0	5.7
Fumbles: Number Lost	0-0	2-1
Penalties: Number-Yards	2-10	1-5
Punts-Yards	7-256	4-159
Average Yards Per Punt	36.6	39.8
Punt Returns-Yards	0-0	3-24
Kickoff Returns-Yards	5-97	3-31
Interception Returns-Yards	1-0	2-9

Notre Dame's Individual Statistics

Rushing: Barz 10-49, Theismann 11-48, Allan 7-47, Huff 11-39, Yoder 2-4, Crotty 2-2

Passing: Theismann 27-17-2-231-2

Receiving: Gatewood 6-112-1, Allan 3-43, Crotty 3-19, Huff 2-15, Yoder 1-24-1, Poskon 1-22, Barz 1-7

Texas's Individual Statistics

Rushing: Worster 20-155, Bertelsen 18-81, Koy 12-40, Street 10-31, Speyrer 1-13, Dale 6-11

Passing: Street 11-6-1-107-0

Receiving: Speyrer 4-70, Bertelsen 1-21, Peschel 1-16

Notre Dame 49 • USC 19
OCTOBER 22, 1977, AT NOTRE DAME STADIUM

Irish Turn Blue to Green to Knock Off USC

The Run-Up: Notre Dame came in 4–1 (a 20–13 road loss at the University of Mississippi) and ranked 11th, after starting the year as the preseason number-three team.

USC came in 5–1 (a 21–20 loss to number-seven ranked Alabama after the Trojans had risen to number one in the polls) and ranked fifth by AP and fourth by UPI.

The Pertinent Details: Puzzled by basketball coach Digger Phelps's exhortations of "Green machine! Green machine!" at the pep rally the night before, the Irish quickly understood after finding green jerseys in their lockers moments before kickoff.

A wooden, student-built Trojan horse that barely fit through the tunnel led the Irish players onto the field.

Students surround the USC Trojan Horse on the field, celebrating Notre Dame's victory over the Trojans in October 1977.

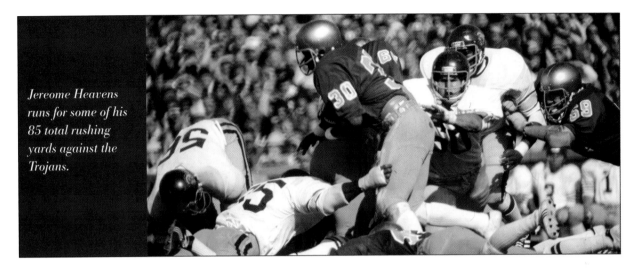

Jereome Heavens runs for some of his 85 total rushing yards against the Trojans.

Irish quarterback Montana ran twice for scores and threw twice to tight end Ken MacAfee for touchdowns. Charles White, who two years later would win the Heisman Trophy, paced the visitors with 135 rushing yards.

Both teams turned the ball over five times, and Notre Dame enjoyed only a minimal advantage in total yards (386–347). But the Irish converted 14 of 19 third downs (compared to three of 14 for USC), and the Irish made great use of the element of surprise to set up two different touchdowns.

From a 7–7 tie, Notre Dame made quick work of USC after White fumbled, Montana scoring from the 1. After a Luther Bradley interception, Ted Burgmeier faked the field goal, and Montana zeroed in on MacAfee for 13 yards and a 22–7 halftime lead.

Bob Golic's punt block turned into a third-period touchdown for Jay Case, and when Montana found MacAfee again on fourth down, the Irish were off to the races at 35–7.

The Determining Factor: The Irish took the field moments before kickoff in green jerseys, their first time in that color since 1963.

The crowd roared its approval. "You could feel the noise on your face," said USC coach John Robinson.

The Stars of the Show: Unheralded defensive back Burgmeier ran for 21 yards on a fake field goal, intercepted a pass, forced a fumble, and turned a bobbled point-after-touchdown snap into a throw for a two-point conversion.

Case returned a blocked USC punt attempt 30 yards for a third-period score, and the Irish led 35–7 after three periods.

Montana was the *ABC Sports* selection. Golic made 11 tackles and blocked a punt.

What the Headlines Said: "Maybe it was the wearin' of the green. Maybe it was just the luck of the Irish, who once again looked Irish. Maybe it was that the real Notre Dame stood up to be counted."–*The New York Times*

"Leave it to Ted Burgmeier to put a little zest into what could be a rather boring job of holding the football. Or at least planning or pretending to hold the ball for kicker Dave Reeve. During his four years at Notre Dame, Burgie has played quarterback, halfback, split

Joe Montana ran for two scores and also threw two touchdown passes to Ken MacAfee.

Scoring Summary

Notre Dame	7	15	13	14	49
USC	0	7	0	12	19

First Quarter

Notre Dame: Mitchell 4 run (Reeve kick) (8:22)

Second Quarter

USC: Celleto 5 fumble return (Jordan kick) (10:46)

Notre Dame: Montana 1 run (Domin pass from Burgmeier) (2:37)

Notre Dame: MacAfee 12 pass from Montana (Reeve kick) (0:20)

Third Quarter

Notre Dame: Case 30 return of blocked punt (Reeve kick) (10:45)

Notre Dame: MacAfee 1 pass from Montana (6:02)

Fourth Quarter

USC: Cain 3 run (14:57)

Notre Dame: Montana 1 run (Reeve kick) (6:39)

USC: Sweeney 14 pass from Hertel (4:26)

Notre Dame: Hart 4 pass from Lisch (Reeve kick) (0:12)

Attendance: 59,075

end, and cornerback, but Saturday he showed Southern Cal, 59,075 stadium onlookers, and a national television audience a little more of his 'jack-of-all trades' talent."–*South Bend Tribune*

"Oh, Paddy, dear, and did you hear the news that's going 'round? The shamrock is no longer banned by law from growin' on Irish ground! The 'Wearing of the Green' is in! It's okay to be Irish. If you're Irish, come into the parlor!... The Irish came out for pregame warmups innocently enough in their blue jerseys. Then, they went back in the locker room and when they came out—ta da! Finian's Rainbow! A green so bright it hurt the eyes. A whole squad of 6'6" leprechauns.... Who needs the Gipper? Just give us the Green!"–Jim Murray in the *Los Angeles Times*

"Ted Burgmeier ignited the Fighting Irish with a touch of bizarre, daring hocus-pocus. Ken MacAfee lifted the green-clad Irish even higher by stretching, diving, and leaping to catch eight of Joe Montana's passes, two for TDs. And Bob Golic, feeling 'just wild inside because of the green jerseys,' applied the clincher when he blocked a punt for another touchdown."—*Chicago Tribune*

What the Players and Coaches Said: "I don't know where he (Dan Devine) got the idea, but it was a hell of an idea," said Notre Dame end Willie Fry.

"I saw them come out screaming in those jerseys, and I knew we were in trouble," said USC linebacker Clay Matthews.

"This was perhaps the most well-kept secret on this campus in years. I ordered the jerseys three months ago, and they just arrived last week. Then, on Thursday, I called my captains in and showed them the jerseys and asked them if they thought we should wear them. I told them not to tell anyone, not even our assistant coaches. So after we warmed up in our pregame workouts the players returned to the locker room to find the jerseys in their lockers," said Devine.

"Some people may say it was the jerseys, the crowd, or the spirit that was exhibited here today, but I tell you it was the team. We got the hell beat out of us," said Robinson.

"They have humiliated us the last three years. We just couldn't lose this time," said Burgmeier.

"I hope they have a nice flight back," said Irish center David Huffman.

The Rundown: This game continued what became a 10-game, season-ending win streak for Notre Dame, the consensus national champion at 11–1.

USC went on to lose road games at California and Washington, then defeated number-17 ranked Texas A&M in the Bluebonnet Bowl, ended up 8–4 and ranked 12th by UPI and 13th by AP in the final polls.

Statistics

Team Statistics

Category	Notre Dame	USC
First Downs	24	19
Rushing	7	9
Passing	15	8
Penalty	2	2
Rushing Attempts	62	41
Yards Gained Rushing	209	188
Yards Lost Rushing	17	21
Net Yards Rushing	192	167
Net Yards Passing	194	180
Passes Attempted	27	29
Passes Completed	16	12
Interceptions Thrown	1	2
Total Offensive Plays	89	70
Total Net Yards	386	347
Average Gain Per Play	4.34	4.96
Fumbles: Number Lost	4/4	4/3
Penalties: Number-Yards	3/36	5/50
Punts-Yards	4/167	5/151
Average Yards Per Punt	41.8	30.2
Punt Returns-Yards	2/43	1/9
Kickoff Returns-Yards	3/24	8/150
Interception Returns-Yards	2/16	2/42

Notre Dame's Individual Statistics

Rushing: Heavens 32-85, Mitchell 8-30-1, Eurick 10-22, Montana 3-14-2, Burgmeier 1-21, Ferguson 2-7, Orsini 2-0, Waymer 1-4, Stone 1-3, Knott 1-5, Pallas 1-3

Passing: Montana 24-13-1-167-2, Lisch 3-3-0-27-1

Receiving: MacAfee 8-97-2, Eurick 1-8, Mitchell 2-29, Haines 1-27, Orsini 2-23, K. Hart 1-4-1, Heavens 1-6

USC's Individual Statistics

Rushing: Tatupu 6-20, White 25-135, Cain 5-19-1, Ford 3-10, Hertel 2-(-17)

Passing: Hertel 29-12-2-180-1

Receiving: Simmrin 1-18, Sweeney 5-114-1, Shipp 1-2, Gay 1-0, Studdard 1-14, Ford 1-8, Tatupu 1-7, White 1-17

6 Notre Dame 31, Miami 30
OCTOBER 15, 1988, AT NOTRE DAME STADIUM

Notre Dame Ends 'Canes' 36-Game Regular-Season Streak

The Run-Up: Notre Dame stood at 5–0 and was ranked fourth nationally, after a season-opening home win over number-9 ranked Michigan helped vault the Irish from their number 13 slot coming into the year. Miami came in at 4–0 and ranked first in both polls, while riding a 16-game overall win streak, a 20-game road win streak, and a 36-game regular-season win streak.

The Pertinent Details: This game was all about respect for the Irish, who were only three years removed from the brutal 58–7 loss at Miami that ended the Gerry Faust regime. Miami had beaten Notre Dame four times in a row, by a combined 133–20 count. And Miami quarterback Steve Walsh had yet to lose as a starting college quarterback.

The game had it all—a number-one ranked opponent in Notre Dame Stadium, 10 combined turnovers (seven by the 'Canes: four fumbles and three interceptions), a record-setting performance by Walsh (his 424 passing yards were the most ever against the Irish, and his four touchdown passes tied a Notre Dame opponent mark held by three others), not to mention a heart-stopping ending.

The Irish drove 75 and 80 yards for its first two scores, then saw Pat Terrell run a Walsh interception back 60 yards for a 21–7 lead. But Walsh came back to put the 'Canes on the board twice in the last four minutes for a halftime tie.

From there, Notre Dame took the lead after Miami misfired on a fake punt, and a Jeff Alm interception led to a field goal that made it 31–21 with a period to go. Down 31–24, and with a fourth and 7 ahead, Cleveland Gary caught a pass down to the Irish 1, but he fumbled and Michael Stonebreaker recovered. The 'Canes gained their final shot after recovering a Tony Rice fumble at the Notre Dame 14 with 2:10 on the clock. On the fourth play (fourth and 7), Walsh located Andre Brown for the touchdown, but Miami ended up a point short when its two-point try went awry.

The Determining Factor: Terrell batted down Walsh's two-point attempt in the back of the end zone with 45 seconds to go.

The Star of the Show: There were plenty of outstanding players for the Irish. Rice completed only eight passes, but they went for 195 yards. Terrell scored a touchdown and saved the game. Frank Stams was in Walsh's face all afternoon—and the list went on.

What the Headlines Said: "The edge of the seats in Notre Dame Stadium may be worn thin, but the stadium's magic is alive and well. And so is Notre Dame's football program."—*South Bend Tribune*

"You can gift wrap this one. But you had best nail the lid. Notre Dame and Miami are liable to pop out and go at each other again with meat cleavers. It was a fight to the death here in the Rust Belt. And the bombs exploding nearly bent the girders in this venerable stadium."—*Indianapolis Star*

*Pat Terrell's 60-yard interception return
gave the Irish a 21–7 lead.*

Scoring Summary

Miami	0	21	0	9	**30**
Notre Dame	7	14	10	0	**31**

First Quarter

Notre Dame: Rice 7 run (Ho kick) (3:36)

Second Quarter

Miami: Brown 8 pass from Walsh (Huerta kick) (12:40)

Notre Dame: Banks 9 pass from Rice (Ho kick) (7:34)

Notre Dame: Terrell 60 interception return (Ho kick) (5:42)

Miami: Conley 23 pass from Walsh (Huerta kick) (2:16)

Miami: Gary 15 pass from Walsh (Huerta kick) (:21)

Third Quarter

Notre Dame: Eilers 2 run (Ho kick) (8:09)

Notre Dame: Ho 27 FG (:37)

Fourth Quarter

Miami: Huerta 23 FG (13:07)

Miami: Brown 11 pass from Walsh (pass failed) (:45)

Attendance: 59,075

"This is not the place for interlopers to come looking for miracles. Steve Walsh might be the miracle maker in Tallahassee or in Ann Arbor or Miami, but at Notre Dame he's just another heretic coming to interfere with the Lord's work."—*Orlando Sentinel*

"It was the Gipper and the Four Horsemen. It was Rockne, Leahy, and Parseghian. It was another chapter in the history of college football's most storied school. It was a classic as fourth-ranked Notre Dame

Notre Dame's physical defense, led by Frank Stams (No. 30) and Jeff Alm (No. 9), held the 'Canes to 57 new rushing yards.

got its long-awaited revenge, defeating number-one Miami."–Associated Press

"Outside and above the catacombs of Notre Dame Stadium, beyond sight or hearing of Steve Walsh, leprechauns leaped and bass drums boomed. Seven Miami turnovers had greased the emerald-green midway for the Irish to dethrone the number-one ranked Hurricanes."–*Miami Herald*

What the Players and Coaches Said: "I woke up at 4:45, and I was sorta like the guy who was drunk and he said to his wife, 'I did *what* last night? I said *what?*' I couldn't believe I said that," said Holtz, of his Friday night pep rally prediction that the Irish would win.

"It was rough out there. It was probably the most physical game I've ever been in," said Irish defensive tackle Chris Zorich.

"The play was the right call. The halfback was open for a split second, but the ball didn't get there in time," said Walsh of the missed two-point play.

"The game my freshman year (a 58–7 defeat) was the most embarrassing game I'd ever played in. To beat these guys was probably a goal ever since that game. It's always been a bitter pill to swallow, and it just stuck in my throat until this moment right now," said Stams.

"The further I get away from it all, the more I appreciate what happened at the end. I think about it now, and it makes me nervous. What if I hadn't made that play? The whole thing has stuck with me," said Terrell.

The Rundown: This victory immediately elevated the Irish to second in the polls, behind UCLA, and they later knocked off number-two ranked USC to end the regular season, then number-three ranked West Virginia in the Fiesta Bowl to end up 12–0 and consensus national champions.

Miami won its final six games of the regular season, knocked off number-six ranked Nebraska 23–3 in the Orange Bowl, and finished second in both polls.

Statistics

Team Statistics

Category	Notre Dame	Miami
First Downs	16	26
Rushing	8	2
Passing	7	23
Penalty	1	1
Rushing Attempts	49	28
Yards Gained Rushing	162	73
Yards Lost Rushing	49	16
Net Yards Rushing	113	57
Net Yards Passing	218	424
Passes Attempted	18	50
Passes Completed	10	31
Interceptions Thrown	1	3
Total Offensive Plays	67	78
Total Net Yards	331	481
Average Gain Per Play	7.9	6.2
Fumbles: Number Lost	3–2	4–4
Penalties: Number-Yards	5–39	6–34
Punts-Yards	4–151	1–25
Average Yards Per Punt	37.8	25.0
Punt Returns-Yards	0–0	2–21
Kickoff Returns-Yards	2–41	6–74
Interception Returns-Yards	3–72	1–0
Time of Possession	31:01	28:59
Third Down Conversions	8–16	7–14

Notre Dame's Individual Statistics

Rushing: Brooks 13–56, Rice 21–20–1, Banks 7–21, Green 4–6, Watters 1–5, Johnson 2–3, Eilers 1–2–1

Passing: Rice 16–8–1–195–1, K. Graham 2–2–0–23–0

Receiving: Ismail 4–96, Brown 2–46, Watters 1–44, Green 1–21, Banks 1–9–1, K. Graham 1–2

Miami's Individual Statistics

Rushing: Gary 12–28, Conley 10–27, Crowell 3–7, Britton 1–(-1), Walsh 2–(-4)

Passing: Walsh 50–31–3–424–4

Receiving: Gary 11–130–1, Brown 8–125–2, Chudzinski 6–85, Conley 3–41–1, Dawkins 2–35, Hill 1–8

A view of the Golden Dome at the University of Notre Dame.

Three Games That Framed the Tradition of Irish Football

The Four Horsemen. Win one for the Gipper. Rudy. All three say "University of Notre Dame." All three say "Notre Dame football." And yet all three transcend Notre Dame, transcend football, transcend athletics. They've become iconic connections with the university based on their adaptation to our everyday culture.

You may not consider yourself anything close to an expert on college football. Stuhldreher? Layden, Miller, and Crowley? Who are those guys? But mention the Four Horsemen, and the light goes on. Writer Grantland Rice, whose reputation became significantly enhanced by the staying power of his descriptive prose and the name he hung on those four Notre Dame seniors, could never have known the term would live on for decades. George Gipp was one of the great players of his era, and his coach, Knute Rockne, arguably rates at (or at least very near) the top of the list of the greatest ever in his field. Rockne's 1928 effort to motivate his troops—combined with a motion picture produced in his name and featuring a future president of the United States—made "winning one for Gipper" a phrase that lived on and on and on.

On the gridiron, Dan "Rudy" Ruettiger was nowhere near the player Gipp was. Yet, decades later, Ruettiger's life became part of another feature film that has become forever linked with Notre Dame—and yet had a life message that went so far beyond sports.

Do you spend your Saturdays cheer, cheering for Notre Dame? No matter. You can't help but remember the *Rudy* music and the Sean Astin characterization that made Irish fans out of countless moviegoers who previously couldn't have told you a thing about Notre Dame.

You may not know a zone blitz from a Tampa two-pass defense. You not be able to tell Harry Stuhldreher from Harry Oliver. But odds are you've run into the Four Horsemen, or you've exhorted someone to "win one for the Gipper," or you've relived the moral of Rudy's persistent approach not only to his own life but also to making the movie about his life. And odds are it won't be the last time.

Notre Dame 13 • Army 7
OCTOBER 19, 1924, AT THE POLO GROUNDS

Grantland Rice Christens the Four Horsemen

The Run-Up: Notre Dame came in at 2–0, having shut out Lombard College (40–0) and Wabash College (34–0) in South Bend, Indiana, the previous two Saturdays.

Army came in at 2–0, having shut out St. Louis University (17–0) and the University of Detroit (20–0) to open the season.

The Pertinent Details: It's one thing to know that Army had long been the established Eastern power in college football (they'd already had 12 seasons with either one or zero losses, and 1924 would become the 13th). It's another to know that this Notre Dame team would go on to win the first of Knute Rockne's national titles. But who might have guessed that this game would be best remembered for a media-coined nickname that became the best-known tag in the history of college football?

The sportswriter responsible: Grantland Rice of the *New York Herald Tribune.*

The name: Notre Dame's "Four Horsemen"—none other than backfield mates Harry Stuhldreher, Jim Crowley, Elmer Layden, and Don Miller, all them eventual Hall of Fame members. Layden and Crowley accounted for the two Notre Dame scores in this particular game.

Notre Dame center Adam Walsh already had one broken hand coming into the game then suffered another during the contest—and still made a late

interception that preserved the victory. He's also credited with coming up with the "Seven Mules" tagline to identify the linemen who blocked for the Four Horsemen.

The game was watched by the largest crowd ever to see Notre Dame play up to that point.

The Determining Factor: The Notre Dame team returned to South Bend, and Rockne's student publicity aide, George Strickler (later sports editor of the *Chicago Tribune*), posed the four players, dressed in their uniforms, on the backs of four horses from a livery stable in town. The wire services picked up the now-famous photo, and the legendary status of the Four Horsemen was ensured.

The Stars of the Show: The stars were, of course, Stuhldreher, Layden, Miller, Crowley, Rice, and, ultimately, Strickler as well.

What the Headlines Said: "Notre Dame's Cyclone Beats Army, 13-7"–headline in the *Herald Tribune.*

"Outlined against a blue, gray October sky, the Four Horsemen rode again. In dramatic lore they are known as famine, pestilence, destruction, and death. These are only aliases. Their real names are Stuhldreher, Miller, Crowley, and Layden. They formed the crest of the South Bend cyclone before which another fighting Army team was swept over the precipice at the Polo Grounds this afternoon as 55,000 spectators peered

The Four Horsemen: Don Miller, Harry Stuhldreher, Jim Crowley, and Elmer Layden pose on horses.

down upon the bewildering panorama spread out upon the green plain below."—Rice in the *Herald Tribune*

"Moving with speed, power, and precision, Knute Rockne's Notre Dame football machine, 1924 model, defeated the Army, 13 to 7, before 60,000 at the Polo Grounds yesterday. The Hoosiers scored a touchdown in the second period and another in the third, and the Army's only rebuttal was a touchdown shortly after the fourth period had begun. But at that late hour the soldiers were tired and battered, and the machine went on to win. For three periods Miller, Crowley, Layden, and Stuhldreher ripped and tore and swooped, and when the cadets finally checked the grinding machine it was too late."—*The New York Times*

"And while Grantland Rice, perched in the press boxes, was having the great idea of the 'Four Horsemen,' Stuhldreher, Layden, Crowley, and Miller did everything a backfield could do, and did it perfectly."—Notre Dame *Scholastic*

"It (Army) played first-class football against more speed than it could match; those who have tackled a cyclone can understand."—Rice from the *Herald Tribune*

What the Players and Coaches Said: "Now, that Crowley. He's like lightning. You'd better put two men on him. And that Layden! Makes yardage every time. Put two men on him! Then there's Miller. I don't have to tell you that I advise putting two men on him. And that quarterback–Stuhldreher! He's the most dangerous of 'em all. He can think! Have three men on him!" wrote captain Pat Mahoney in his scouting report submitted to the Army coaches.

The Rundown: The Irish finished 10–0 for the season, defeated Stanford in the Rose Bowl, and gave up only 54 points all season (three shutout wins and two others where opponents managed only a field goal). Notre Dame was the consensus national champion–and the only team in the nation that ended up unbeaten and untied (Dartmouth University was 7–0–1, California 8–0–2, and Yale University 6–0–2).

Army finished 5–1–2, tying Yale and Columbia University before shutting out Navy 12–0 to end the year.

Scoring Summary

Notre Dame	**0**	**6**	**7**	**0**	**13**
Army	**0**	**0**	**0**	**7**	**7**

Second Quarter
Notre Dame: Layden 1 run (kick failed)

Third Quarter
Notre Dame: Crowley 20 run (Crowley kick)

Fourth Quarter
Army: Harding 15 run (Garbisch kick)

A reported 55,000 fans watched the Army–Notre Dame matchup at the Polo Grounds in New York.

Notre Dame 12 • Army 6
NOVEMBER 10, 1928, AT YANKEE STADIUM

Rockne Prompts Win Over Army with "Win One for the Gipper"

The Run-Up: In what turned out to be the only time Rockne lost more than two games in a season, his Irish came in at 4–2, having won consecutive games against Drake University and Penn State University after earlier losses against the University of Wisconsin and Georgia Institute of Technology.

Army came in 6–0, including shutout wins against Boston University, Harvard University, and Providence College.

The Pertinent Details: Rockne seldom was at a loss for motivational material for his football teams. This was the afternoon when he apparently outdid himself, summoning up the image of a dying George Gipp from eight years earlier to help prod his Notre Dame team against the unbeaten Army. Said Rockne, "The day before he died George Gipp asked me to wait until the situation was hopeless some game and then ask the team to go and win one for him. This is the day, and you are the team."

Rockne, supposedly at halftime, quoted Gipp's final deathbed words: "Sometime, Rock, when the team is up against it, when things are wrong, and the breaks are beating the boys, ask them to win one for the Gipper. I don't know where I'll be then, Rock, but I'll know about it and I'll be happy."

Jack Chevigny scored the first Irish touchdown, supposedly saying, "That's one for Gipp," as he crossed the goal. With the score tied at 6–6 in the fourth period, the Irish drove to the Cadets' 16. But an errant pass from center produced a 16-yard loss. Rockne then subbed sophomore Johnny O'Brien for Johnny Colrick at left end with fewer than two minutes on the clock. On third and 26, John Niemiec looped a pass toward O'Brien, who made his way past Army star Chris Cagle and made a lunging catch as he fell over the goal line. O'Brien then returned to the bench, thus earning the nickname "One-Play" O'Brien.

The Determining Factors: The final whistle blew after Army had driven to the Notre Dame 1-yard line (after a 55-yard Cagle return of the Notre Dame kickoff after Rockne's men had taken the lead).

The Star of the Show: Gipp? Rockne? O'Brien? Take your pick.

What the Headlines Said: "Battered, outweighed, twice defeated, an underdog, the burning flame that is the 1928 edition of the Notre Dame football team fought and smashed its way to a 12–6 victory over Army's greatest team, to accomplish the most startling

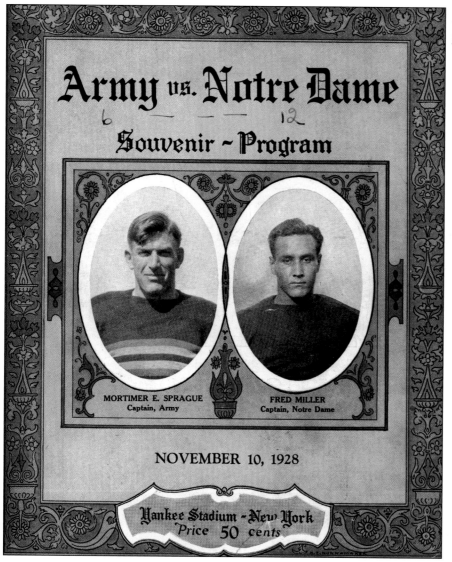

Notre Dame-Army game program cover from 1928.

upset of the season last Saturday at Yankee Stadium."
—Notre Dame *Scholastic*

"From the opening minutes of play when Eddie Collins threw (Chris) Cagle for a 15-yard loss, to the last play when an exhausted Irish line stopped Hutchinson on its six inch marker, the men of Notre Dame played like supermen. The tradition of Salmon, of Eichenlaub, and of Brandy was with this team, and the spirit of the immortal Gipp seemed to have inspired every man. No words of ours can tell you how this team fought. All we can say is that it fought as no Notre Dame team ever has, and for you who know the traditions of your school, no more need be said."
—Notre Dame *Scholastic*

Johnny O'Brien crosses the Army goal for the winning touchdown. (Photo courtesy of the Scholastic Football Review*)*

What the Players and Coaches Said: "There was no one in the room that wasn't crying. There was a moment of silence, and then all of a sudden those players ran out of the dressing room and almost tore the hinges off the door. They were all ready to kill someone," said Irish line coach Ed Healey.

"You could see a great big smile on his (Rockne's) face. He was happy when things created during the week were used to perfection in the ballgame," said Notre Dame quarterback Frank Carideo.

The Rundown: Notre Dame went on to lose its last two games against Carnegie Institute of Technology, Notre Dame's first home loss since 1905, and at the University of Southern California. The Irish's overall

5–4 record marked Notre Dame's worst since an identical mark in 1905 and qualified as the most losses in a season ever at Notre Dame.

Army ended up 8–2, after losing its final contest 26–0 to Stanford.

Scoring Summary

Notre Dame	0	0	6	6	12
Army	0	0	6	0	6

Third Quarter
Army: Murrell 1 run (kick failed)
Notre Dame: Chevigny 1 run (kick failed)

Fourth Quarter
Notre Dame: O'Brien 38 pass from Niemiec (kick failed)

3 Notre Dame 24 • Georgia Tech 3
NOVEMBER 8, 1975, AT NOTRE DAME STADIUM

They Called It the "Rudy Game"

The Run-Up: In Dan Devine's first season as head coach, Notre Dame finished with a 6–2 record, with losses to Michigan State University and number-three ranked University of Southern California. The Irish were rated number 12 in the AP poll.

Georgia Tech also came in with a 6–2 record, with losses to the University of South Carolina and Auburn University.

The Pertinent Details: Many of the details of this contest probably didn't matter. What did matter came in the final minute when Devine inserted a senior walkon named Daniel "Rudy" Ruettiger into the football game.

A Joliet, Illinois, native who had transferred into Notre Dame from Holy Cross Junior College across the street, Ruettiger actually sacked Georgia Tech quarterback Rudy Allen on the final play of the game and was carried off the field by his Irish teammates.

All that became part of the feature movie *Rudy* that was filmed on the Notre Dame campus and debuted in 1993, with scenes from the game filmed at halftime of an Irish home game against Penn State in '92. What's noteworthy about the movie is that, for many people who have never been to campus, it defines their impression of Notre Dame. (The year after the movie debuted, applications to the university increased 20 percent.)

What actually happened in the real game? It was an artistic masterpiece for the Notre Dame defense. The Yellow Jackets came in averaging more than 376 rushing yards per game from their wishbone attack, but Notre Dame limited them to 143 (67 of those on a run from punt formation, a 38-yard gain on the first play from scrimmage, and a 17-yard scramble by the quarterback). Georgia Tech did not complete a pass all day (it tried four). The only reason Tech managed to get as far as the Notre Dame 18 was because the Irish dropped a fumbled punt on their own 21-yard line. It marked only the second time in 21 games Georgia Tech was held without a touchdown.

Freshman Jerome Heavens scored a pair of touchdowns, as the Irish turned the tables with 311 rushing yards of their own.

The Determining Factor: Heavens ran 73 yards for a touchdown in the third period (the second Irish offensive play of the second half), making the score 17–0 in favor of the home team and giving Ruettiger a chance to get into the game. Heavens finished with 148 yards on the ground.

The Star of the Show: It was Ruettiger that day—and then again 18 years later when *Rudy* hit the big screen.

What the Headlines Said: "Notre Dame's disciplined defense shut off Georgia Tech's heralded wishbone attack, and the Irish rediscovered a running

Daniel "Rudy" Ruettiger is carried off the field by teammates after his only game appearance.

game of their own to wipe out the visiting Yellow Jackets Saturday. Tech came to South Bend for the Irish home finale sporting the best rushing record in the nation—376.4 yards a game. But after Pat Moriarty rambled 38 yards almost to midfield on the first play, the defense stopped Tech at almost every turn."—*South Bend Tribune*

"Heavens's run, for all practical purposes, ended the game. But it didn't end the drama. Not, at least, where Frank Allocco and Dan Ruettiger were concerned.... Ruettiger, a 27-year-old senior, a live-in security guard at the A.C.C., a veteran of two years in the navy, and

Actor Sean Astin portrayed Daniel Ruettiger in the 1992 movie Rudy.

Jerome Heavens scores a touchdown in the third period of the Notre Dame-Georgia Tech game.

Scoring Summary

	1	2	3	4	T
Georgia Tech	0	0	0	3	3
Notre Dame	7	3	7	7	24

First Quarter
Notre Dame: Heavens 16 run (Reeve kick) (5:59)

Second Quarter
Notre Dame: Reeve 29 field goal (9:28)

Third Quarter
Notre Dame: Heavens 73 run (Reeve kick) (14:13)

Fourth Quarter
Georgia Tech: Whealler 40 field goal (8:52)
Notre Dame: Knott 3 run (Reeve kick) (:28)
Attendance: 59,075

unlikeliest of all a 5'7", 184-pound defensive end, entered the game after the Irish scored with 28 seconds remaining. The veteran of three years with the prep team made the most of his opportunity, too, sacking Tech quarterback Rudy Allen for a five-yard loss on the game's final play."—Notre Dame *Scholastic*

"Some of his Notre Dame teammates don't even know his name is Dan Ruettiger. It has always been just 'Ruetty.'"—*South Bend Tribune*

What the Players and Coaches Said: "Let me put it this way. Everything we tried didn't work. I knew Notre Dame would be good, but they were fantastic. They have more size and speed than anybody. They are the best defensive team we've played. We have no alibis. Notre Dame beat us fair and square," said Tech coach Pepper Rodgers.

"It's a dream that came true. I've been waiting 27 years for this. All I wanted to do was be a part of this great tradition, to prove to people that it can be done. It's persistence that counts. What happened to me only happens in the movies," said Ruettiger.

"Can you imagine lining up across from Ross Browner or Willie Fry all day and suddenly seeing Rudy across from you? He finessed his man on the giggle," said Irish assistant coach Joe Yonto.

"There are bigger players, but none with bigger hearts," said Browner.

The Rundown: The Irish lost the following Saturday at the University of Pittsburgh, dropped out of the rankings, then defeated the University of Miami (Florida) in the season finale. Notre Dame finished 8–3 for the season, ended up 17th in the final United Press International poll (12th in the Associated Press poll), and did not play in a bowl game.

Georgia Tech finished with a 7–4 record after dropping its finale at Georgia.

Ruettiger graduated from Notre Dame in 1976, became a motivational speaker, and ultimately convinced Tri-Star Pictures, director David Anspaugh, and screenwriter Angelo Pizzo to make his story into a feature film. *Rudy* became the first film for theatrical release to be shot on the Notre Dame campus since *Knute Rockne: All American* in 1940.

Statistics

Team Statistics

Category	Notre Dame	Georgia Tech
First Downs	21	7
Rushing	16	5
Passing	5	0
Penalty	0	2
Rushing Attempts	64	48
Yards Gained Rushing	330	172
Yards Lost Rushing	19	29
Net Yards Rushing	311	143
Net Yards Passing	74	0
Passes Attempted	16	4
Passes Completed	7	0
Interceptions Thrown	0	0
Total Offensive Plays	80	52
Total Net Yards	385	143
Average Gain Per Play	4.8	2.7
Fumbles: Number Lost	4–2	2–1
Penalties: Number-Yards	4–45	1–8
Punts-Yards	6–265	11–412
Average Yards Per Punt	44.2	37.5
Punt Returns-Yards	4–36	4–19
Kickoff Returns-Yards	2–63	3–37
Interception Returns-Yards	0	0
Time of Possession	24:50	35:10

Notre Dame's Individual Statistics
Rushing: Slager 7–5, Hunter 12–54, Heavens 18–148–2, McLane 4–20, Knott 4–17–1, J. Browner 11–43, Eurick 6–20, Allocco 2–4

Passing: Slager 16–7–0–74–0

Receiving: MacAfee 4–43, Kelleher 2–25, Heavens 1–6

Georgia Tech's Individual Statistics
Rushing: Moriarty 6–53, Head 6–28, Rucker 6–6, Shamburger 10–27, Crowley 6–7, Myers 2–3, Brown 1–16, Hill 2–4, Yeager 2–5, Allen 7–0

Passing: Myers 1–0–0–0–0, Allen 3–0–0–0–0

10 Irish Bowl Victories That Can't Be Beat

For years, postseason bowl games in college football weren't much more than glorified exhibitions. For years, the final polls were taken and national champions were crowned at the end of the regular season.

In some ways, that made it easier for the University of Notre Dame to remain detached from the bowl scene for some 45 years after the Irish brought home a Rose Bowl victory at the end of the 1924 season.

Then the picture changed. The 1965 season marked the first in which the Associated Press waited until after the bowl games to offer its final ratings. United Press International followed suit, beginning with the 1974 season. Now, all of the sudden, the bowls had taken on new meaning.

Enter Ara Parseghian on the Notre Dame football scene in 1964. His presence immediately thrust the Irish back into the national title picture. Notre Dame, at 9–1, claimed the Grantland Rice Trophy from the National Football Foundation as its '64 champion. Parseghian's '66 team, after its ballyhooed 10–10 tie with Michigan State University, dispatched USC 51–0 a week later and earned a consensus crown.

So, when Notre Dame opted to return to the bowl scene in 1969, it made all the sense in the world. Part of the rationale involved the fact that the bowls, now more than ever, were affecting the national championship race. The university made it clear that part of the idea of playing in January was to have a chance to improve the football team's final poll slot. That meant playing a more highly ranked opponent as often as possible.

That turned into playing top-ranked University of Texas in 1969, and another number-one Texas team a year later in 1970. Then there was number-one ranked University of Alabama in '73 and second-ranked Alabama in '74 (in Parseghian's final game with the Irish). Parseghian's teams played in five bowl games: three times versus a first-ranked team, once versus number-two ranked team, and once versus number nine.

The list went on and on. Another number-one ranked Texas team in '77. Number-one ranked University of Georgia in 1980. Number-three ranked West Virginia University in '88. Top-ranked University of Colorado teams in both '89 and '90. Number-three ranked Florida, number-four ranked Texas A&M University, number-four Colorado—and so on and so on and so on.

That mix of lots of unbeaten and highly ranked (and regarded) if not top-ranked opponents, combined with plenty of blue-chip Irish teams, has made for some memorable New Year's Day (and beyond) assignments.

As the Bowl Alliance and Bowl Coalition have morphed into the Bowl Championship Series, the postseason rules of engagement continue to change.

Count on this chapter expanding in future editions of this book if future Irish squads have anything to say about it.

1 Notre Dame 27 • Stanford 10
JANUARY 1, 1925, AT PASADENA IN THE ROSE BOWL

Final Four Horsemen Appearance Leads Rose Bowl Win

The Run-Up: Notre Dame had finished a perfect regular season, going 9–0 and outscoring its opposition 258–44 behind the talented Four Horsemen and Seven Mules.

Stanford University came into the game with a 7–0–1 record for the season, after tying its regular-season finale against California (20–20).

The Pertinent Details: Notre Dame found itself outgained nearly two to one in total yards (316–186)

and first downs (16–7). But that didn't stop Knute Rockne's unbeaten squad from breaking open a close game with three defensive touchdowns (a fumble return by Ed Hunsinger and two Elmer Layden interception returns of 63 and 78 yards) to ruin Stanford's second appearance in Pasadena, California.

Stanford kicked a field goal midway through the opening period—then Notre Dame scored the next 20 points. Rockne's unit drove 46 yards to take the lead on the first of Layden's touchdowns, this one a

The 1925 Notre Dame football team in Pasadena, California, for the Rose Bowl game against Stanford.

three-yard rush. Later in the period, Layden's interception of an Ernie Nevers throw turned into a 78-yard return and a 13–3 lead. Finally, late in the third period, the Cardinal mishandled a Layden punt, and Hunsinger's 20-yard return made the score 20–3. Later, Layden added yet another long interception return.

The game marked Notre Dame's first bowl game—its only one until 45 years later in 1969—and its lone trip to the Rose Bowl Game. It also marked the first appearance by a Notre Dame football team on the West Coast, with the game played in 89-degree conditions.

The Determining Factors: Stanford couldn't hold on to the football. Eight turnovers (five interceptions and three lost fumbles) did in the Cardinal.

The Star of the Show: Layden, who did it all on both sides of the line, was the star of the game, scoring once on a rushing play, running back a pair of interceptions for touchdowns, and punting, too.

What the Headlines Said: "Dempsey, knocked out of the ring battered and banged about, lingered to knock Luie Firpo loose from his underpinning; Notre Dame, out-charged, out-passed, and wobbly through inferior physical condition, stuck through four periods of hair-raising football here yesterday and accomplished the ruin of the Cardinal, 27 to 10."—*San Francisco Call and Post*

"When Blasco Ibanez penned his yarn about 'The Four Horsemen' he automatically reserved parking space in anybody's five-foot shelf, but who is the soul brave enough to rise and say creations of the Spanish novelist will ride down to posterity with louder hoofbeats than the galloping buccaneers turned out by Knute Rockne on the banks of the Wabash far away? Two thousand miles from home, in a strange setting of

Football program for the 1925 Rose Bowl.

golden tinted orange groves and winter blooming beds of crimson poinsettias, Rockne's four horsemen rode wild to the end of the trail here in the annual New Year's Day East-West football clash, and with a 27 to 10 score defeated fullback Ernie Nevers and 10 other Leland Stanford men."—*San Francisco Call and Post*

What the Players and Coaches Said: "It is one thing to get the breaks and another to take advantage of them. Some might say that we were lucky, but you

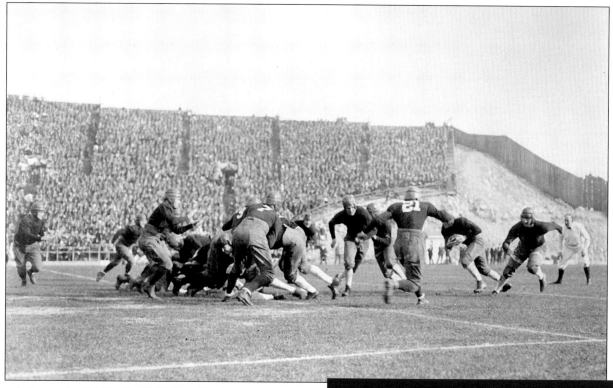

Action on the field in the 1925 Rose Bowl.

will admit that it takes a smart team to know what to do with the breaks after it gets them," said Rockne.

The Rundown: Notre Dame claimed its first consensus national title by virtue of its Rose Bowl victory and a 10-0 final slate. Four Horsemen Harry Stuhldreher, Jim Crowley, and Elmer Layden joined Illinois's Red Grange in the consensus All-America backfield.

Stanford ended up 7-1-1 and the Pacific Coast Conference champion in its first season under Glenn "Pop" Warner.

Scoring Summary

Notre Dame	0	13	7	7	27
Stanford	3	0	7	0	10

First Quarter
Stanford: Cuddeback 27 field goal (8:00)

Second Quarter
Notre Dame D: Layden 3 run (kick blocked) (13:30)
Notre Dame: Layden 78 interception return (Crowley kick) (8:00)

Third Quarter
Notre Dame: Hunsinger 20 fumble return (Crowley kick) (5:00)
Stanford: Shipkey 6 pass from Walker (Cuddeback kick) (1:00)

Fourth Quarter
Notre Dame: Layden 70 interception return (Crowley kick) (:30)

2 Notre Dame 24 • Texas 11
JANUARY 1, 1971, AT DALLAS IN THE COTTON BOWL

Notre Dame Defense Throttles Worster and Number One Texas's Streak

The Run-Up: Notre Dame came into the matchup with at 9–1 record for the season and ranked sixth, despite having been ranked at number one for a week prior to a 10–7 win against the Georgia Institute of Technology. The Irish later lost their regular-season finale 38–28 in the rain at the University of Southern California, despite Joe Theismann's 526 passing yards.

The University of Texas boasted a 30-game winning streak overall (the third longest in history) and had a 10–0 record for the season. It was ranked first in both polls, after moving into the top slot in the Associated Press poll in late October.

This matchup marked only the third time in history the same two teams had faced each other in bowl games in consecutive years. Formerly, Louisiana State University and Santa Clara University had clashed in the 1937–38 Sugar Bowls, and the University of Nebraska and the University of Alabama had fought in the 1966 Orange Bowl and 1967 Sugar Bowl.

The Pertinent Details: The Irish hadn't been able to slow down the Texas express the previous year on the same field in the same Cotton Bowl contest. This time, it went Notre Dame's way.

All the scoring came in the first half, with Theismann (Heisman Trophy runner-up) setting the tone for the Irish when he hit Tom Gatewood for 26 yards and a touchdown to finish off an 80-yard drive. After Texas fumbled away the kickoff at its own 13,

Theismann ran the ball in from the 3 on the sixth play. Early in the second quarter, Theismann ended a 53-yard drive with a 15-yard run that made the score 21–3 for the Irish.

Five lost fumbles doomed the Longhorns' winning streak (they fumbled nine times altogether). Three of the fumbles were by All-American Steve Worster, who managed only 42 rushing yards. Texas counted up 216 rushing yards, but that was far below its average of 374 per game.

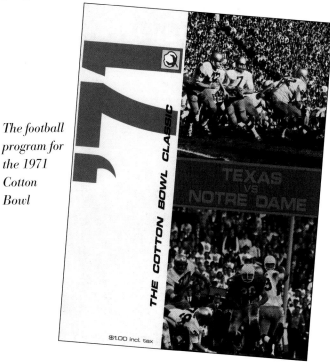

The football program for the 1971 Cotton Bowl

Heisman Trophy runner-up Joe Theismann ran for two scores and threw another to help beat the Longhorns.

The Determining Factor: The Longhorns made enough mistakes to manage only 11 points despite 426 total yards, 82 offensive plays, and 20 first downs.

The Stars of the Show: Texas quarterback Eddie Phillips won the offensive vote, thanks to his 164 rushing yards and 199 passing yards (nine of 17 throwing).

But Theismann, with one touchdown pass and two rushing touchdowns, was the winning signal-caller. The defensive Most Valuable Player was Notre Dame's Clarence Ellis. He helped hold the Longhorns to only 10 completions on 27 tries, and he also caught a 37-yard pass while playing offense.

Scoring Summary

Notre Dame	14	10	0	0	24
Texas	3	8	0	0	11

First Quarter
Texas: Feller 23 field goal (11:28)
Notre Dame: Gatewood 26 pass from Theismann (Hempel kick) (7:58)
Notre Dame: Theismann 3 run (Hempel kick) (5:11)

Second Quarter
Notre Dame: Theismann 15 run (Hempel kick) (13:28)
Texas: Bertelsen 2 run (Lester pass from Phillips) (1:52)
Attendance: 73,000

What the Headlines Said: "It was, first of all, the day Darrell Royal either lost the meat in his wishbone or found a Woo in his soup, a day when the Texas Longhorns, who had been number one, 1A, or 1B since before the midi, bombarded Notre Dame with so many fumbles the Cotton Bowl looked like an Easter egg hunt for leprechauns."—Dan Jenkins in *Sports Illustrated*.

"Time arched on into another new year Friday but without a traveling companion which had been almost as certain for nearly three long years. For the University of Texas's proud and seemingly enduring winning streak of 30 consecutive games finally crumbled at the Cotton Bowl, the victim of a masterfully designed and executed performance by Notre Dame, 24–11."—*Dallas Morning News*

"[Ara] Parseghian made the good defensive move, and Royal made the good offensive preparations. In between was Joe Theismann getting the points that mattered, and that was the difference."—*Sports Illustrated*

"After almost five decades of winning football games for the Gipper, the Fighting Irish of Notre Dame stampeded onto the Cotton Bowl's AstroTurf today and won the biggest one of all for themselves. They hog-tied the national champions from the University of Texas, 24 to 11. The Fighting Irish decisively and dramatically won the game that pride and prestige dictated that they must win."—*Chicago Tribune*

"Notre Dame put in a new defense that choked the Texas wishbone."—*Dallas Times Herald*

"The eyes of Texas are turning black today from the shiners hung on 'em by Notre Dame. Getting beat was one thing, but having its famed 'wishbone' offense, with its triple-option privileges, styled down to the status of a miniskirt is like adding insult to injury." —*Chicago Daily News*

What the Players and Coaches Said: "Angry people win football games, and Notre Dame was angrier than we were," said Royal.

"This is one of the big moments in Notre Dame football history," said Parseghian.

"I guess a defeat is good for you now and then, but I don't really recommend it," said Royal.

"We tried to make them play left-handed. We knew they wanted to run 90 percent of the time. So we wanted to make them pass instead of run. With our interior secondary, our people lined up in a wishbone, too, with the secondary and the middle linebacker keying on the Texas halfbacks and fullback. They did what we wanted to make them do. When they spread, their lead blocker was gone for the runs," said Parseghian.

The Rundown: This marked Notre Dame's first bowl victory since the 1925 Rose Bowl. At 10–1, Notre Dame finished second in the final AP poll (behind 11–0–1 Nebraska, which beat fifth-ranked LSU 17–12 in the Orange Bowl) and fifth in the UPI standings taken before the bowls. At 10–1, Texas was third in the final AP standings and won the prebowl UPI title.

Statistics

Team Statistics

Category	Notre Dame	Texas
First Downs	20	16
Rushing	10	9
Passing	9	7
Penalty	1	0
Rushing Attempts	55	43
Yards Gained Rushing	260	192
Yards Lost Rushing	44	46
Net Yards Rushing	216	146
Net Yards Passing	210	213
Passes Attempted	27	19
Passes Completed	10	10
Interceptions Thrown	1	1
Total Offensive Plays	82	72
Total Net Yards	426	359
Average Gain Per Play	5.2	5.0
Fumbles: Number Lost	9–5	1–1
Penalties: Number-Yards	3–33	5–52
Punts-Yards	5–163	8–366
Average Yards Per Punt	32.6	45.7
Punt Returns-Yards	4–26	0–0
Kickoff Returns-Yards	4–41	3–58
Interception Returns-Yards	1–0	1–0

Notre Dame's Individual Statistics

Rushing: Cieszkowski 13–52, Parker 13–48, Gulyas 9–24, Theismann 18–22
Passing: Theismann 16–9–1–176–1, Bulger 2–1–0–37–0, Steenberge 1–0–0–0–0
Receiving: Yoder 2–96, Gatewood 2–43–1, Cieszkowski 2–11, Parker 2–7, Ellis 1–37, Creaney 1–19

Texas's Individual Statistics

Rushing: Phillips 23–164, Worster 16–42, Wiggington 6–10, Bertelsen 8–5, Dale 1–2, Lester 1–(-7)
Passing: Phillips 17–9–0–199–0, Wiggington 10–1–1–11
Receiving: Comer 4–67, Bertelsen 3–85, Lester 2–17, Dale 1–41

Notre Dame 24 • Alabama 23
DECEMBER 31, 1973, AT TULANE STADIUM IN THE SUGAR BOWL

Irish Prevail Over Bear's Tide in a Sugar Bowl for the Ages

The Run-Up: The Irish came in at 10–0, having outscored their opponents 358–66 and defeated sixth-ranked USC and number-20 University of Pittsburgh along the way. The Irish came into the Sugar Bowl ranked third by the AP and fourth by UPI in the two polls.

Alabama was 10–0, ranking first in both polls (moving into the top slot only after Ohio State University tied unbeaten University of Michigan in the teams' final regular-season contest). It marked the first meeting in history between Notre Dame and Alabama.

The Pertinent Details: It's hard to manage a more back-and-forth, entertaining football game between unbeaten teams—with a national championship at stake to boot. The lead changed hands six times, going to 7–6 for the Tide after Wayne Bullock scored late in the opening period for the Irish to start the point-making (Alabama had zero net yards in the first 15 minutes). Then freshman Al Hunter produced a dazzling 93-yard kick return to make the score 14–7.

'Bama drove 93 yards to start the second half and to regain the edge at 17–14, then Eric Penick's one-play, 12-yard possession followed a Drew Mahalic fumble recovery in midair to make it 21–17 for the Irish.

A Bullock fumble gave the ball back to Alabama at the Irish 37, and the Tide came through with some dipsy-doo, as Mike Stock flipped a 25-yard option throw to a wide-open quarterback Richard Todd (only to miss the Bill Davis point-after-touchdown try). Notre Dame needed 11 plays to go 79 yards, and reached the 3, where Bob Thomas knocked through what turned out to be the winning field goal at the 4:26 mark.

Alabama forced the Irish to start at their own 1-yard line after a 69-yard punt, but Tom Clements came through with a clutch throw, ending in only the second reception of the year by tight end Robin Weber.

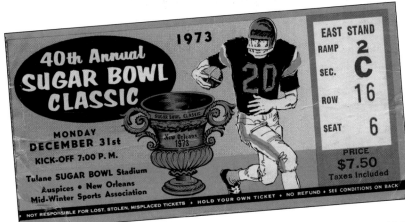

A ticket stub to the 40th annual Sugar Bowl, held in New Orleans on New Years Eve, 1973, pitting Notre Dame against Alabama

The Determining Factors: Irish quarterback Clements connected with little-used tight end Weber on a game-saving, third-down-and-8 throw from Notre Dame's own end zone. The play was immortalized in a still photograph taken from the end zone by Rich Clarkson for *Sports Illustrated*.

The Star of the Show: Clements won the popular vote (and the Miller-Digby Memorial Trophy), thanks to his 74 rushing yards, his 169 passing yards, and the huge 35-yarder to Weber.

What the Headlines Said: "Coach Paul (Bear) Bryant may have stopped the rain that threatened to turn Tulane Stadium into a little Lake Pontchartrain Monday night. He may have breathed on the artificial turf and helped make it dry. But that's where he ran out of miracles. Because the Bear didn't have a kicker who could make an extra point under pressure, and because he had no defense for a simply sensational quarterback named Tom Clements, he lost the Sugar Bowl and a national college football championship to Notre Dame's Fighting Irish, 24–23."–*Los Angeles Times*

"Pro football will stage its annual 'Super' Bowl game in a couple of weeks, but the adjective surely has been stolen by Notre Dame and Alabama in a New Year's Eve game that was one of football's all-time greatest games."–*South Bend Tribune*

"Bob Thomas, a 5'10", 171-pound midget amongst a mountain of men, kicked a field goal late in the fourth quarter and etched his name forever in football lore in tumultuous, trembling Sugar Bowl Stadium Monday night. They talk of Gipp, of the Four Horsemen, of Crowley and Rockne, Leahy and Lujack. Forget them. The legend of Notre Dame lives still because quarterback Tom Clements gave Thomas a chance of a lifetime and he met the challenge." –*Montgomery Advertiser*

Tom Clements passes to Robin Weber in the 1973 Sugar Bowl. (Photo courtesy of Rich Clark, NCAA Photos)

Drew Mahalic (No. 45) returned an Alabama fumble to the Tide 12, then Eric Penick scored on the next play for a 21–17 Irish third-period lead.

What the Players and Coaches Said: "I don't really feel like we lost, just that time ran out on us. The long pass at the end beat us. If we get the ball back we're going to win the game. When we had them backed up to the 1-yard line, if I'd been a betting man I'd have bet you we were going to win," said Bryant.

"I definitely feel we're the national champion. We beat the leading scoring team in the nation and the team that was leading in offensive yardage. We beat a great football team and they lost to a great football team. What has been demanded of us, we have satisfied. This doesn't imply that the other teams are not good teams, but I think a premium is placed on

going totally unscathed," said Irish coach Ara Parseghian.

"I've been watching Notre Dame for 43 years and this is one of our greatest victories. The only other one that compares with it is the 18–13 upset of Ohio State in 1935," said Notre Dame athletics director Moose Krause.

"[Dave] Casper was the primary receiver. But Alabama was so run-conscious when they had us that deep that I was able to freeze their defense with a running fake to Eric Penick. Weber was so open I didn't even look at Casper. But I couldn't see what happened on the play until I looked over at our sideline," said Clements.

Scoring Summary

Notre Dame	6	8	7	3	24
Alabama	0	10	7	6	23

First Quarter

Notre Dame: Bullock 1 run (kick failed) (5:51)

Second Quarter

Alabama: Billingsley 6 run (Davis kick) (10:10)

Notre Dame: Hunter 93 kickoff return (Demmerle pass from Clements) (7:17)

Alabama: Davis 39 field goal (0:39)

Third Quarter

Alabama: Jackson 5 run (Davis kick) (11:02)

Notre Dame: Penick 12 run (Thomas kick) (2:30)

Fourth Quarter

Alabama: Todd 25 pass from Stock (kick failed) (9:39)

Notre Dame: Thomas 19 field goal (4:26)

Attendance: 85,161

Statistics

Team Statistics

Category	Notre Dame	Alabama
First Downs	20	23
Rushing	12	15
Passing	6	7
Penalty	5–45	3–32
Rushing Attempts	59	52
Yards Gained Rushing	252	190
Yards Lost Rushing	5	43
Net Yards Rushing	252	190
Net Yards Passing	169	127
Passes Attempted	12	15
Passes Completed	7	10
Interceptions Thrown	0	1
Total Offensive Plays	71	67
Total Net Yards	421	317
Fumbles: Number Lost	4–3	5–2
Penalties: Number-Yards	5–45	3–32
Punts-Yards	3	6
Punt Returns-Yards	3	6
Kickoff Returns-Yards	150	159
Interception Returns-Yards	0	0
Time of Possession	31:06	28:54

Notre Dame's Individual Statistics

Rushing: Bullock 19-79-1, Clements 15-74, Best 12-45, Penick 9-28-1, Bullock 19-79-1, Hunter 4-26

Passing: Clements 12-7-0-169-0

Receiving: Demmerle 3-59, Casper 3-75, Weber 1-35

Alabama's Individual Statistics

Rushing: Jackson 11-62-1, Billingsley 7-54-1, Beck 2-5, Spivey 11-44, Stock 3-13, Culliver 2-5, Todd 3-32, Shelby 3-1, Rutledge 10-(-25)

Passing: Rutledge 12-7-1-88-0, Todd 2-2-0-14-0, Stock 1-1-0-25-1

Receiving: Pugh 2-28, Jackson 2-22, Stack 1-15, Wheeler 1-13, Sharpless 2-22, Todd 1-25-1, Billingsley 1-2

"It was like two heavyweight champions meeting for the first time," said Irish offensive lineman Frank Pomarico.

"I may have been a little surprised. I do remember asking Coach Parseghian if he was sure he wanted that play," said Clements of the end-zone pass call known as the "tackle trap pass."

The Rundown: Notre Dame's triumph over top-rated Alabama pushed the Irish to number one in the final AP poll and left the Irish the consensus number-one team.

After its bowl-winless streak reached seven games, the Tide dropped to number four in the AP voting. Notre Dame received 33 of 60 first-place votes (Oklahoma had 16, Ohio State 11) and finished more than 100 total points ahead of runner-up Ohio State.

Notre Dame 13 • Alabama 11
JANUARY 1, 1975, AT MIAMI IN THE ORANGE BOWL

Notre Dame Holds Off Unbeaten Tide in Parseghian's Finale

The Run-Up: Notre Dame came in at 9–2, with losses to Purdue University and sixth-ranked USC. The Irish ranked number one following their season-opening win over Georgia Tech, were number five heading into their regular-season finale at USC, and then stood at number nine in the AP poll coming into the bowl season.

The University of Alabama came in with an 11–0 record and as number one in the United Press International poll and number two according to AP (behind unbeaten University of Oklahoma).

The Pertinent Details: For the second straight season, Notre Dame faced an unbeaten and top-rated Alabama team in the postseason. And, once again, Bear Bryant came up empty against the Irish, this time in Parseghian's final game as Notre Dame head coach (he announced his retirement after the end of the regular season).

The Irish played it close to the vest, throwing only eight times all night. They grabbed an early lead after recovering an Alabama fumble (the Tide dropped a punt at their own 16), then made great use of a 77-yard, 17-play touchdown march that took up more

Tom Clements runs for some of his 26 rushing yards in the 1975 Orange Bowl against Alabama.

than seven minutes of the second period. That made the score 13–0, and the Irish held on from there, with four 'Bama turnovers making life tough for the top-rated team.

Bryant's squad threw for an un-Tide-like 223 yards through the air (194 by Richard Todd), with Todd's 48-yard touchdown throw making it a two-point game with just a little more than three minutes left. Alabama held and forced an Irish punt, and a couple of completions put them in enemy territory—until a Reggie Barnett pickoff ended it for the Irish (after an earlier interception by safety John Dubenetzky).

The Determining Factors: The Irish showed their share of grit in proving that the one-sided regular-season-ending loss at USC was a distant memory and that they had no intention of letting Parseghian leave on a losing note. The same Notre Dame defense that in its most recent outing had seen USC light up the board for 55 points this time limited Alabama's running game to 62 yards.

The Star of the Show: The hero of the day was Irish fullback Wayne Bullock, the Notre Dame workhorse back with 24 carries and 83 yards, plus the first Notre Dame touchdown.

What the Headlines Said: "Somebody up there smiles on French Armenian Presbyterian football coaches and frowns on good ole boys."—*Fort Lauderdale News*

"Alabama players cried unashamedly after their dreams of an undefeated football season and national championship were ruined for the second straight year by Notre Dame in a bowl game. There was no solace available to the Crimson Tide after Wednesday night's 13–11 defeat in the Orange Bowl."—Associated Press

Scoring Summary

Notre Dame	7	6	0	0	13
Alabama	0	3	0	8	11

First Quarter
Notre Dame: Bullock 4 run (Reeve kick) (6:41)

Second Quarter
Notre Dame: McLane 9 run (kick failed) (8:29)
Alabama: Ridgeway 21 field goal (1:45)

Fourth Quarter
Alabama: Schamun 48 pass from Todd (Pugh pass from Todd) (3:13)
Attendance: 71,801

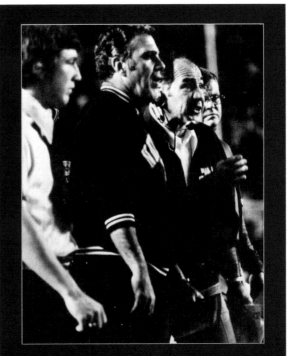

Ara Parseghian and Tom Pagna coaching from the sidelines at the 1975 Orange Bowl.

"The locker room was nearly empty when Paul Bryant finally made his exit. The Bear, walking ever so slowly, appeared older than his 81 years. Someone said he looked as old as Methuselah, but that wasn't true. He looked older… In his hands he held a half-dozen manila folders. Drawn in black ink on the outside of the folders was the Alabama game plan, the plan that was supposed to beat Notre Dame in last night's Orange Bowl game, the plan that was to win a national championship. But it didn't do either of those things."—*Miami News*

What the Players and Coaches Said: "It was almost like a carbon copy of last year's game," said Parseghian.

"We just didn't get it done. They just whipped us," said Bryant.

"After the game I came into the locker room and I wanted to say a lot of things to the team. It all hit me at that moment. This was my last game. I could not find the words to say what I was really feeling. What I said was so inadequate. I just told them I was proud of them and that I appreciated their effort and that I was pleased to go out a winner," said Parseghian.

"It was the most emotional game we've played all year long," said Bullock.

"I'm sure that Ara will enjoy his vacation a lot more now," said Bryant.

The Rundown: This season marked the first time the final UPI poll of coaches took place after the bowl games. Notre Dame's win vaulted the Irish to number four in the UPI poll and number six in the AP. Alabama ended up 11–1 and ranked second by UPI and fifth by the AP after the Tide's eighth consecutive bowl defeat.

Statistics

Team Statistics

Category	Notre Dame	Alabama
First Downs	15	14
Rushing	14	3
Passing	0	11
Penalty	1	0
Rushing Attempts	66	33
Yards Gained Rushing	215	107
Yards Lost Rushing	30	45
Net Yards Rushing	185	62
Net Yards Passing	19	223
Passes Attempted	8	29
Passes Completed	4	15
Interceptions Thrown	2	2
Total Offensive Plays	74	62
Total Net Yards	204	285
Average Gain Per Play	2.77	4.60
Fumbles: Number Lost	1/1	5/2
Penalties: Number-Yards	1/5	1/15
Punts-Yards	6	7
Average Yards Per Punt	38	40
Punt Returns-Yards	0	34
Kickoff Returns-Yards	54	32
Interception Returns-Yards	2/26	2/0

Notre Dame's Individual Statistics

Rushing: Bullock 24-83-1, Samuel 10-39, McLane 8-30-1, Clements 11-26, Penick 6-15, Parise 3-4, Goodman 1-2, Allocco 3-(-14)

Passing: Clements 7-4-1-19-0, Goodman 1-0-1-0-0

Receiving: Demmerle 2-12, McLane 1-9, Goodman 1-(-2)

Alabama's Individual Statistics

Rushing: Culliver 11-60, Shelby 5-25, Todd 9-4, Billingsley 2-3, Taylor 1-1, Pugh 1-(-8), Stock 1-(-9), Rutledge 3-(-14)

Passing: Todd 24-13-2-194-1, Rutledge 5-2-0-29-0

Receiving: Newsome 6-68, Schamun 5-126-1, Billingsley 3-17, Brown 1-12

Notre Dame 38 • Texas 10
JANUARY 2, 1978, AT DALLAS IN THE COTTON BOWL

Irish Handle Campbell and Top-Ranked Texas to Claim Title

The Run-Up: Notre Dame came in 10–1, ranked fifth by both AP and UPI, with eight straight wins to its credit.

Texas came in 11–0 and ranked first in both polls, with a 12-game overall win streak, having given up but 114 regular-season points. The Longhorns jumped into the top spot at midseason after previous number-one teams University of Oklahoma, University of Michigan, and USC all lost games.

The Pertinent Details: The Irish national title apparently had been quashed in a second-game-of-the-season loss at Mississippi. But after Joe Montana took over for good as Irish quarterback, Notre Dame rolled into championship form.

Still, winning the championship appeared to be a reach, with four teams ranked ahead of Dan Devine's squad heading into the bowls. But fourth-ranked Michigan cooperated by losing to 13th-ranked Washington in the Rose Bowl, and second-ranked Oklahoma fell to sixth-ranked Arkansas in the Orange Bowl. Third-rated Alabama defeated ninth-place Ohio State in the Sugar Bowl, and at last there was a window of opportunity for the Irish. And, boy, did they make the most of it in front of a Cotton Bowl–record crowd.

The Determining Factors: Notre Dame put three scores on the board in fewer than eight minutes in the second period to take a 21–3 lead, and the Irish were

never really headed. First, Texas fumbled the ball away at its own 27 (Jim Browner recovered), and Terry Eurick (he made the cover of *Sports Illustrated* the next week) ran it in on the fifth play. Three minutes later, Eurick scored again to finish off a 35-yard drive after a Willie Fry fumble recovery. Four minutes later, a Doug Becker interception put Notre Dame at the Texas 17, and Montana promptly threw to Vagas Ferguson to make it 24–3.

The Longhorns made it awfully tough on themselves by committing six turnovers (Randy McEachern threw three interceptions). Notre Dame proved to be the dominant running team with 243 yards (101 by Jerome Heavens) to 131 by Texas (the 'Horns had been averaging 300). Plus, Irish guard Ernie Hughes did yeoman's work against Texas's Outland Trophy–winner and defensive tackle Brad Shearer.

The Stars of the Show: Ferguson, with his 100 rushing yards, three receptions, two rushing scores, and a third touchdown on a pass from Montana, got the offensive nod. Bob Golic won the defensive award after 17 tackles, a blocked field goal, and a major role in holding Heisman Trophy–winner Earl Campbell to a relatively harmless 116 rushing yards on 29 carries (Campbell never had a gain longer than 18 yards).

What the Headlines Said: "There is a story about a dentist who was renowned for the speed of his work.

As a patient would settle into the chair for a crucial extraction, the dentist would lean forward and say, 'This won't take long...did it?' In less than eight minutes in the second period, Notre Dame performed surgery on Texas that was, if not painless, exquisitely deft. From a 3–3 tie, the practically perfect Irish did some remarkable operating, and before 76,701 chilled Cotton Bowl spectators could say, bye-bye, national championship, the score was 24–3. Though it would eventually mount to 38–10, the game was over right there."—*Sports Illustrated*

"The Texas Longhorns helped eliminate one team from the conglomeration now clamoring for the final number-one ranking in college football Monday afternoon in the 42nd Cotton Bowl—itself. Cinderella has a glass jaw."—*Dallas Morning News*

Scoring Summary

Notre Dame	**3**	**21**	**7**	**7**	**38**
Texas	**3**	**7**	**0**	**0**	**10**

First Quarter
Notre Dame: Reeve 47 field goal (11:35)
Texas: Erxleben 42 field goal (6:07)

Second Quarter
Notre Dame: Eurick 6 run (Reeve kick) (14:56)
Notre Dame: Eurick 10 run (Reeve kick) (11:37)
Notre Dame: Ferguson 17 pass from Montana (Reeve kick) (7:28)
Texas: Lockett 13 pass from McEachern (Erxleben kick) (0:00)

Third Quarter
Notre Dame: Ferguson 3 run (Reeve kick) (6:49)

Fourth Quarter
Notre Dame: Ferguson 26 run (Reeve kick) (9:41)
Attendance: 76,701

Statistics

Team Statistics

Category	Notre Dame	Texas
First Downs	26	16
Rushing	15	6
Passing	11	9
Penalty	0	1
Rushing Attempts	53	50
Yards Gained Rushing	250	190
Yards Lost Rushing	7	59
Net Yards Rushing	243	131
Net Yards Passing	156	160
Passes Attempted	32	24
Passes Completed	14	11
Interceptions Thrown	1	3
Total Offensive Plays	85	74
Total Net Yards	399	291
Average Gain Per Play	4.7	3.9
Fumbles: Number Lost	0-0	3-3
Penalties: Number-Yards	4-37	1-5
Punts-Yards	5-152	3-120
Average Yards Per Punt	30.4	40.0
Punt Returns-Yards	0-0	1-1
Kickoff Returns-Yards	1-17	8-81
Interception Returns-Yards	3-20	1-0

Notre Dame's Individual Statistics
Rushing: Heavens 22-101, Ferguson 21-100-2, Eurick 4-16-2, Lisch 2-16, Stone 2-4, Mitchell 1-3, Montana 1-3
Passing: Montana 25-10-1-111-1, Lisch 7-4-0-45-0
Receiving: MacAfee 4-45, Waymer 3-38, Ferguson 3-23-1, Haines 2-29, Eurick 1-12, Pallas 1-9

Texas's Individual Statistics
Rushing: Campbell 29-116, H. Jones 11-63, Thompson 1-2, Johnson 1-2, McEachern 8-(-52)
Passing: McEachern 24-11-3-160-0
Receiving: Harris 4-57, Jackson 3-33, L. Jones 1-34, Miksch 1-18, Lockett 1-13-1, H. Jones 1-5

"Football carries a lot of weight in Texas. So do sidearms, cattle spreads, Dr. Pepper franchises, and oil exploration rights. The University of Texas linemen do not. All the beef for Texas was standing just outside the end zone, a genuine longhorn steer who kept dropping tokens of displeasure at the outcome of the Cotton Bowl yesterday afternoon. Out there on the field the former number-one team in the nation, the University of Texas, was doing a tumbleweed imitation in a 38–10 loss to Notre Dame."—*Boston Globe*

What the Players and Coaches Said: "We attacked and attacked and attacked. We didn't give them time to breathe," said Irish linebacker Doug Becker.

"Our offensive plan was very basic. The linemen were to take their man wherever he wanted to go, and the backs simply had to cut off the blocks," said Irish offensive tackle Tim Foley.

"We were ticked off. People weren't giving us any credit," said Irish defensive tackle Willie Fry.

"Texas is a good football team, and we beat them every way possible. This game puts us where Texas was," said Devine.

Running back Vagas Ferguson was instrumental in the 1978 Cotton Bowl.

"This was their day. I'd like to play them tomorrow but that's not the way it works," said Texas coach Fred Akers.

The Rundown: The Irish received all kinds of help from teams rated ahead of them, as Notre Dame's win jumped the Irish to first place in both final polls, while Texas fell to fourth in the AP and fifth by UPI. It marked Notre Dame's 10th consensus national title.

Notre Dame 34 • West Virginia 21
JANUARY 2, 1989, AT SUN DEVIL STADIUM IN THE FIESTA BOWL

Rice's Passing Show Gives Notre Dame Its 11th Consensus Title in the Fiesta Bowl

The Run-Up: Notre Dame came in with an 11–0 record for the season and ranked at number one by both AP and UPI. West Virginia also stood at 11–0 and ranked third in both polls.

The Pertinent Details: Having already defeated top-rated University of Miami at midseason and then second-ranked USC on the road in the regular-season finale, the Irish came to Tempe, Arizona, in search of the triple versus third-ranked West Virginia University.

Meanwhile, coach Lou Holtz, in an effort to make his players approach the game like any other, asked the Fiesta Bowl staff if his team could skip the traditional uniform bowl patch, so the blue Irish jerseys would look like they would on any other Saturday.

Whatever the motivation, it worked. Quarterback Tony Rice averaged 30 yards per pass completion, the Notre Dame running game rumbled for 242 yards, and the physical Irish defense kept the Mountaineers at bay most of the day.

The Determining Factor: West Virginia quarterback Major Harris suffered a limiting shoulder injury on the third play from scrimmage—at the same time Notre Dame's offense was exploding on touchdown drives of 61, 63, and 84 yards. The Mountaineers didn't manage a first down until five minutes into the second period. Then, when West Virginia pulled within

26–13 and took an interception back to the Irish 26, Notre Dame responded with a 12-yard tackle for loss on third down and forced a punt. Holtz's charges then drove 80 yards for a score, 57 of those yards on a throw to Ricky Watters.

The Stars of the Show: Rice, who never threw the ball as well as he did that afternoon in Tempe, claimed the offensive honors, while Frank Stams's two sacks and harassment of Harris handed Stams the defensive MVP trophy.

What the Headlines Said: "Those probably weren't echoes reverberating across Sun Devil Stadium on Monday. Only cheers. And it wasn't thunder that shook down from above. Just a few raindrops. But if Notre Dame's Fighting Irish didn't wake up the echoes and shake down the thunder, they did about everything else."—*Arizona Republic*

"It's as if the Four Horsemen—this time accompanied by a nervous, lisping, sandy-haired groom—were at it again. Like a gang of highwaymen, Notre Dame trampled previously undefeated West Virginia 34–21 in the Fiesta Bowl to finish 12–0 and win its 11th national championship. Notre Dame came out running and smoking and talking more trash than the cast of that old Gipper movie. Behind junior quarterback Tony Rice's game-high 75 yards rushing and

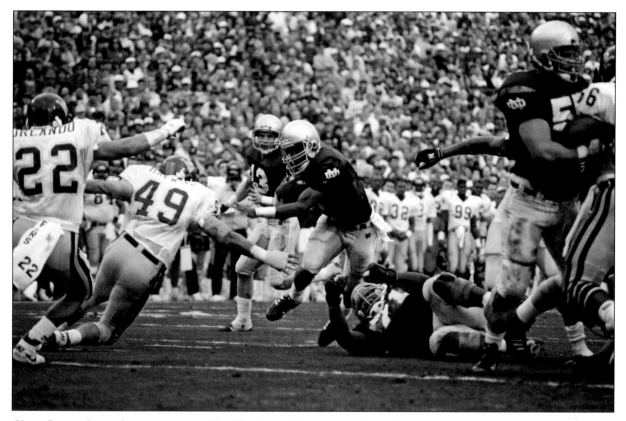

Notre Dame charged to victory over West Virginia with a top-notch passing and running game.

career-high 213 yards passing, the Irish rolled up 455 net yards while holding the erstwhile explosive Mountaineers to just 282 yards, their lowest total in 19 games."—*Sports Illustrated*

"One-dimensional? Can't throw? Come on, Lou. What in the name of Knute Rockne were you talking about all week? Notre Dame quarterback Tony Rice, the player Irish coach Lou Holtz said couldn't throw, completed seven of 11 for a career-high 213 yards and two touchdowns Monday."—*Arizona Republic*

"A football team seldom given its just due tapped destiny on the shoulder Monday afternoon and took its special place in history. First Notre Dame made Major Harris mortal, then it made its fairy-tale season complete by rolling over West Virginia, 34–21."—*South Bend Tribune*

"The man with the magic touch—and tongue—has tried to play down his team's abilities, if not its effort, all year long. He's done it to take the pressure off—that pressure of playing a number-one, a number-two, and a number-three team all in one season. And the pressure of just being Notre Dame, the most inviting target in all of college football. One Phoenix sports columnist even called him Coach Houdini. 'Only a wizard could

Irish captains Mark Green (No. 24) and Andy Heck (No. 66) celebrate Rodney Culver's second-period touchdown run that gave the Irish the 16–0 advantage.

make the top-ranked college football team appear to be an underdog.'"—*South Bend Tribune* on Holtz

What the Players and Coaches Said: "When we pass when we want to, we can get it done," said Irish tackle Andy Heck.

"I think I may have underestimated this team. This is a great football team because nobody proved otherwise," said Holtz.

"Great teams seize the moment and that's exactly what Notre Dame did today," said West Virginia coach Don Nehlen.

"Sometimes it seemed like they had about 16 players on the field," said West Virginia center Kevin Koken.

"I had nothing to lose. I was in a great situation. I was in Major Harris's shadow the whole week leading up to the game. Anything positive Tony Rice did was going to be a surprise, so I had no pressure on me at all. We thought we could throw on West Virginia. They did a lot of one-on-one coverage and we felt we had the receivers who could beat their guys. All week we worked on that," said Rice.

The Rundown: Notre Dame's victory moved the Irish to 12–0 and earned them their 11th consensus national title thanks to a number-one finish in both final polls. West Virginia ended up 11–1 and ranked fifth in both major polls.

Scoring Summary

Notre Dame	9	14	3	8	34
West Virginia	0	6	7	8	21

First Quarter
Notre Dame: Hackett 45 field goal (10:25)
Notre Dame: Johnson 1 run (run failed) (4:34)

Second Quarter
Notre Dame: Culver 5 run (Ho kick) (9:41)
West Virginia: Baumann 29 field goal (6:18)
Notre Dame: Ismail 29 pass from Rice (Ho kick) (1:48)
West Virginia: Baumann 31 FG (2:00)

Third Quarter
Notre Dame: Ho 32 field goal (5:34)
West Virginia: Bell 17 pass from Harris (3:32)

Fourth Quarter
Notre Dame: Jacobs 3 pass from Rice (Rice run) (13:05)
West Virginia: Rembert 3 run (Rembert run) (1:14)
Attendance: 74,911

Statistics

Team Statistics

Category	Notre Dame	West Virginia
First Downs	19	19
Rushing	13	4
Passing	6	10
Penalty	0	5
Rushing Attempts	59	37
Yards Gained Rushing	245	141
Yards Lost Rushing	3	33
Net Yards Rushing	242	108
Net Yards Passing	213	174
Passes Attempted	11	30
Passes Completed	7	14
Interceptions Thrown	1	1
Total Offensive Plays	70	67
Total Net Yards	455	282
Average Gain Per Play	6.5	4.2
Fumbles: Number Lost	2–0	0–0
Penalties: Number-Yards	11–102	3–38
Punts-Yards	4–147	7–318
Average Yards Per Punt	36.8	45.1
Punt Returns-Yards	3–28	2–35
Kickoff Returns-Yards	2–3	6–107
Interception Returns-Yards	1–0	1–14

Notre Dame's Individual Statistics
Rushing: Johnson 5-20-1, Brooks 11-36, Rice 13-75, Green 13-62, Banks 5-12, Watters 3-6, Culver 3-20-1, Eilers 1-2, Belles 3-10, Mihalko 1-2
Passing: Rice 11-7-1-213-2
Receiving: Brown 2-70, Johnson 1-19, Ismail 1-29-1, Green 1-35, Jacobs 1-3-1, Watters 1-57

West Virginia's Individual Statistics
Rushing: Harris 13-42, Brown 11-49, Taylor 6-12, Johnson 1-5, Tyler 2-21, Napoleon 3-9, Rembert 1-3-1
Passing: Harris 26-13-1-166-1, Jones 4-1-0-8-0
Receiving: Winn 3-31, Taylor 3-34, Bell 4-44-1, Rembert 2-40, Brown 1-17, Tyler 1-8

Notre Dame 21, Colorado 6
JANUARY 1, 1990, AT MIAMI IN THE ORANGE BOWL

Irish Run Roughshod Over Top-Rated Buffaloes in Miami

The Run-Up: Notre Dame came in at 11–1 and ranked fourth in both polls, its lone loss coming in the regular-season finale at Miami (ending a Notre Dame record 23-game win streak) after the Irish had been rated number one in the polls all season long. Colorado came in 11–0 and ranked first in both polls.

Pertinent Details: Notre Dame used a staunch defense, 106 rushing yards by Raghib Ismail, plus 89 more rushing yards, and two scoring runs by Anthony Johnson to knock off top-ranked Colorado in the Orange Bowl.

The Buffaloes had three very legitimate first-half scoring chances, but Notre Dame thwarted them one after another. That left room for Notre Dame's running game to take over in the final 30 minutes (177 yards worth), on touchdown drives of 69, 46, and 82 yards. Those three drives combined to include 31 plays, notably 17 straight runs on the final Notre Dame scoring march. Colorado suffered through three turnovers, compared to none for the Irish.

Psychologically, the Buffs had to be shaking their heads when they couldn't score after having first and goal at the Notre Dame 1-yard line midway through

Two scoring runs (four and seven yards) by Anthony Johnson propelled the Irish to their 21–6 victory over number-one-ranked Colorado in '90 Orange Bowl.

The most impressive play of the night came when Raghib Ismail stormed down the right sideline for the 35 yards and a score to make it 14–0 for Notre Dame in the third period.

the second period. The Irish held off three straight runs (two by Eric Bieniemy, one by Darian Hagan), then squashed a fake field-goal attempt on fourth down when Stan Smagala and Troy Ridgley combined to nail holder Jeff Campbell.

The Determining Factor: The number-one team in the country was held by the Irish to a single touchdown, that one coming one second short of three full periods into the football game. By then, Notre Dame held a 14–0 lead, and a nearly nine-minute touchdown drive by Notre Dame in the final period left no time for a Buffalo comeback.

The Star of the Show: The voters said the day's champion was Ismail, who led all ball-carriers with 108 rushing yards (on 16 carries). He put the Irish in

great position at 14–0 on the scoreboard when he dashed down the right sideline for 35 yards and a touchdown midway through the third period after a Ned Bolcar interception. Normally a flanker, Ismail actually ended up playing mostly at tailback because of an early injury to Watters, who was limited to two carries.

What the Headlines Said: "For once the Orange Bowl turf was someone else's bad dream. One incredible goal-line stand plus one punishing end-to-end zone drive exorcised ghosts and expelled doubts that Notre Dame's football team could indeed rev it up and serve up a sweet Orange Bowl toast."–*South Bend Tribune*

"The fourth-ranked Fighting Irish clogged up top-ranked Colorado's high-octane offense and went turnover free in powering to a 21–6 Orange Bowl victory. And the Irish can thank sore-shouldered flanker Raghib 'Rocket' Ismail, bulldozing fullback Anthony Johnson, and fifth-year linebacker Ned Bolcar for it, too."–Fort Wayne *Journal-Gazette*

"The story of this game occurred in the first two periods. Three times Colorado appeared destined to score touchdowns as it marched seemingly at will through the Irish defense, and three times the Buffaloes came up empty at or within the 20-yard line, including failure after a sensational goal-line stand for four downs at the Irish 1."–*Chicago Tribune*

Scoring Summary

Notre Dame	0	0	14	7	21
Colorado	0	0	6	0	6

Third Quarter

Notre Dame: Johnson 4 run (Hentrich kick) (11:48)

Notre Dame: Ismail 35 run (Hentrich kick) (7:19)

Colorado: Hagan 39 run (kick failed) (0:01)

Fourth Quarter

Notre Dame: Johnson 7 run (Hentrich kick) (1:32)

Attendance: 81,191

Irish coach Lou Holtz can't help but smile as his Irish players enjoy the postgame celebration after beating Colorado in the '90 Orange Bowl.

"Never one to pass up an opportunity for overstatement, Notre Dame coach Lou Holtz practically made the second half of Monday night's Orange Bowl game a life-or-death proposition for his Fighting Irish. With that, the luck of the Irish became the pluck of the Irish. Showing they are very fluent in smashball—the language of preference in the Big Eight Conference—they beat top-ranked and previously unbeaten Colorado at its own game."—*St. Louis Post-Dispatch*

What the Players and Coaches Said: "We had the opportunity of a lifetime and we let it slip away. Coming away from the first half without any points after controlling the game for a while was too much to overcome. I didn't think anybody could keep us out of the end zone like they did, but they did," said Buffalo coach Bill McCartney.

"I don't know how you can decide on anybody else being number one—that's my personal opinion—unless you want to say who's the best team on November 25 (when Notre Dame lost to Miami). We were number one for 11 weeks and the one week we were out of number one we beat the number-one team by 15 points. I just believe we have the best record against the toughest schedule. Case rests," said Irish coach Lou Holtz.

"If you try a fake field goal, that means that you've gone away from your game plan. Once they did not score on that, we knew that we were in good shape," said Irish defensive lineman Chris Zorich.

The Rundown: Notre Dame's victory and final 12–1 record left the Irish second in the final AP poll and third in the final UPI poll (behind number one Miami). Colorado, also at 12–1, finished fourth in both polls.

Statistics

Team Statistics

Category	Notre Dame	Colorado
First Downs	18	16
Rushing	14	12
Passing	4	4
Penalty	0	0
Rushing Attempts	52	46
Yards Gained Rushing	295	239
Yards Lost Rushing	16	22
Net Yards Rushing	279	217
Net Yards Passing	99	65
Passes Attempted	9	13
Passes Completed	5	4
Interceptions Thrown	0	2
Total Offensive Plays	61	59
Total Net Yards	378	282
Average Gain Per Play	6.2	4.8
Fumbles: Number Lost	0-0	1-1
Penalties: Number-Yards	3-35	1-5
Punts-Yards	5-204	3-118
Average Yards Per Punt	40.1	39.3
Punt Returns-Yards	0-0	3-36
Kickoff Returns-Yards	2-24	3-43
Interception Returns-Yards	2-0	0-0
Time of Possession	32:43	27:17
Third Down Conversions	7/12	5/13
Sacks By-Yards	1/5	1/6

Notre Dame's Individual Statistics

Rushing: Ismail 16-108-1, Johnson 15-89-2, Rice 14-50, Culver 5-29, Watters 2-3

Passing: Rice 9-5-0-99-0

Receiving: Eilers 2-47, Smith 1-27, Johnson 1-13, Brown 1-12

Colorado's Individual Statistics

Rushing: Hagan 19-106-1, Bieniemy 11-66, Flannigan 12-45, Kissick 2-6, Campbell 2-(-6)

Passing: Hagan 13-4-2-65-0

Receiving: Kissick 2-33, Pritchard 1-16, Perak 1-16

Notre Dame 39 • Florida 28
JANUARY 1, 1992, AT THE SUPERDOME IN THE SUGAR BOWL

Bettis Runs Wild, Irish Clip Gators in Sugar Bowl

The Run-Up: Notre Dame came in at 9–3, having lost to number three Michigan, number 13 University of Tennessee, and number eight Penn State University. The Irish ranked 18th in both polls.

Florida came in 10–1, its lone loss to number 18 Syracuse University. The Southeastern Conference champion Gators were third in the AP and fourth in the *USA Today*/CNN polls.

The Pertinent Details: Notre Dame upset third-rated Florida 39–28 thanks to 245 second-half team rushing yards and 150 overall and three touchdowns by Jerome Bettis as the Irish overcame a 17–7 halftime deficit.

This one was all about respect, with critics saying the Irish wouldn't be able to play with third-rated Florida. Irish coach Lou Holtz played right into that hype, suggesting that an Orlando, Florida, restaurant's waiter had offered him a joke: "What's the difference between Cheerios and Notre Dame? Cheerios belong in a bowl."

Holtz even pulled out the green connection. Though the Irish wore white jerseys, they were trimmed in green, with green numbers and green socks.

Florida led 13–0 and appeared to be moving the ball at will against the Irish defense. But the Gators also found themselves frustrated by reaching the Notre Dame 9, 13, 15, and 12 on four different possessions, only to settle for field goals on all four attempts.

Bettis had only four first-half carries for 23 yards. All that changed in the second half, mainly because Notre Dame went to the run. The Irish first half: 10 runs, 11 passes (while the Gators were running off 51 plays). The Irish second half: 39 runs, eight passes.

The last of Arden Czyzewski's five field goals (after a lost Irish fumble) gave Florida its last lead at 22–17. From there, Notre Dame drove 64 yards on 14 plays (11 of them runs), with five straight running plays from the 19 giving Notre Dame the lead for good.

Florida set Sugar Bowl records for first downs (29), passing yards (370), pass attempts (58), and completions (28 by Shane Matthews, beating the previous mark held by his coach, Steve Spurrier, by one). But none of it was enough.

The Determining Factor: Notre Dame's running game went crazy in the second half, and Florida never did figure out how to effectively score touchdowns against an Irish defense that disdained the rush and seemed to drop everyone into coverage.

The Star of the Show: Bettis was simply unstoppable. In the second half alone, he bulldozed the Gators for 127 yards and game-clinching touchdowns runs of five, 49, and 39 yards in the final five minutes

Rodney Culver's 93 rushing yards proved pivotal as Notre Dame's second-half offensive dominance thwarted third-ranked Florida.

alone. Notre Dame's entire team managed only 34 rushing yards in the opening two periods.

What the Headlines Said: "With critics saying that the school had been invited here only because of past achievements, Notre Dame decided to pull out all the tradition and unfurl all the glory in preparation for its Sugar Bowl meeting with the University of Florida. So while Florida players went to the movies (*The Last Boy Scout*) on Tuesday, Coach Lou Holtz made his Notre Dame team watch *Wake Up the Echoes*, an inspirational film about the school's fabled football history."—*The New York Times*

"Ask any Fighting football Irishman worth his shamrock today, and he'll tell you the sledgehammer is mightier than the slingshot. Sledgehammer as in Jerome Bettis, a 247-pound sophomore. Sledgehammer as in Rodney Culver, a 226-pound senior. Sledgehammer as in Tony Brooks, a 223-pound senior.... Whereas those legendary Four Horsemen of

Irish fullback Jerome Bettis led the charge in the second half, finishing with 123 rushing yards and three touchdowns in the final two periods alone to beat Florida.

the '20s did it with sleight of hand, these Three Horsemen did it with in-your-face brute force."—New Orleans *Times-Picayune*

What the Players and Coaches Said: "We didn't put a lot of pressure on Matthews, but we tightened up inside the 20, changed our coverage and came away feeling very good when they were only able to get the threes," said Holtz.

"When we heard it, we got real upset. We felt like nobody liked us and we wanted to go out and prove them wrong," said Bettis about the Cheerios joke.

"When crunch time comes, you go back to what you do best. At halftime we said we're going back to the basics, power, off tackle, et cetera. I told the team Florida's awfully good on defense, but I think we're a pretty good offensive football team, too. If they can stop us, we'll walk across the field and shake their hands. But let's give our players a chance," said Holtz.

"I think we proved we belonged," said Holtz.

The Rundown: The Irish win left them at 10–3 and rated 12th by *USA Today*/CNN and 13th by the AP.

Florida dropped to seventh in the AP and eighth in the *USA Today*/CNN polls.

When Notre Dame's team returned to campus, it found a large box that had been delivered to the football offices by General Mills. The box contained dozens of smaller boxes of Cheerios.

Scoring Summary

Notre Dame	0	7	10	22	39
Florida	10	6	0	12	28

First Quarter

Florida: Jackson 15 pass from Matthews (Czyzewski kick) (10:40)

Florida: Czyzewski 26 field goal (3:36)

Second Quarter

Florida: Czyzewski 24 field goal (10:29)

Notre Dame: Dawson 40 pass from Mirer (Hentrich kick) (8:01)

Florida: Czyzewski 36 field goal (0:20)

Third Quarter

Notre Dame: Pendergast 23 field goal (10:03)

Notre Dame: Smith 4 pass from Mirer (Pendergast kick) (2:12)

Fourth Quarter

Florida: Czyzewski 37 field goal (13:42)

Florida: Czyzewski 24 field goal (11:21)

Notre Dame: Bettis 3 run (Brooks pass from Mirer) (4:48)

Notre Dame: Bettis 49 run (Pendergast kick) (3:32)

Florida: Houston 36 pass from Matthews (pass failed) (2:28)

Notre Dame: Bettis 39 run (Pendergast kick) (2:04)

Attendance: 76,447

Statistics

Team Statistics

Category	Notre Dame	Florida
First Downs	23	29
Rushing	18	13
Passing	4	16
Penalty	1	0
Rushing Attempts	49	33
Yards Gained Rushing	324	162
Yards Lost Rushing	45	21
Net Yards Rushing	279	141
Net Yards Passing	154	370
Passes Attempted	19	58
Passes Completed	14	28
Interceptions Thrown	1	2
Total Offensive Plays	68	91
Total Net Yards	433	511
Average Gain Per Play	6.4	5.6
Fumbles: Number Lost	4–3	0–0
Penalties: Number-Yards	3–15	4–40
Punts-Yards	2–68	2–105
Average Yards Per Punt	34.0	52.5
Punt Returns-Yards	0–0	0–0
Kickoff Returns-Yards	7–188	6–90
Interception Returns-Yards	2–31	1–4
Time of Possession	29:00	31:00
Third Down Conversions	8/13	11/20
Sacks By-Yards	3	2

Notre Dame's Individual Statistics

Rushing: Bettis 16-150-3, Culver 13-93, Brooks 13-68, Failla 1-(-2), Mirer 6-(-30)

Passing: Mirer 19-14-1-154-2

Receiving: T.Smith 7-75, Dawson 2-49-1. Brown 1-11, Culver 1-6, Bettis 1-5, I.Smith 1-4-1, Pollard 1-4

Florida's Individual Statistics

Rushing: Rhett 15-63, McClendon 7-34, Matthews 7-27, McNabb 4-17

Passing: Matthews 58-28-2-370-2

Receiving: Jackson 8-148-1, Houston 3-52-1, Sullivan 4-47, Hill 3-41, Rhett 4-38, McClendon 3-19, Everett 2-18, McNabb 1-7

9 Notre Dame 28, Texas A&M 3
JANUARY 1, 1993, AT DALLAS IN THE COTTON BOWL

Irish Run Game More Than Enough to Whip Aggies in Dallas

The Run-Up: Notre Dame came in 9–1–1 and ranked fifth in both polls after an early season tie with number-six Michigan and a loss versus number 19 Stanford University. The Irish defeated three straight ranked foes to end the regular season: number nine Boston College, number 22 Penn State, and number 19 USC.

Texas A&M came in at 12–0 and rated third by *USA Today*/CNN and fourth by AP.

The Pertinent Details: Notre Dame simply dominated the football game, finishing with huge advantages in first downs (28–11), rushing yards (290–78), total yards (439–165), plays run (82–51), and time of possession (38:01–21:59).

At least the Aggies hung in on the scoreboard until Rick Mirer connected with Lake Dawson on a perfectly blocked middle screen that accounted for the first Irish points 36 seconds before halftime. Notre Dame was even more dominant in the second half, holding the football for more than 22 minutes and limiting five of A&M's six possessions to 19 yards or fewer. The Aggies' longest second-half drive lasted six plays and led to their field goal.

Notre Dame's offensive line proved so impressive that the Irish ran the ball 34 straight times down the stretch (throwing only three times after intermission), as the combination of Mirer, Reggie Brooks, Bettis, and the defense made life impossible for A&M.

The Irish wore "Moose" stickers on the fronts of their helmets, in memory of former athletics director Edward "Moose" Krause, who passed away a few weeks before the game.

The Determining Factor: Notre Dame's defense threw the Aggies for losses on four of their first six offensive plays (two by Devon McDonald, two by Brian Hamilton). That set the tone.

The Stars of the Show: Mirer won the MVP award on offense, completing eight of 16 passes for 119 yards and netting 55 yards rushing, but one also could make a case for Brooks (115 rushing yards), Bettis (75 rushing yards and a 26-yard touchdown reception), and McDonald (he won the defensive MVP honor after making 10 tackles, four for losses, one sack).

What the Headlines Said: "Texas A&M officially withdrew from the national championship race less than a minute into the Cotton Bowl's fourth quarter. The fourth-ranked Aggies kicked a field goal just to avoid a shutout by number five Notre Dame.… The Aggies' bid for a national championship had faded after entering the game as one of only three remaining unbeaten, untied teams. A&M failed to answer skeptics' claims that its undefeated record was a result of playing just one ranked opponent before meeting the Irish.… It was A&M's worst loss in (R.C.) Slocum's

This Jerome Bettis touchdown run was one of two on the day for the Irish fullback (he also scored a third time on a touchdown pass) on his way to a 75-yard rushing afternoon.

four-year tenure and the largest margin of defeat for the school in a bowl game."—*Dallas Morning News*

"For the second straight January 1, Notre Dame quieted the critics who felt there should be more deserving teams in its place. And for the second straight year, the Texas A&M Aggies came away from their New Year's Day bowl with cotton mouth."—*Blue and Gold Illustrated*.

What the Players and Coaches Said: "We're not accustomed to being beaten like that. You at least like to see some points on the board," said Slocum.

"Rick is the most underrated quarterback in America. He was almost perfect and this just may be the best game we've played since I've been coach at Notre Dame. In the last seven games, this may be the best team I've been around. I think today we could

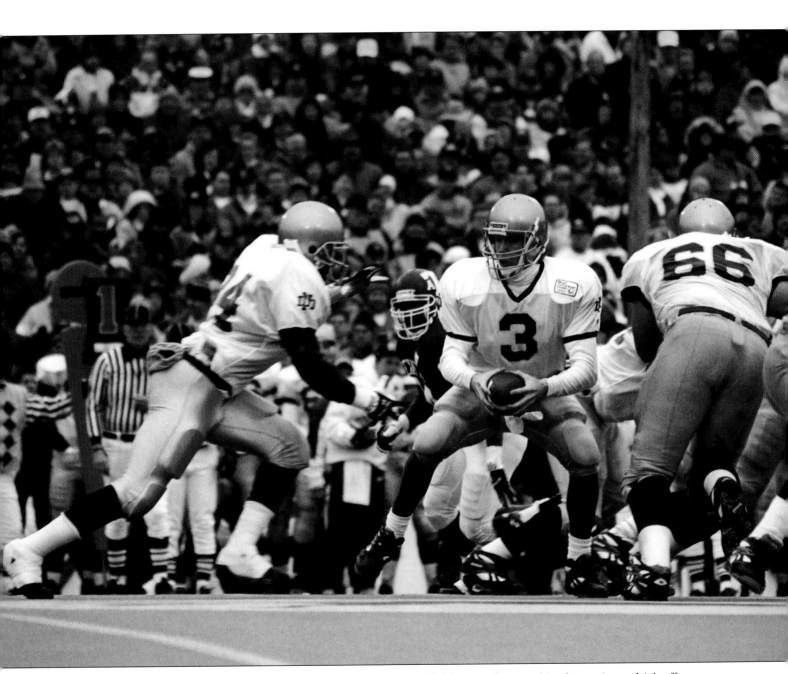

Fullback Ray Zellars receives a handoff from quarterback Rick Mirer, as they combined to assist an Irish offense that piled up 439 yards.

have beaten any team in the country," said Irish coach Lou Holtz.

"We couldn't run inside, we couldn't run outside, we couldn't run anywhere. It wouldn't have made a whole lot of difference if we had Greg [Hill, suspended A&M back]," said Slocum.

"I've been on some good teams in my years at Notre Dame, but this team over the last seven games is the best. It's too bad we started too late," said Mirer.

"You saw our philosophy work to perfection. It was the other team doing it," said Slocum.

The Rundown: The Notre Dame win left the Irish at 10–1–1, good for the number-four slot in both final polls.

Texas A&M's first loss of the year left the Aggies at 11–1 and rated sixth by *USA Today*/CNN and seventh by AP.

Scoring Summary

Notre Dame	0	7	14	7	**28**
Texas A&M	0	0	0	3	**3**

Second Quarter
Notre Dame: Dawson 40 pass from Mirer (Hentrich kick) (0:36)

Third Quarter
Notre Dame: Bettis 26 pass from Mirer (Hentrich kick) (7:17)
Notre Dame: Bettis 1 run (Hentrich kick) (0:33)

Fourth Quarter
Texas A&M: Venetoulias 41 field goal (14:27)
Notre Dame: Bettis 4 run (Hentrich kick) (5:03)
Attendance: 71,615

Statistics

Team Statistics

Category	Notre Dame	Texas A&M
First Downs	28	11
Rushing	20	8
Passing	6	2
Penalty	2	1
Rushing Attempts	64	33
Yards Gained Rushing	308	122
Yards Lost Rushing	18	44
Net Yards Rushing	290	78
Net Yards Passing	149	87
Passes Attempted	18	18
Passes Completed	9	7
Interceptions Thrown	0	0
Total Offensive Plays	82	51
Total Net Yards	439	165
Average Gain Per Play	5.4	3.2
Fumbles: Number Lost	3–3	2–2
Penalties: Number–Yards	3–30	7–42
Punts–Yards	4–152	6–243
Average Yards Per Punt	38.0	40.5
Punt Returns–Yards	1–9	2–8
Kickoff Returns–Yards	1–13	5–98
Interception Returns–Yards	0–0	0–0
Third Down Conversions	12–17	3–12

Notre Dame's Individual Statistics
Rushing: Brooks 22–115, Bettis 20–75–2, Mirer 13–55, Becton 5–26, Burris 2–8, Davis 1–8, Zellars 1–3
Passing: Mirer 16–8–0–119–2, Failla 1–1–0–30–0, Bettis 1–0–0–0–0
Receiving: Smith 3–38, Dawson 2–46–1, Miller 1–30, Bettis 1–26–1, Brooks 1–5, Griggs 1–4

Texas A&M's Individual Statistics
Rushing: Thomas 20–50, Mitchell 1–12, Pullig 9–11, Carter 3–5
Passing: Pullig 18–7–0–87–0
Receiving: Harrison 3–59, Schorp 2–14, Mitchell 1–12, Groce 1–2

10 Notre Dame 24, Texas A&M 21
JANUARY 1, 1994, AT DALLAS IN THE COTTON BOWL

Late Field Goal in Cotton Bowl Gives Irish Shot at Number One

The Run-Up: Notre Dame came in 10–1, following a loss to Boston College that ended the regular season. The Irish stood at fourth in both polls.

Texas A&M came in 10–1 and rated number six by the *USA Today*/CNN poll and seventh by AP. The Aggies' lone loss came the second week of the season versus Oklahoma.

The Pertinent Details: Notre Dame battled back from 14–7 and 21–14 deficits after a sluggish first half in which the Irish did little right after taking the opening kickoff, producing a 91-yard drive, and running 13 plays that took up one second short of seven minutes on the clock.

The Irish answered with touchdowns on their first two possessions after the break. With Lee Becton rushing for 32 of the 51 yards, Notre Dame tied it on a two-yard Ray Zellars run. A&M drove 80 yards to make it 21–14, and the Irish responded again with a 65-yard touchdown march that featured 31 more yards from Becton.

Pete Bercich's interception at his own 44 came at 8:42 of the final period. After Michael Miller's 38-yard punt return four minutes later arranged for Kevin Pendergast's lead-grabbing field goal, A&M fumbled the ball away to Bobby Taylor on its first play from scrimmage. After the Irish had to punt with a little more than a minute left, A&M tried a fourth-down,

hook-and-ladder play but fumbled that one away to Renaldo Wynn.

The Determining Factors: Pendergast, who came to the football roster from the Notre Dame soccer team, booted a 31-yard field goal with 2:22 left to break a 21–21 tie and give the victory to the Irish.

The Stars of the Show: Becton earned offensive MVP honors from the media after his game-high 138 rushing yards on 26 carries.

The defensive version went to A&M's Antonio Shorter, who had eight tackles and three sacks.

What the Headlines Said: "Making plays makes the difference. Coming up with two fumbles and an interception in the final nine minutes of the football game stated Notre Dame's case for a national championship. The much-maligned Irish defense responded at crunch time during Notre Dame's 24–21 Cotton Bowl victory over Texas A&M Saturday night."—*South Bend Tribune*

"Notre Dame's Michael Miller fielded two punts Saturday. He fumbled the first one, but he recovered. Did he ever recover. The second time, his return turned the game around. Miller, a junior from Missouri City, Texas, ran back a punt 38 yards to the Texas A&M 22-yard line with 3:55 left in the Mobil Cotton Bowl

Veteran Irish tailback Lee Becton runs for some of his game-high 138 ground yards as Notre Dame defeated Texas A&M in the Cotton Bowl.

Classic. The play set up the deciding points, a 31-yard field goal by Kevin Pendergast with 2:17 remaining in Notre Dame's 24–21 victory against A&M."–*Dallas Morning News*

"Most coaches use the locker-room blackboard at halftime to make adjustments in their offenses or defense. Notre Dame's Lou Holtz used his Saturday in the Cotton Bowl to make one in his team's attitude.

With the Irish trailing by seven points, Holtz told the players who were ready to accept the challenge posed by a motivated Texas A&M team to write their names on the board. 'All I need is 22,' Holtz said. He got all 92 players on the roster, and Notre Dame needed all the extra effort they could muster to win...."–*Los Angeles Times*

Irish kicker Kevin Pendergast, shown here kicking off, made the difference with his 31-yard field goal with 2:22 left.

What the Players and Coaches Said: "I'm not at all happy about just coming in here and playing them close. We had plays to make and we didn't make them," said A&M coach Slocum.

"After that first drive I did not think we played a good first half. I challenged the players more at half-time. I challenged them to go back to Notre Dame football," said Holtz

"A lot of people doubted our ability to bounce back from the Boston College game. Guess what, we did," said Irish safety Jeff Burris.

"The main thing is we won the game. We didn't have many missed assignments in the second half," said Becton.

"If there are no undefeated teams, and everybody uses the head-to-head as the first tiebreaker, we beat the only other team (Florida State) up for the national championship that has a loss," said Holtz.

"If we're not able to win the title, I think winning this game was gratifying enough. It was the perfect scenario after Boston College with the defense coming through to bail us out and Pete Bercich having an interception," said Irish tackle Aaron Taylor.

The Rundown: The Irish victory pushed Notre Dame to second in both final polls, behind 12–1 Florida State, the team the Irish beat in the 10th week of the regular season.

Texas A&M dropped to eighth in both polls.

Scoring Summary

Notre Dame	7	0	14	3	24
Texas A&M	7	7	7	0	21

First Quarter

Notre Dame: McDougal 19 run (Pendergast kick) (8:01)

Texas A&M: Hill 8 run (Venetoulias kick) (3:56)

Second Quarter

Texas A&M: Smith 15 pass from Pullig (Venetoulias kick) (2:56)

Third Quarter

Notre Dame: Zellars 2 run (Pendergast kick) (10:21)

Texas A&M: Thomas 1 run (Venetoulias kick) (6:50)

Notre Dame: Edwards 2 run (Pendergast kick) (3:48)

Fourth Quarter

Notre Dame: Pendergast 31 field goal (2:22)

Attendance: 69,855

Statistics

Team Statistics

Category	Notre Dame	Texas A&M
First Downs	19	20
Rushing	13	11
Passing	5	9
Penalty	1	0
Rushing Attempts	51	37
Yards Gained Rushing	236	147
Yards Lost Rushing	30	44
Net Yards Rushing	206	103
Net Yards Passing	105	238
Passes Attempted	15	31
Passes Completed	7	17
Interceptions Thrown	0	1
Total Offensive Plays	66	68
Total Net Yards	311	341
Average Gain Per Play	4.7	5.0
Fumbles: Number Lost	1-0	4-2
Penalties: Number-Yards	5-34	3-15
Punts-Yards	7-266	4-149
Average Yards Per Punt	38.0	37.3
Punt Returns-Yards	2-35	0-0
Kickoff Returns-Yards	3-59	5-117
Interception Returns-Yards	1-1	0-0
Third Down Conversions	5-13	6-14

Notre Dame's Individual Statistics

Rushing: Becton 26-138, McDougal 9-13-1, Zellars 9-25-1, Edwards 3-6-1, Miller 2-20, Burris 1-4, Kinder 1-0

Passing: McDougal 15-7-0-105-0

Receiving: Dawson 2-41, Mayes 2-27, Becton 1-3, McBride 1-16, Zellars 1-18

Texas A&M's Individual Statistics

Rushing: Hill 16-38-1, Groce 1-2, McElroy 4-45, Thomas 9-33-1, Pullig 7-(-15)

Passing: Pullig 31-17-1-238-1

Receiving: Groce 4-45, Shrop 3-53, Harrison 3-52, Mitchell 2-29, Smith 2-24-1, McElroy 1-7, Hill 1-7, Thomas 1-21

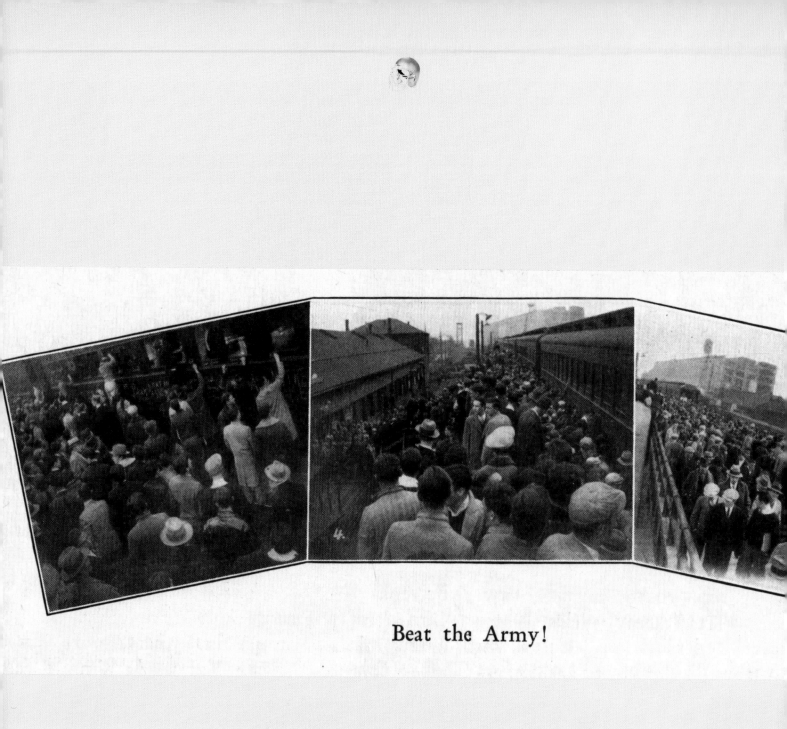

Beat the Army!

Four "Games of the Century" of Their Eras

These days, so-called "games of the century" are a dime a dozen. In fact, the Bowl Championship Series arguably tries to produce at least one each year in its first week of January slot, not to mention any regular-season clashes that merit that sort of designation. Several of Notre Dame's bowl games (the '73 Sugar Bowl versus the University of Alabama comes to mind) easily could have been shifted to this category.

But four regular-season games in particular all had something in common—they all were played in November (the second, ninth, 19th, and 13th of the month), so there was little question about the merits of these teams.

Notre Dame and Ohio State University, two of the glamorous names in college football, had never met until the Irish and Buckeyes did battle in 1935. The Notre Dame–Army rivalry dominated the 1940s, and the '46 meeting may still rank as the most talked-about scoreless tie in college history.

The '66 Irish-Michigan State University clash in East Lansing, Michigan, basically determined by itself the national champion, and it represented one of the more amazing collections of talented players ever assembled.

Then the 1993 visit by Florida State University to Notre Dame Stadium without question marked the most-hyped event to be played on the South Bend campus. Never had two unbeaten teams faced off so late in the season with so much at stake in the Irish home facility. Several dozen media members received game tickets in the top rows of seats in the stands after the press box sections were full.

The annual Bowl Championship Series title matchup between the top two teams in the final regular-season poll means the potential for these sorts of games is far greater than it used to be.

But this quartet of Saturdays—two Notre Dame victories and a pair of ties—remains unmatched.

1 Notre Dame 18 • Ohio State 13
NOVEMBER 2, 1935, AT COLUMBUS

Underdog Irish Knock Off "Unbeatable" Buckeyes Team

The Run-Up: In Elmer Layden's second season as head coach, Notre Dame came in at 5–0, having outscored its opponents by a combined 92–16.

Ohio State came in at 4–0, having outscored its foes 160–26 to that point, with a 10-game overall win streak.

The Pertinent Details: In the first-ever matchup between the Irish and Buckeyes, Notre Dame defeated top-ranked Ohio State 18–13 in Ohio Stadium in the contest dubbed the "Game of the Century" and voted the most thrilling game of the first half of the 20th century. It also qualified as one of the all-time great Notre Dame comebacks, thanks to three Irish final-period touchdowns.

The powerful Buckeyes still led 13–0 heading into the final period. An Andy Pilney punt return 53 yards to the Ohio State 13 helped set up Notre Dame's first touchdown. But after the Irish fumbled the ball away at the Buckeyes' goal line, it appeared Ohio State would hold on.

After regaining the ball at their own 20 with three minutes left, Notre Dame needed only four plays to reach the end zone. A second missed point after

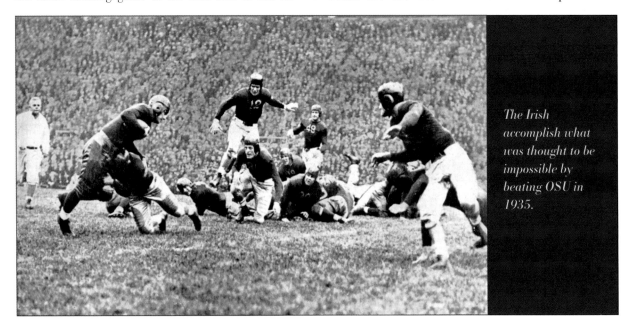

The Irish accomplish what was thought to be impossible by beating OSU in 1935.

William "Bill" Shakespeare threw the pass that scored the final points for the Irish in the Notre Dame-Ohio State game.

touchdown left the score at 13–12 for Ohio State. After Dick Beltz fumbled the ball away for the Buckeyes, Notre Dame had one more chance from its own 45. Pilney scrambled to the Ohio State 19 but suffered a knee injury on the play and was carried from the field. In came Bill Shakespeare with 50 seconds on the clock, and on his second play he found Wayne Millner in the end zone for the game-winning points. Notre Dame's defense limited the potent Buckeyes to two net second-half yards.

The Determining Factor: Millner grabbed the winning throw in the final minute.

The Stars of the Show: Shakespeare needed two plays (his first pass was nearly intercepted by Beltz) off the bench to become an Irish legend. And, until he was hurt, Pilney did it all for the Irish, setting up the initial touchdown with a punt return, throwing for the second, forcing a fumble, and running to set up the third.

What the Headlines Said: "Then, the incredible happened and so fast and furiously, as the lion-hearted blue-shirted players from South Bend became so many swirling, insensate fire-eaters, as to leave the vast assemblage stunned."—*The New York Times*

"Some sort of magic must have entered the Notre Dame locker room between the halves and something surely went out of the Ohio State dressing room at the same time because when the two teams met in the second half Notre Dame had found itself and Ohio State was floundering."—Notre Dame *Scholastic*

"I had never seen a Notre Dame offense so completely stopped. When the Irish passed, the ball was intercepted and turned into a touchdown. It was difficult to get a running play started against the

Scoring Summary

Notre Dame	0	0	0	18	18
Ohio State	7	6	0	0	13

First Quarter
Ohio State: Boucher 70 run with lateral after interception (Beltz kick)

Second Quarter
Ohio State: Williams 3 run (kick failed)

Fourth Quarter
Notre Dame: Miller 2 run (kick failed)
Notre Dame: Layden 15 pass from Pilney (kick failed)
Notre Dame: Millner 19 pass from Shakespeare (kick failed)
Attendance: 81,018

hard-charging Ohio State line. It was even hard to get a punt away."—author Francis Wallace

What the Players and Coaches Said: "I heard the crowd and the trainer says to me, 'Andy, it's over. We won.' That's the last thing I remember. Then, I went out. There were a lot of heroes. A lot of our players found something special that day," said Pilney.

"I've thought a lot about the pass. But I wake up nights dreaming about the one before it—the one the Ohio State guy had in his hands and dropped. If he'd held it, Wayne (Millner) and I both would have been bums," said Shakespeare.

The Rundown: Notre Dame lost the next Saturday at home against Northwestern University, tied Army at Yankee Stadium, then defeated the University of Southern California to finish 7–1–1.

Ohio State won its last three games, including shutout wins over the University of Illinois and the University of Michigan, to end up 7–1.

Notre Dame 0 • Army 0
NOVEMBER 9, 1946, AT YANKEE STADIUM

Lujack Tackles Blanchard to Preserve Top Teams' Tie

The Run-Up: Notre Dame came in 5–0, outscoring its opponents 177–18 to that point in the season. The Irish were third in the first poll of the season and rated second by the AP coming into the game.

Behind eventual Heisman Trophy winner Glenn Davis, Army came in at 7–0, with a 25-game overall win streak and consecutive national titles.

The Pertinent Details: Second-ranked Notre Dame and top-rated Army finished in a 0–0 tie in Yankee Stadium, as John Lujack made a saving tackle on a Doc Blanchard run late in the game. That was

drastically different than the two previous seasons, when Army had vanquished the Irish 59–0 and 48–0 (with Irish coach Frank Leahy serving during World War II).

The game had been sold out since June, and tickets were being scalped for $200 (versus the $4.80 face value). Notre Dame students created their own organization: SPATNC—the Society for the Prevention of Army's Third National Championship.

The statistics were essentially a wash. Neither team came close to scoring on many occasions. Notre Dame once reached the Army 3-yard line in the second

Notre Dame coach Frank Leahy and injured members of his grid squad in a practice session November 8, 1946. From left to right: George Strohmeyer, center; Johnny Lujack, quarterback; Leahy; Bob McBride, guard; Ziggy Czarobski, tackle; Floyd Simmons, back; and Terry Brennan, back.

Bill Gompers (arrow) on the way through center to Army's 5-yard line.

Scoring Summary

Notre Dame	0	0	0	0	0
Army	0	0	0	0	0

Attendance: 74,121

Statistics

Team Statistics

Category	Notre Dame	Army
First Downs	10	9
Net Yards Rushing	173	138
Net Yards Passing	52	52
Passes Attempted	17	16
Passes Completed	5	4
Interceptions Thrown	4	2
Fumbles: Number-Lost	5-3	3-2
Penalties: Number-Yards	1-5	2-30
Punts	8	7
Average Yards Per Punt	40	40

period, but the Irish gave up the ball on downs. The Cadets got to the Irish 14 after a Notre Dame fumble but also lost it on downs. When Blanchard headed to the left sideline from his own 37 later in the game, Lujack cut him down on the Notre Dame 37. That threat ended when Terry Brennan intercepted an Army pass inside the 10.

The Irish held Davis to 24 yards on 18 carries and Blanchard to 59 yards on 19 attempts. Arnold Tucker intercepted three passes for the Cadets and also had a 30-yard gain on a fake pass play.

The Determining Factor: Lujack, who played every down both ways, lassoed Blanchard. He also made another saving tackle on Tucker on the last play of the first half.

The Star of the Show: Lujack was the star in a game in which defense was king.

What the Headlines Said: "The Heisman Trophy winner of 1945 was tackled by the Heisman Trophy winner of 1947, and that was the ballgame. There was no winner."—*Football News*

What the Players and Coaches Said: "I suppose I should be elated over the tie. After all, we didn't lose. But I'm not," said Leahy.

"They said Blanchard couldn't be stopped one on one in the open field. I really can't understand all the fuss. I simply pinned him against the sideline and dropped him with a routine tackle," said Lujack.

"There is no jubilation in this dressing room. It was a vigorously fought, terrific defensive game. Both teams played beautifully on the defense and that affected both teams' attacks," said Army coach Red Blaik.

The Rundown: After the tie with Army, the Irish won their final three games against Northwestern, Tulane University, and number-16 USC to finish 8–0–1 and number one in the final poll. Notre Dame moved from number two to number one in the final week by virtue of its 26–6 win over USC, coupled with Army's 21–18 win over a Navy team that finished 1–8.

Army finished 9–0–1, defeating Pennsylvania and Navy in its final two outings, good for number two in the last AP poll.

3 Notre Dame 10 • Michigan State 10
NOVEMBER 19, 1966, AT EAST LANSING

Top Two Unbeaten Teams Play to Most Talked-About 10–10 Tie Ever

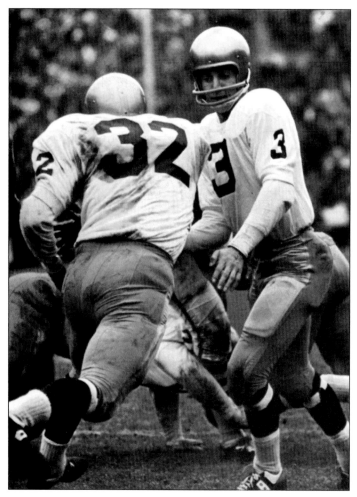

Irish quarterback Coley O'Brien (No. 3) hands off the ball to Larry Conhar (No. 32) in the 1966 game against the Spartans.

The Run-Up: Notre Dame came in with a record of 8–0 and ranked first in both polls. The Irish jumped past Michigan State University in the polls in early October after a 32–0 Irish win over the University of North Carolina, coupled with an 11–8 Michigan State win over an Ohio State University team that would finish 4–5. The Irish defense had shut out five of its last six foes coming into the game.

Michigan State came in at 9–0 and ranked second in both polls, having already won a second straight unbeaten Big Ten title, and with a 19-game regular-season win streak.

The game marked the 10th time in the history of the Associated Press poll that the number-one and number-two teams had faced each other since the poll began in 1936. The game originally was slated to be televised live only regionally by *ABC Sports*, but fans' outcry prompted ABC to show it live in additional areas and on tape delay to still others.

The Pertinent Details: At the time this game was played, it may well have been the most hyped regular-season contest in college football history. It also may have been as brutal and hard-hitting a defensive game as anyone might ever have anticipated.

The Irish lost both center George Goeddeke and quarterback Terry Hanratty (to a separated shoulder on a big hit from Bubba Smith) during the game itself, and All-America running back Nick Eddy never played

John Pergrine attacks Michigan State quarterback Jimmy Raye, whose pass attempt sails toward the ground.

at all after reinjuring a shoulder while getting off the train in East Lansing, Michigan, the day before the game (the Irish football team never again traveled by train to a game). *Sports Illustrated* ran a photo of Irish linebacker Jim Lynch completely upside down after intercepting a pass.

The game received so much attention—maybe in part due to the end result—that it became the subject of an entire book, *The Game of the Century: The Biggest Game of Them All*, by Notre Dame graduate Mike Celizic.

On the field played more than two dozen All-Americans, notably Notre Dame's Alan Page and Michigan State's Bubba Smith and George Webster.

Michigan State grabbed a 10–0 lead in the contest, and Notre Dame came back to tie it. Sophomore Coley O'Brien came off the bench to replace Hanratty, and O'Brien connected with Bob Gladieux for a 34-yard touchdown pass, then directed a 70-yard drive that led to Joe Azzaro's tying field goal (on first play of the final period).

Tom Schoen's late interception set up Notre Dame at the Michigan State 18, but Azzaro's eventual 41-yard kick attempt at the 4:39 mark missed. When the Irish got the ball back at their own 30 with 1:24 left, they ran out the clock.

The Determining Factor: Notre Dame white-washed USC the next Saturday, 51–0, thus ensuring that the Irish would finish at number one.

The Star of the Show: The game's big hero was not that easy to determine. The *Detroit Free Press* thought it might be O'Brien: "It was magnificent the way this little Coley O'Brien immediately rallied the Irish for their touchdown, because, simply, ask yourself this question—who is Coley O'Brien? He looks like a tumbleweed being blown across the flat prairie lands, no bigger than the quarterback at North Farmington High. And certainly, no cover boy. The people at *Time* probably never heard of him. But he fused the spark in his team and before you could utter the magic words, 'We're number one,' the Irish were on the scoreboard and back in the game."

What the Headlines Said: "Bless me, Father for I have sinned...I rooted for Michigan State. But now I would like to repent. The winner, and it hurts to say it, was Notre Dame. On Monday morning the vote will go out to the Associated Press in New York: 1—Notre Dame, 2—Michigan State, etc., etc. And let's not hear any of that tripe from Birmingham that Alabama is the best team in the nation. Bear Bryant's boys snuck in the back door when the AP held that ridiculous poll last January. Make no mistake about it—the two best

Scoring Summary

Michigan State	0	10	0	0	10
Notre Dame	0	7	0	3	10

Second Quarter
Michigan State: Cavender 4 run (Kenney kick)
Michigan State: Kenney 47 field goal
Notre Dame: Gladieux 34 pass from O'Brien (Azzaro kick) (10:30)

Fourth Quarter
Notre Dame: Azzaro 28 field goal
Attendance: 80,011

teams in the country were on display here Saturday and our grudging admiration goes to the Fighting Irish."—Joe Falls in the *Detroit Free Press*

"It would have been far better to see the Irish making an all-out effort to break the tie. But there is a time to gamble, and there isn't a time to gamble. This wasn't the time."— *Detroit Free Press*

"Coach Ara Parseghian of top-ranked Notre Dame, lashing at the widespread criticism for not making what he called 'a stupid gamble' against number two Michigan State, says his Fighting Irish still rate as the number-one college football team in his book."—*South Bend Tribune*

"It was like an unremembered song that spins round and round your brain and then it's gone. It will never be back and you will never know what it was. Michigan State wanted an answer today. Instead it got a tie and a great group of seniors will leave school never knowing if they could beat Notre Dame." —*Chicago Tribune*

Statistics

Team Statistics

Category	Notre Dame	Michigan State
First Downs	16	13
Rushing	5	7
Passing	5	6
Penalty	0	0
Rushing Attempts	38	46
Yards Gained Rushing	122	165
Yards Lost Rushing	31	26
Net Yards Rushing	91	142
Net Yards Passing	128	142
Passes Attempted	24	20
Passes Completed	8	7
Interceptions Thrown	1	1
Total Offensive Plays	62	66
Total Net Yards	219	284
Average Gain Per Play	3.5	4.3
Fumbles: Number Lost	3-1	2-1
Penalties: Number-Yards	1-5	5-32
Punts-Yards	8-336	8-304
Average Yards Per Punt	42	38
Punt Returns-Yards	2-5	3-(-8)
Kickoff Returns-Yards	3-64	3-63
Interception Returns-Yards	-38	1-0

Notre Dame's Individual Statistics

Rushing: Hanratty 2-12, Bleier 13-53, Conjar 11-32, Gladieux 1-1, O'Brien 9-(-3), Haley 2-(-4)

Passing: Hanratty 4-1-0-26-0, Hardy 1-0-0-0-0, O'Brien 19-7-1-102-1

Receiving: Gladieux 3-71-1, Bleier 3-16, Conjar 1-18, Haley 1-23

Michigan State's Individual Statistics

Rushing: Raye 21-75, Lee 6-17, Jones 10-13, Cavender 7-36-1, Apisa 2-1

Passing: Raye 20-7-3-142-0

Receiving: Washingon 5-123, Lee 1-11, Brenner 1-8

What the Players and Coaches Said: "Time will prove everything that has happened here today," said Parseghian.

"It was a titanic game. Almost like a Super Bowl. Everyone wanted a conclusion. Neither Duffy Daugherty nor I wanted a tie. But that's the way it ended," said Parseghian.

"Ara did the smart thing and the right thing—because we still had another game to play," said O'Brien.

"We told them they were sissies not to go for it," said Smith.

The Rundown: The tie ended the season for Michigan State, leaving the Spartans at 9-0-1 and second in the polls. Duffy Daugherty's team was ineligible for the Rose Bowl after playing in Pasadena the previous season.

The Irish had one game remaining and made the most of it by beating number 10 USC 51-0, leaving the Irish at number one in both final polls.

4 Notre Dame 31 • Florida State 24
NOVEMBER 13, 1993, AT NOTRE DAME STADIUM

Notre Dame Tops Florida State in South Bend Battle of 16-Game Streaks

An Irish defender makes a shoestring tackle on Florida State's Tamarick Vanover after one of Vanover's four receptions.

The Run-Up: Notre Dame came in ranked second in the country in both polls, with a perfect 9–0 record and a 16-game overall win streak.

Florida State University also came in 9–0 and with a 16-game win streak. The Seminoles had been ranked first in both polls all season long.

The Pertinent Details: Never had a game in Notre Dame Stadium received such pregame hype, thanks in part to the fact that it marked only the third time in the month of November that a number-one ranked opponent had come to South Bend (Northwestern in '36 and Michigan State in '65).

Notre Dame issued a record number of media credentials, and Irish coach Lou Holtz invited the burgeoning media contingent to his house for a barbeque dinner on the Thursday night before the game. The game marked the first in which the ESPN *College Gameday* show left Bristol, Connecticut, and traveled to a game site. Regis Philbin, Spike Lee, Roger Clemens—they all showed up. Fans filled the Joyce Center so quickly Friday night for the pep rally that the building was full two hours before the rally began.

The Irish sent a message early that they would win this game on the ground. Florida State had been allowing only 97 ground yards per game. By the end of the first period, Notre Dame already had 99. By the third period, the Irish had built a 24–7 advantage on their way to piling up 239 rushing yards.

Notre Dame drove 80 yards to make it 31–17 on the second of Burris's touchdown runs with 6:53 remaining, but the Seminoles weren't finished. Irish safety Brian Magee saw a potential fourth-down interception slide into the hands of Kez McCorvey to make it 31–24 at the 2:26 mark. Ward's 50th and final pass attempt from the Irish 14 went into Shawn Wooden's hands (he knocked it down) near the goal line as the clock ticked down to 0:00. The Seminole defense had given up only two rushing touchdowns all season long—but Notre Dame managed four.

The Determining Factor: Wooden ended Florida State's final threat by knocking Ward's final attempt to the ground as the game ended.

The Stars of the Show: There were plenty of outstanding players for the Irish: defensive tackle Jim Flanigan (he made the cover of *Sports Illustrated*), safety John Covington (he intercepted a Charlie Ward pass after 159 Ward throws without a mistake and made the cover of *The Sporting News*), safety Jeff Burris (he scored two touchdowns on his three rushing carries), tailback Lee Becton (he ran for 122 yards), and cornerback Wooden (he thwarted Ward's last-gasp pass attempt to end the game).

What the Headlines Said: "It had been more than a year since the road-running front-runners had had to play catch-up, and they were playing on unfamiliar turf—both their predicament and against a ground game as rapacious as Notre Dame's."—*TIME* magazine

"The Notre Dame mystique remains abstract. But it's easier to find than the Notre Dame mistake. The Irish put a sledgehammer in one hand and a football in the other and dropped neither in Saturday's flam-

Scoring Summary					
Florida State	7	0	7	10	24
Notre Dame	7	14	3	7	31

First Quarter
Florida State: Knox 12 pass from Ward (Bentley kick) (7:09)
Notre Dame: Jarrell 32 run (Pendergast kick) (4:30)

Second Quarter
Notre Dame: Becton 26 run (Pendergast kick) (10:42)
Notre Dame: Burris 6 run (Pendergast kick) (7:48)

Third Quarter
Notre Dame: Pendergast 47 field goal (9:41)
Florida State: Dunn 6 pass from Ward (4:45)

Fourth Quarter
Florida State: Bentley 24 field goal (10:40)
Notre Dame: Burris 11 run (Pendergast kick) (6:53)
Florida State: McCorvey 20 pass from Ward (Bentley kick) (2:26)

Attendance: 59,075

boyant 31–24 victory over Florida State."—*Orange County Register*

"It cannot end like that, without a breath, with time expired and a country mesmerized and the Game of Any Millennium drawing within one completed pass of actual confirmation. No, they must do it again. Too much suspense remains, too many grudges, too much limbo about who truly is better."—*Chicago Sun-Times*

What the Players and Coaches Said: "They have a spirit here that helps them. They played like they were possessed. They won the game today on execution," said Florida State coach Bobby Bowden.

Irish defensive tackle Jim Flanigan (No. 44) set the tone for a Notre Dame defense that limited top-rated Florida State to 96 net rushing yards.

"This is one game that lived up to the hype. I think this is the best football team we've beaten since I've been in coaching," said Holtz

"They didn't know what Notre Dame was about, and after being here I hope they do," said Burris, referring to Ward's pregame reference to Notre Dame's "Rock Knuteny."

"To me the mystique of Notre Dame is faith in belief. The biggest problem with this team, I thought, was getting them to believe," said Holtz.

"We had 30 minutes to do it, and I said if Notre Dame scored 21 points in a half, we could, too. That kind of thing. The same thing Knute would have told them," said Bowden on his halftime approach.

The Rundown: The Irish win moved them to number one for a week, but they lost 41–39 to number 16 Boston College the next Saturday. A Cotton Bowl win over Texas A&M left Notre Dame 11–1 and at number two on the AP list behind the same Florida State team they beat on November 13.

Florida State's loss dropped the Seminoles only to number two in the AP poll, but the Irish loss a week later, coupled with a 62–3 Florida State win over North Carolina State University, put the 'Noles back at number one. Florida State then defeated seventh-ranked Florida to finish the regular season and second-ranked University of Nebraska (18–16) in the Orange Bowl to claim the national title.

Holtz was left to wonder why the late-season, head-to-head argument that carried the day in 1989 didn't count in '93.

Statistics

Team Statistics

Category	Notre Dame	Florida State
First Downs	20	26
Rushing	12	6
Passing	7	17
Penalty	1	3
Rushing Attempts	49	27
Yards Gained Rushing	258	143
Yards Lost Rushing	19	47
Net Yards Rushing	239	96
Net Yards Passing	108	307
Passes Attempted	18	53
Passes Completed	9	32
Interceptions Thrown	0	1
Total Offensive Plays	67	80
Total Net Yards	347	403
Average Gain Per Play	5.2	5.0
Fumbles: Number Lost	0-0	1-1
Penalties: Number-Yards	4-38	7-70
Punts-Yards	7-238	6-221
Average Yards Per Punt	34.0	36.8
Punt Returns-Yards	1-1	2-19
Kickoff Returns-Yards	1-33	3-64
Interception Returns-Yards	1-7	0-0
Time of Possession	30:20	29:40
Third Down Conversions	4-13	5-14
Fourth Down Conversions	0-1	1-1
Sacks By-Yards	2-22	1-9

Notre Dame's Individual Statistics

Rushing: Becton 26-122-1, Zellars 11-44, Jarrell 1-32-1, Burris 3-19-2, McDougal 3-12, Failla 1-10, Kinder 1-0

Passing: McDougal 18-9-0-108-0

Receiving: Becton 2-39, Miller 2-30, Johnson 2-22, Dawson 2-20, Zellars 1-(-3)

Florida State's Individual Statistics

Rushing: Ward 11-38, Floyd 5-31, Jackson 7-18, Dunn 3-0, McCorvey 1-9

Passing: Ward 50-31-1-297-3, Jackson 2-1-0-10-0, McCorvey 1-0-0-0-0

Receiving: McCorvey 11-138-1, Jackson 5-26, Frier 4-46, Vanover 4-30, Dunn 3-18-1, Knox 2-30-1, Floyd 2-9, Ward 1-10

Oklahoma's 47-game winning streak from 1953-57 remains the longest in major-college football history—and Notre Dame holds the distinction of defeating the Sooners at both ends of the streak, including providing the end of the 47-game skein in a victory in '57 in Norman, Oklahoma.

Nine Games That Featured Unbelievable Endings

Remember that line from the Notre Dame "Victory March"? Sure you do. It goes, "What though the odds be great or small, old Notre Dame will win over all." Catchy phrasing, as it turned out—and more than a little apropos.

What it means is that Notre Dame football teams, seemingly since the dawn of time, have displayed a penchant for winning games they weren't supposed to win, often in sense-defying fashion, and just as often the very last. Either the other team was supposed to be unbeatable, or "the breaks were beating the boys" as Knute Rockne would have suggested, or it's time to "win another one for the Gipper," or time to break out the green jerseys, or an occasion to play a tape of another Rockne or Lou Holtz pep talk.

We don't even remember the final scores of most of these games. All we remember is that somebody defied the odds and came through to make a play (or two) in the most unlikely circumstances, with the clock scarily heading toward the double-zero mark, and so somehow, amazingly, Notre Dame won the game. And every time it happens again (like Jeff Samardzija's romp through the UCLA secondary in 2006), it gives us a reason to trot out all the stories from the times it happened before.

You could argue that there should be lots more of these games on this particular list—and you're probably right. But, in that regard, sometimes the Irish were their own worst enemy. Their teams were so good that there wasn't much drama involved.

Take 1966, for example. The Irish were so dominant that they finished the season averaging 32.4 points per game more than their opponents. Throw out the 10–10 tie with Michigan State University, and the margin goes to 36.0. See what we mean?

However, in great tribute to the reputation of Notre Dame's program over the years, the appearance of the Irish on the schedule generally elicited stunningly competent performances from opponents. And on more than a few occasions, that made for great drama right down to the very end.

Here are the best we can recall.

Notre Dame 7 • Oklahoma 0
NOVEMBER 16, 1957, AT NORMAN

Irish Put Sooners' 47-Game Streak in Past Tense

The Run-Up: Notre Dame came in with a 4–2 record for the season, having dropped out of the Associated Press rankings for the first time that season after consecutive losses to number 16 Navy and number four Michigan State.

The University of Oklahoma came in as an 18-point favorite and rated second in both polls (behind unbeaten Texas A&M University), with a 47-game overall win streak (and a 123-game scoring streak) dating back to its loss to Notre Dame in the 1953 season opener in Norman, Oklahoma.

The Pertinent Details: Notre Dame defeated Oklahoma 7–0 on a touchdown run by Dick Lynch with 3:50 remaining, and the win ended what is still the longest success streak in college football history. This result came only a year after the number-one ranked Sooners had whitewashed the Irish 40–0 in South Bend.

Notre Dame's defense broke up a Sooner fourth-down pass attempt from the Irish 13 on the first series of the game—and that seemed to set the tone for an afternoon in which Terry Brennan's defenders held the

Dick Lynch scores the only point for the Irish in the 1957 face-off with the previously undefeated Sooners.

home team to nine first downs, 98 rushing yards, and 145 total yards.

The Irish traversed as far as the Oklahoma 3 and later the 6 in the opening half but could not score. Then, Sooner second-half punts left the Irish to start from their own 3, 4, 7, and 15 on four different possessions.

The winning drive, which started with 12:51 on the clock, covered 80 yards and took 20 plays. With the Sooners keying on Irish back Nick Pietrosante, on fourth down from the 3, Bob Williams pitched the ball to Lynch, who took it around the right side to score with fewer than four minutes remaining.

The Determining Factor: Lynch scored.

The Stars of the Show: Pietrosante and Lynch combined to dominate the Notre Dame rushing attack. Irish line coach Bernie Witucki, formerly a coach at the University of Tulsa, received the game ball.

What the Headlines Said: "The game was over. The usually dry Okie terrain was moist with the rain of Wednesday and the tears of the 11,000 Sooner students. They stood in the stands for a long time. Most of them had never seen their heroes lose. They stamped their feet nervously, punched each other to see if it was true, and even cried a little."—Notre Dame *Scholastic*

"Russia's two Sputniks collided in midair above the 50-yard line here Saturday afternoon. The sun set in the east. Hitler was discovered alive in Washington, D.C. And almost equally as incredible, University of Oklahoma lost a football game."—*Daily Oklahoman*

"Notre Dame gained football immortality on the red clay flats of Oklahoma Saturday."—*Chicago Sun-Times*

Nick Pietrosante tackles Brewster Hobby in the 1957 Notre Dame-Oklahoma game.

Scoring Summary

Notre Dame	0	0	0	7	0
Oklahoma	0	0	0	0	0

Fourth Quarter
Notre Dame: Lynch 7 run (Stickles kick) (3:50)
Attendance: 63,170

"The so-aptly named Fighting Irish returned to their old habit of rising to astounding heights against enormous odds, putting a dull edge to Oklahoma's offense and eventually winning while looking every inch the champion."—*Daily Oklahoman*

What the Players and Coaches Said: "I will never forget the effort and the determination you showed me today," said Brennan to his team after the game.

"I was willing to settle for a scoreless tie in the third period. I felt at the start of the second half we had a good chance. But after we couldn't get going, even with our tremendous punting to their goal, I was ready to settle for a scoreless tie," said Sooner coach Bud Wilkinson.

"They were in tight, real tight, just waiting for me to give the ball to Pietrosante. Well, I just faked to him and tossed out to Lynch and it worked like a charm," said Williams.

"There were only four or five basic plays—and if you stopped them you had a chance to win. The big thing was to stop their running game," said Brennan.

"Come back next Saturday, folks. That's when the new winning streak starts," said Oklahoma public address announcer Jack Ogle.

The Rundown: A wild celebration in downtown South Bend ensued when the Irish squad arrived home that night. Notre Dame lost the next week at home to eighth-ranked Iowa, then finished by beating fifth-place USC and SMU for a final 7–3 record.

Oklahoma beat Nebraska and Oklahoma State to finish the regular season, then defeated 16th-ranked Duke in the Orange Bowl for a final 10-1 mark. The Sooners finished fourth in both the AP and UPI polls, behind unbeaten Auburn and once-beaten OSU and Michigan State.

Statistics

Team Statistics

Category	Notre Dame	Oklahoma
First Downs	17	9
Rushing	9	5
Passing	8	3
Penalty	0	1
Rushing Attempts	60	47
Yards Gained Rushing	199	134
Yards Lost Rushing	31	36
Net Yards Rushing	168	98
Net Yards Passing	79	47
Passes Attempted	20	11
Passes Completed	9	4
Interceptions Thrown	1	1
Total Offensive Plays	80	58
Total Net Yards	247	145
Average Gain Per Play	3.1	2.5
Fumbles: Number Lost	5–4	2–1
Penalties: Number-Yards	5–45	5–35
Punts	8	10
Average Yards Per Punt	38.5	36.5
Punt Returns-Yards	2–10	6–49
Kickoff Returns-Yards	1–19	2–40

Notre Dame's Individual Statistics

Rushing: Pietrosante 17-56, Lynch 17-54, Reynolds 7-29, Doyle 4-26, Just 2-17, Williams 8-1, Lima 3-3, Izo 2-10

Passing: Williams 19-8-70, Izo 1-1-9

Receiving: Colisimo 3-30, Royer 2-19, Pietrosante 1-10, Just 1-10, Wetoska 1-9, Lynch 1-1

Oklahoma's Individual Statistics

Rushing: Thomas 10-36, Boyd 4-17, Morris 6-17, Baker 7-14, Carpenter 3-5, Sandefer 8-3, Dodd 8-3, Rolle 1-3,

Passing: Watts 3-2-31, Dodd 3-2-16, Sherrod 1-0-0, Carpenter 1-0-0, Sandefer 1-0-0, Thomas 1-0-0, Hobby 1-0-0

Receiving: Pellow 2-31, Morris 1-11, Rector 1-5

Notre Dame 17 • Syracuse 15
NOVEMBER 18, 1961, AT NOTRE DAME STADIUM

Second-Time Field Goal the Charm for Perkowski

The Run-Up: Notre Dame came in at 4–3, after winning its first three games and rising as high as sixth in the AP poll, only to lose its next three games to number-one ranked Michigan State, the Ara Parseghian–coached Northwestern team, and Navy.

Syracuse University stood at 6–2, having ranked as high as fifth in the AP listings after the first Orange win of the year.

The Pertinent Details: It looked like Syracuse would wake up some of its own echoes in Notre Dame Stadium. The Orange battled back from a 14–0 Irish lead, as tight end John Mackey hauled in a 57-yard touchdown pass on fourth and one. When reserve quarterback Bob Lelli came in for the injured Dave Sarette, Lelli connected on a touchdown pass to Dick Easterly for a 15–14 advantage (Easterly had caught a two-point conversion throw after the first Syracuse score).

Meanwhile, Orange back Ernie Davis was on his way to leading both teams in rushing with his 95 yards, only a few weeks before he was awarded the Heisman Trophy.

The Irish squandered two chances to score by throwing interceptions twice in the final five minutes. The scene was bleak when the Irish took over at their own 30 with 17 seconds left. But sophomore Frank Budka scrambled for 20 yards and completed an 11-yard pass to George Sefcik. That set up Joe Perkowski

Kicker Joe Perkowski (No. 38) kicking his second attempt, a 42-yard field goal.

for a 56-yard field-goal try. Syracuse's Walt Sweeney crashed into holder Sefcik and was called (controversially) for roughing the kicker. With no time on the clock, the kick became a 42-yarder, and this time it was good.

The Determining Factor: Perkowski gained a second chance at a game-winning field goal and made the most of it.

The Star of the Show: Perkowski.

What the Headlines Said: "Notre Dame beat Syracuse 17–15 in overtime here this afternoon. The Orange won in the regulation 60 minutes, 15–14, staging one of the most heroic comebacks in the history of Notre Dame Stadium. But, the Fighting

Scoring Summary

Notre Dame	0	7	7	3	17
Syracuse	0	0	8	7	15

Second Quarter
Notre Dame: Dabiero 41 pass from Budka (Perkowski kick) (2:58)

Third Quarter
Notre Dame: Traver 25 pass from Budka (Perkowski kick)
Syracuse: Mackey 57 pass from Sarette (Easterly pass from Sarette) (8:35)

Fourth Quarter
Syracuse: Easterly 2 pass from Lelli (Ericson kick)
Notre Dame: Perkowski 42 field goal (0:00)
Attendance: 49,246

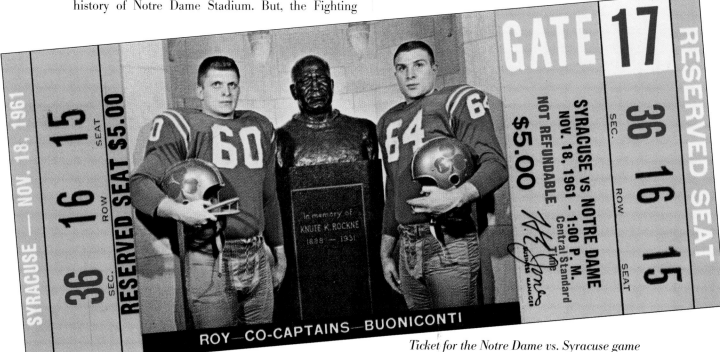

Ticket for the Notre Dame vs. Syracuse game picturing co-captains Norb Roy and Nick Buonicoti standing next to the bust of Knute Rockne.

Irish, thanks to a delayed call on the part of head linesman F.G. Skibbie, unbelievably won by booting a 42-yard field goal after the final gun had sounded."— *Syracuse Herald American*

"In an unbelievable finish to a rip-roaring game, Notre Dame beat Syracuse long after time had officially run out."—Syracuse *Post-Standard*

"'It just couldn't have happened.' That was the unbelievable comment heard over and over again in the Syracuse University locker room here late Saturday afternoon as a downcast group of Orange gridders looked back on their 17–15 loss to Notre Dame." —Syracuse *Post-Standard*

What the Players and Coaches Said: "We lost and what more can you really say? There's no use complaining. We lost," said Syracuse coach Ben Schwartzwalder.

The Rundown: Notre Dame lost its last two games of the season on the road at Iowa and Duke to end up 5–5.

Syracuse defeated Boston College the following Saturday, then knocked off Florida's University of Miami 15–14 in the Liberty Bowl to finish 8–3 and rated 14th in the last AP poll.

Statistics

Team Statistics

Category	Notre Dame	Syracuse
First Downs	14	10
Rushing	7	6
Passing	7	3
Penalty	0	1
Rushing Attempts	34	47
Yards Gained Rushing	140	194
Yards Lost Rushing	56	18
Net Yards Rushing	84	176
Net Yards Passing	199	132
Passes Attempted	27	20
Passes Completed	12	7
Interceptions Thrown	3	1
Total Offensive Plays	61	67
Total Net Yards	283	308
Average Gain Per Play	4.6	4.5
Fumbles: Number Lost	1-0	4-1
Penalties: Number-Yards	50	80
Punts-Yards	9	9
Average Yards Per Punt	38	37
Punt Returns-Yards	1-11	2-9
Kickoff Returns-Yards	2-63	3-83
Interception Returns	1-22	3-54

Notre Dame's Individual Statistics
Rushing: Budka 6-(-13), Sefcik 3-5, Dabiero 7-54, Gray 1-1, Costa 2-(-1), Lind 9-34, O'Hara 5-17, Lamonica 1-(-8)
Passing: Budka 27-12-3-199-2
Receiving: Traver 6-92-1, Kelly 2-37, Goberville 1-16, Dabiero 2-43-1, Sefcik 1-11

Syracuse's Individual Statistics
Rushing: Sarette 5-5, Davis 18-95, Easterly 7-17, Fallon 3-17, Schoonover 5-11, King 3-4, Meyers 3-10, Girardi 1-17, Lelli 2-0
Passing: Sarrette 18-6-1-131-1, Lelli 2-1-0-1-1
Receiving: Mackey 2-80-1, Bowman 1-13, Easterly 4-39-1

3 Notre Dame 12 • Michigan 10
SEPTEMBER 15, 1979, AT ANN ARBOR

Male, Crable Combine to Quash Michigan

The Run-Up: Notre Dame came into its season opener rated ninth in the AP preseason poll, following a 9–3 record and Cotton Bowl victory the previous season.

Michigan came into its season opener rated sixth by the AP.

The Pertinent Details: Notre Dame had only seven first downs and only 179 total yards, but the Irish got a school-record four field goals from Chuck Male. That ended up being enough to upset Michigan. Three of the three-pointers came after Wolverine turnovers, as the Irish shut out Michigan in the second half, with 94 yards and four first downs in those two periods.

The Determining Factor: Bob Crable blocked a potential game-winning field goal by Bryan Virgil from 42 yards out with six seconds left.

The Stars of the Show: The Irish had to thank Crable, with his 10 solo tackles and two assists, and Male.

What the Headlines Said: "For most of the afternoon, it looked as if Notre Dame were hanging on by Male's toenail."–*Sports Illustrated*

"Michigan lined up with :07 to play for a shot at the go-ahead field goal and Notre Dame linebacker Bob Crable wasn't about to take it laying down. So he talked teammate Tim Foley into it. 'I told Tim to keep him (Michigan guard Mike Trgovac) pinned down,' said Crable, 'and then I could step on both of them to get higher.' Foley did, Crable did and Bryan Virgil's kick was blocked to give the Irish a 12–10 opening-game upset victory."–*Peoria Journal-Star*

"Chuck Male's grades weren't good enough when he graduated from Mishawaka Marian High School to be accepted at Notre Dame. He averaged a perfect 4.0 here Saturday."–Fort Wayne *News-Sentinel*

A ticket for the 1979 Notre Dame-Michigan game, which marked Notre Dame's first appearance in Michigan Stadium in 36 years.

What the Players and Coaches Said: "This is the biggest thrill of my coaching career. The coaches kept their cool, the players kept their cool and not one person on the team gave up. You never really make

The 118 rushing yards by Vagas Ferguson (No. 32) helped land him on the cover of Sports Illustrated *the week after the Irish defeated sixth-ranked Michigan.*

Scoring Summary

Michigan	3	7	0	0	10
Notre Dame	3	3	6	0	12

First Quarter
Michigan: Virgil 30 field goal (7:35)
Notre Dame: Male 40 field goal (2:27)

Second Quarter
Michigan: Edwards 1 run (Virgil kick) (10:48)
Notre Dame: Male 44 field goal (4:48)

Third Quarter
Notre Dame: Male 22 field goal (8:21)
Notre Dame: Male 39 field goal (3:46)
Attendance: 105,111

many changes. You just play better," said Irish coach Dan Devine.

"When they snapped the ball, I just jumped over the center and tried to get as high as I could. I felt the ball hit right on my left hip," said Crable.

"We just wanted it more than they did," said Irish back Vagas Ferguson.

"The first one was the toughest. The rest were easy," said Male.

The Rundown: The win landed Ferguson, who had 118 rushing yards, on the cover of *Sports Illustrated* the next week.

The loss was Michigan's first nonconference defeat since 1969, when it fell to the University of Missouri, which was then coached by Devine.

Notre Dame ended up 7–4 overall and unranked; the Irish did not play in a bowl game.

Michigan went on to finish 8–4 overall, ending up third in the Big Ten after losing three straight versus Purdue, Ohio State, and then 17–15 to North Carolina in the Gator Bowl.

Statistics

Team Statistics

Category	Notre Dame	Michigan
First Downs	7	16
Rushing	5	9
Passing	2	7
Penalty	0	0
Rushing Attempts	43	45
Yards Gained Rushing	138	211
Yards Lost Rushing	24	39
Net Yards Rushing	114	172
Net Yards Passing	65	134
Passes Attempted	12	24
Passes Completed	5	12
Interceptions Thrown	2	1
Total Offensive Plays	55	69
Total Net Yards	179	306
Average Gain Per Play	3.2	4.4
Fumbles: Number Lost	3–1	2–2
Penalties: Number-Yards	3–45	4–28
Punts-Yards	7–263	7–207
Average Yards Per Punt	37.6	29.6
Punt Returns-Yards	3–1	3–44
Kickoff Returns-Yards	3–79	2–44
Interception Returns-Yards	1–14	2–0

Notre Dame's Individual Statistics

Rushing: Ferguson 35–118, Lisch 5–(-8), Sweeney 1–3, Barber 1–3, Koegel 1–(-2)

Passing: Lisch 10–5–1–65–0, Stone 1–0–0–0–0, Courey 1–0–1–0–0

Receiving: Masztak 3–30, Hunter 1–31, Ferguson 1–4

Michigan's Individual Statistics

Rushing: Edwards 22–72–1, Dickey 14–68, Reid 7–28, Wangler 1–7, Carter 1–(-3)

Passing: Marsh 18–9–1–106–0, Wangler 6–3–0–28–0

Receiving: Marsh 4–46, Edwards 3–20, Mitchell 2–30, Clayton 2–15, Carter 1–23

Notre Dame 18 • South Carolina 17
OCTOBER 27, 1979, AT NOTRE DAME STADIUM

Lisch Shows That Montana's Not the Only Irish Comeback Kid

The Run-Up: Notre Dame came in at 4–2 and ranked 14th by the AP after losing to fourth-rated USC the previous Saturday.

The University of South Carolina was 5–1, having won five straight after an opening loss at North Carolina.

The Pertinent Details: The Irish somehow led only 3–0 at the break, despite 248 total yards, mainly because South Carolina had completed only one pass. So the Gamecocks promptly exploded, stunning Notre Dame with 17 points on its first three third-period possessions.

A Ferguson scoring run finished off a 73-yard touchdown march to end the third quarter. But Male missed a 34-yard field-goal attempt, and the Gamecocks still led 17–10 when the Irish fielded a punt and took over on their own 20 with 1:36 left.

In a 54-second period, Rusty Lisch threw to Pete Holohan, to Ty Dickerson, to Ferguson, even to himself for three yards on a deflected toss, and finally to Dean Masztak to make it 17–16. His final throw was to Holohan for the win.

The Determining Factor: Holohan hauled in a two-point conversion pass from Lisch with 42 seconds remaining to complete a comeback from a 17–3 second-half deficit.

The Star of the Show: Give the game ball to Lisch, who did his best Joe Montana imitation by hitting both the tying touchdown pass and then the winning two-point throw on his way to 336 passing yards altogether.

What the Headlines Said: "On an overcast Saturday afternoon in late October, Rusty Lisch served notice that Notre Dame's sometimes overzealous football fans would have to find another scapegoat for the team's disappointing 1979 season.... The fifth-year senior had to borrow a page from the man who beat him out of his job two autumns earlier to finally prove that he was worthy of the title he carried—that of Notre Dame's starting quarterback."—Notre Dame *Scholastic*

"He (Lisch) took a team that had done its damnedest to lose, and he wouldn't let it. He took an

Scoring Summary

South Carolina	0	0	17	0	17
Notre Dame	3	0	7	8	18

First Quarter
Notre Dame: Male 40 field goal (4:01)

Third Quarter
South Carolina: McKinney 62 pass from Harper (Leopard kick) (9:45)
South Carolina: Clark 49 run (Leopard kick) (6:50)
South Carolina: Leopard 33 field goal (1:52)
Notre Dame: Ferguson 26 run (Male kick) (:17)

Fourth Quarter
Notre Dame: Masztak 14 pass from Lisch (Holohan pass from Lisch) (:42)
Attendance: 59,075

offense that was its own worst enemy, and force-fed it 80 yards into the South Carolina end zone."—Notre Dame *Scholastic*

"Attention Digger Phelps: forget those cross-country basketball recruiting junkets, trim the budget and recruit in your own backyard. There are a couple of guys on the Notre Dame football team who can handle a ball. Their ball has corners, to be sure, but they're 6'4" and rather healthy youngsters, and they seem rather dedicated to the task at hand, especially in the clutch. For the record, they are Dean Masztak, a sophomore tight end, and Pete Holohan, a junior flanker. Saturday, they caught a few footballs—two in particular—and were, for a moment, as important as the Gipper and Rockne and all those other people Notre Dame has sainted."—*Greenville News*

"For the sixth time in Coach Dan Devine's five years here, a Notre Dame football team pulled one of those one-in-a-hundred comeback victories out of the fire Saturday. The victim this time was South Carolina, a strong physical team that did everything but win. The flight home to Columbia must have seemed like 50,000 miles to the Gamecocks."—Fort Wayne *News-Sentinel*

What the Players and Coaches Said: "Rusty told Dean to hook at the goal line and we sent both of our tailbacks out to control the linebackers. That helped Dean get open," said Devine.

"Rusty called the play in the huddle, but then he gave me different instructions. He told me to hook up in the end zone and the ball would be there," said Masztak.

"I've never gone for a tie in my life and I never will. I didn't come to Notre Dame to tie," said Devine.

The Rundown: The Irish closed out 1979 at 7–4; they did not participate in a bowl game and did not qualify for the final polls.

Statistics

Team Statistics

Category	Notre Dame	South Carolina
First Downs	24	15
Rushing	7	13
Passing	17	1
Penalty	0	1
Rushing Attempts	36	62
Yards Gained Rushing	158	299
Yards Lost Rushing	11	29
Net Yards Rushing	147	270
Net Yards Passing	383	68
Passes Attempted	44	9
Passes Completed	25	2
Interceptions Thrown	1	0
Total Offensive Plays	80	71
Total Net Yards	530	338
Average Gain Per Play	6.6	4.8
Fumbles: Number Lost	1–1	2–0
Penalties: Number-Yards	5–63	2–12
Punts-Yards	7–210	10–392
Average Yards Per Punt	30.0	39.2
Punt Returns-Yards	3–(-1)	1–(-1)
Kickoff Returns-Yards	2–26	2–35
Interception Returns-Yards	0–0	1–0
Fumble Returns-Yards	0	1
Time of Possession	28:28	31:32
Third Down Conversions	5–15	6–20

Notre Dame's Individual Statistics

Rushing: Ferguson 21-94-1, Barber 5-22, Carter 4-16, Lisch 4-14, J. Stone 2-1

Passing: Lisch 43-24-1-336-1, Holohan 1-1-0-47-0

Receiving: Masztak 6-78-1, Dickerson 4-111, Holohan 4-53, Hunter 3-72, Ferguson 3-24, Barber 2-29, Vehr 1-10, J. Stone 1-3, Lisch 1-3

South Carolina's Individual Statistics

Rushing: Rogers 30-113, Clark 14-116-1, Dorsey 8-28, Harper 9-10, McKinney 1-3

Passing: Harper 9-2-0-68-1

Receiving: McKinney 1-62-1, Rogers 1-6

The Gamecocks ended up 8–4 overall, losing to Missouri in the Hall of Fame Classic.

5 Notre Dame 29 • Michigan 27
SEPTEMBER 20, 1980, AT NOTRE DAME STADIUM

Oliver's Kick Produces High Drama in Win over Wolverines

The Run-Up: Notre Dame came into the game eighth in the AP poll, coming off a 31-10 win over Purdue in the season opener, after a 7–4 mark the previous campaign in '79.

Michigan rated 14th in the AP, coming off a season-opening win over Northwestern University. Michigan had an 8–4 mark in '79.

The Pertinent Details: Holder Tim Koegel swears the wind stopped at just the right time (as opposed to the 20-mile-per-hour gusts that helped produce a 69-yard Irish punt earlier). And with that, junior Harry Oliver (Koegel's high school teammate)—whose best had been a 38-yard field goal in a junior varsity game (he'd missed a point after touchdown earlier in the game)—kicked a 51-yard field goal as time expired to give Notre Dame a 29–27 win over Michigan.

After the Irish led early, 14–0, and Michigan came back with three straight touchdowns, the final three minutes proved to be as good as it gets. Crable recovered a Wolverine fumble, and his Irish then drove 74 yards to take a 26–21 lead with 3:03 remaining. Then Michigan responded with a 78-yard drive of its own to retake the advantage at 27–26 with 41 seconds to go

Harry Oliver kicks the game-winning field goal in the 1980 Notre Dame-Michigan game.

(the missed two-point conversion left the Irish in striking distance).

That left it to freshman Blair Kiel, who had come off the bench and needed five plays out of the shotgun to get the Irish in position (plus a pass interference penalty)—one of them a fourth-down throw to Tony Hunter in front of the Notre Dame bench.

Westwood One announcer Tony Roberts created a particularly memorable radio call of Oliver's game-winner.

The Determining Factor: Oliver did his thing.

The Star of the Show: Oliver, who claimed he made one from 65 in warmups, earned his acclaim by a landslide.

What the Headlines Said: "There have been many memorable Notre Dame victories down through the years, and the Irish latest win will probably earn a place among the most dramatic."—United Press International

"Call it the luck of the Irish if you want to, but somebody somewhere must be Notre Dame's good-luck charm as another legendary chapter was added to the school's storied football history."—Associated Press

What the Players and Coaches Said: "This is the all-time, all-time, all-time moment. I've never seen Harry kick one that far but it went through today and that's all I care about. No win was more emotional than this one. Of course, the last one is always the best," said Irish coach Dan Devine.

Irish tailback Phil Carter (No. 22) gains some of his game-best 103 rushing yards in Notre Dame's heart-stopping win over Michigan.

Scoring Summary

Michigan	0	14	7	6	27
Notre Dame	0	14	6	9	29

Second Quarter
Notre Dame: Carter 6 run (Oliver kick) (13:05)
Notre Dame: Holohan 10 pass from Courey (Oliver kick) (5:00)
Michigan: Ricks 8 pass from Wangler (Haji-Sheikh kick) (1:50)
Michigan: Betts 9 pass from Wangler (Haji-Sheikh kick) (:31)

Third Quarter
Michigan: Edwards 2 run (Haji-Sheikh kick) (11:57)
Notre Dame: Krimm 49 interception return (kick failed) (1:03)

Fourth Quarter
Notre Dame: Carter 4 run (pass failed) (3:03)
Michigan: Dunaway 1 pass from Wangler (pass failed) (:41)
Notre Dame: Oliver 51 field goal (:00)
Attendance: 59,075

"I didn't look up until I heard everyone screaming and I knew Harry had made it," said Crable.

"It crossed my mind that I can't make this. But there really wasn't time to think," said Oliver.

"This is the type of game you win 20 times and lose 20 times," said Michigan coach Bo Schembechler.

The Rundown: Notre Dame went on to win its first seven games and rose to number one in the AP poll (before a tie against Georgia Institute of Technology), ending up 9–2–1 after a Sugar Bowl loss to national champion and number-one ranked University of Georgia. The Irish finished ninth in the AP poll and 10th in the two polls.

Michigan lost the next week to South Carolina, then won its final nine games, including a Rose Bowl win over Washington,) to finish 10–2 and rated fourth in both polls.

Statistics

Team Statistics

Category	Notre Dame	Michigan
First Downs	14	17
Rushing	9	11
Passing	4	5
Penalty	1	1
Rushing Attempts	42	47
Yards Gained Rushing	136	243
Yards Lost Rushing	9	22
Net Yards Rushing	127	221
Net Yards Passing	107	109
Passes Attempted	19	24
Passes Completed	9	12
Interceptions Thrown	2	1
Total Offensive Plays	60	71
Total Net Yards	234	330
Average Gain Per Play	3.9	4.6
Fumbles: Number Lost	0-0	2-1
Penalties: Number-Yards	5-39	3-47
Punts-Yards	6-261	5-221
Average Yards Per Punt	43.5	44.2
Punt Returns-Yards	4-30	2-17
Kickoff Returns-Yards	1-26	3-110
Interception Returns-Yards	1-49	2-20
Fumble Returns-Yards	1	0
Time of Possession	29:27	30:33
Third Down Conversions	10-16	10-17

Notre Dame's Individual Statistics
Rushing: Carter 30-103-2, Sweeney 2-11, Buchanan 3-6, J. Stone 2-4, Courey 6-3
Passing: Courey 13-6-2-62-0, Hunter 1-1-0-31-0, Kiel 4-2-0-14-0
Receiving: Hunter 3-32, Masztak 3-25, Holohan 2-41-1, Carter 1-9

Michigan's Individual Statistics
Rushing: Ricks 14-83, Woolfolk 9-70, Edwards 12-40-1, Hewlett 9-28, Ingram 1-2, Wangler 2-(-9), Powers *0-7 (* credited with gain of seven on fumble recovery)
Passing: Hewlett 5-1-0-11-0, Wangler 19-11-1-98-3
Receiving: Carter 2-30, Edwards 2-22, Betts 2-17-1, Ricks 2-17-1, Ingram 2-10, Woolfolk 1-12, Dunaway 1-1-1

Notre Dame 17 • Penn State 16
NOVEMBER 14, 1992, AT NOTRE DAME STADIUM

Mirer, Bettis, and Brooks Are Stars of Snow Bowl

The Run-Up: Notre Dame came in with a record of 7–1–1 and ranked eighth by AP, thanks to four straight wins, including a 54–7 thrashing of ninth-ranked Boston College the previous Saturday.

Penn State came in ranked 22nd, with a 6–3 record that included losses to Miami, Boston College, and BYU in three of its last four games.

The Pertinent Details: Notre Dame's series against Penn State ended (at least temporarily, with Penn State headed to the Big Ten the next year) with a 17–16 Irish win in the snow. The victory came when Rick Mirer threw to Jerome Bettis for the touchdown, then

hit Reggie Brooks for the two-point conversion with 20 seconds left.

After the two teams had struggled to a 9–9 tie, Penn State took advantage of an Irv Smith fumble to drive 44 yards in six plays to take a 16–9 lead at the 4:25 mark. From there, Mirer led a 64-yard drive for the ages, throwing to Bettis for 21 yards, scrambling for 15 yards on second and 16, finding Ray Griggs on a 17-yard pass play, and scrambling seven more yards to the Penn State 8.

On fourth and goal from the 4, with 25 seconds on the clock, Lou Holtz called a play from a formation Notre Dame had never run. With Smith covered, Mirer

Neither the snow nor Penn State defenders could prevent Irish fullback Jerome Bettis (No. 6) from running for 68 yards on 14 carries.

Reggie Brooks (No. 40) runs for daylight on his way to a game-high 78 ground yards in the victory over Penn State in 1992.

yelled, "Go." Bettis snuck into the end zone, and Mirer found him. Next came the far-fetched result on the conversion on a play Mirer said he'd run hundreds of times, just never to Brooks.

The Determining Factor: Brooks, who would go on to rush for a season total of 1,343 yards and an awesome average of 8.0 yards per carry, had caught only one pass all season long. However, he became the unlikely recipient of Mirer's two-point throw after the Irish quarterback was flushed out of the pocket, and Brooks qualified as the fourth option.

The Stars of the Show: It's a tie for first between Mirer, Bettis, and Brooks. And the happy ending might not have happened had Bobby Taylor not blocked Penn State's first-period point-after-touchdown attempt.

What the Headlines Said: "Hollywood producers already may be scrambling for the rights to the script

Scoring Summary

Notre Dame	3	3	3	8	17
Penn State	6	0	0	10	16

First Quarter
Notre Dame: Hentrich 26 field goal (9:57)
Penn State: Anderson 1 run (kick blocked) (1:26)

Second Quarter
Notre Dame: Hentrich 31 field goal (0:09)

Third Quarter
Notre Dame: Hentrich 37 field goal (5:27)

Fourth Quarter
Penn State: Muscillo 22 field goal (8:35)
Penn State: O'Neal 13 run (Muscillo kick) (4:25)
Notre Dame: Bettis 3 pass from Mirer (Brooks pass from Mirer) (0:20)
Attendance: 59.075

that was written in the Notre Dame–Penn State game at Notre Dame Stadium. Notre Dame's 17–16 football win over Penn State was that good."–*South Bend Tribune*

"A stone-fingered running back barely hauled in a conversion pass to give Notre Dame its biggest victory of the season."—Associated Press

"It was a storybook conclusion to one of college football's most recognized rivalries."—*Grand Rapids Press*

What the Players and Coaches Said: "Don't worry about it. We're going to win this thing," said Mirer to his defensive teammates after Penn State scored to take the lead with 4:25 left.

"Someone stepped on my ankle and someone else stepped on my back and Irv (Smith) plopped all over me after I got the ball. I said, 'Please get off of me, I can't breathe.' They just kept piling on. It was just the greatest feeling I ever had," said Brooks.

"Usually, we hit one of the two wideouts from the left that are crossing. Lake [Dawson] was open but I was slow getting there so I worked my way across, looked at Irv [Smith] but couldn't get it to him. Reggie just kept moving and got to the corner. I just laid it out and let him go and get it," said Mirer of the game-wining two-point play.

"You wouldn't believe this but Reggie Brooks has bad hands. He wouldn't be the first guy I'd want to throw to," said Holtz.

The Run-Down: Notre Dame went to play 19th-ranked USC and won its regular-season finale, then defeated fourth-ranked Texas A&M University in the Cotton Bowl for a final 10–1–1 record and a fourth-place ranking in both final polls.

Penn State defeated the University of Pittsburgh the next Saturday, then fell to Stanford University in the Blockbuster Bowl for a final 7–5 mark.

Statistics

Team Statistics

Category	Notre Dame	Penn State
First Downs	17	14
Rushing	8	8
Passing	9	6
Penalty	0	0
Rushing Attempts	53	40
Yards Gained Rushing	230	130
Yards Lost Rushing	50	23
Net Yards Rushing	180	107
Net Yards Passing	164	131
Passes Attempted	24	28
Passes Completed	12	7
Interceptions Thrown	1	1
Total Offensive Plays	77	68
Total Net Yards	344	238
Average Gain Per Play	4.5	3.5
Fumbles: Number Lost	3-2	1-1
Penalties: Number-Yards	4-32	2-10
Punts-Yards	4-155	6-216
Average Yards Per Punt	38.8	36
Punt Returns-Yards	0-0	0-0
Kickoff Returns-Yards	2-21	5-100
Interception Returns-Yards	1-0	1-13
Third Down Conversions	6-17	5-16

Notre Dame's Individual Statistics

Rushing: Bettis 14-68, Brooks 23-78, Lytle 3-35, Becton 2-5, Zellars 1-3, Mirer 10-(-9)

Passing: Mirer 23-12-1-164-1, Hentrich 1-0-0-0-0

Receiving: I. Smith 4-59, Dawson 2-39, Bettis 2-24-1, Jarrell 2-13, Griggs 1-17, Mayes 1-12

Penn State's Individual Statistics

Rushing: Anderson 26-73-1, O'Neal 6-30-1, McDuffie 1-12, Archie 2-1, Collins 5-(-9)

Passing: Collins 28-7-1-131-0

Receiving: McDuffie 3-46, Drayton 2-29, T. Thomas 1-46, O'Neal 1-10

7 USC 34 • Notre Dame 31
OCTOBER 15, 2005, AT NOTRE DAME STADIUM

"Bush Push" Puts End to Irish's Bid to Upset Number-One Ranked USC

The Run-Up: Notre Dame came in with a record of 4–1 and rated ninth by the AP, thanks to road wins over third-ranked Michigan and 22nd-ranked Purdue.

USC came in 5-0 and ranked number one, as the defending national champion and with a 27-game overall win streak.

The game was so big Notre Dame issued a record number of media credentials (948) for a game in Notre Dame Stadium. Approximately 45,000 fans attended the Friday night pep rally held in Notre Dame Stadium, where Dan "Rudy" Ruettiger served as master of ceremonies. Tim Brown, Chris Zorich, and Joe Montana also spoke at the pep rally.

The Pertinent Details: This game had it all, and was headlined by an All-America–caliber performance (160 rushing yards and three touchdowns) by the man who ultimately would win the Heisman Trophy, Reggie Bush. But Notre Dame, in its green jerseys, managed to rebound from deficits of 7–0, 14–7, and 28–24 to take the lead after a Brady Quinn run finished off an 87-yard scoring drive that made it 31–28 for the Irish with 2:04 left on the clock. That's when it really got interesting.

Backed up and facing fourth and 9 from his own 26, Matt Leinart connected on a 61-yard throw and run to Dwayne Jarrett down the USC sideline. With no timeouts remaining, Leinart scrambled inside the 10, only to have Notre Dame's Corey Mays separate him from the football.

The clock ran out, and Irish fans stormed the field. But officials ruled the ball went out at the 1 and put six seconds back on the clock. (USC coach Pete Carroll did not approve replay, so there was no look from above.) From there, Leinart and Bush concocted the game-winning (and saving) play.

The Determining Factor: Leinart managed to sneak over the goal line with a helpful (and likely illegal) push from Bush with three seconds to go.

The Stars of the Show: Take your pick—Leinart, Bush, and Jarrett all could make a claim.

What the Headlines Said: "Matt Leinart's head was in his hands. He was not thinking of the sudden, dramatic expansion of an already-enduing legend at the University of Southern California. There had been enough time to manufacture a Hollywood ending here on the Gipper's campus, perhaps the most gripping in the 77-game series between the Trojans and Notre Dame, but not nearly enough to grasp its wonder."– *USA Today*

"About 30 inches separated everything for Southern California from nothing. The distance to the Notre Dame end zone covered by quarterback Matt Leinart on the final snap of the best game of the season meant Trojans coach Pete Carroll could smile and talk about things such as special players doing

Irish safety Tom Zbikowski looks for an opening against the top-rated Trojans in his 60-yard second-period punt return for a touchdown.

special things.... An inch less, and Carroll couldn't chirp.... Take nothing away from the triumph. This was a moment in time for both programs—a harrowing escape for the Trojans, who kept their three-peat hopes alive, and a this-close loss for a Notre Dame program that looks primed to reclaim its position as a consistent national power. Grand theater, as USC-Notre Dame should be."—*Kansas City Star*

"In a game that will be reviewed by Rockne, Leahy and all of the lads as long as there's a Note Dame

Classic channel up above, the Fighting Irish nudged the echoes on Saturday but couldn't close the thunder."—*Chicago Sun-Times*

"For a fleeting, euphoric moment, the scoreboard looked exactly right to Notre Dame. It registered 31–28 in favor of the Irish with 0:00 on the clock. Enough flashbulbs popped in the undulating final minutes Saturday night at Notre Dame Stadium that somebody must have pictures to prove it.... Irish fans rushed onto the field to celebrate the biggest win here in 12 years, but it turned out to be premature."—*South Bend Tribune*

What the Players and Coaches Said: "You're on the 1-yard line, you know? It's really man on man. It's get in the end zone or go home. This is probably going to go down as one of the greatest games ever played in college football, period." said Leinart.

"I shoved him as hard as I could," said Bush.

"I told our guys we had an opportunity to ice the game on offense, on special teams and win it on defense. When you're going against a team the caliber of USC and you have a chance to end the game, you better do it," said Notre Dame coach Charlie Weis.

"Every time he [Bush] touched the ball, he looked like he could score. And most of the time, it seemed he did. He's the reincarnation of Marshall Faulk," said Weis.

"We learned that we can stand toe to toe with the number-one team in the country," said Irish center Bob Morton.

Quarterback Brady Quinn (No. 10), offensive coordinator Michael Haywood, and head coach Charlie Weis devise the next play call against USC in '05.

Scoring Summary

Notre Dame	7	14	0	10	31
USC	14	0	7	13	34

First Quarter

USC: Bush 36 run (Danelo kick) (8:53)

Notre Dame: Thomas 16 run (Fitzpatrick kick) (3:06)

USC: White 3 run (Danelo kick) (2:02)

Second Quarter

Notre Dame: Samardzija 32 pass from Quinn (Fitzpatrick kick) (12:27)

Notre Dame: Zbikowski 60 punt return (Fitzpatrick kick) (10:23)

Third Quarter

USC: Bush 45 run (Danelo kick) (9:28)

Fourth Quarter

Notre Dame: Fitzpatrick 32 field goal (14:50)

USC: Bush 9 run (Danelo kick) (5:09)

Notre Dame: Quinn 5 run (Fitzpatrick kick) (2:04)

USC: Leinart 1 run (kick failed) (0:03)

Attendance: 80,795

"If you're looking for me to say this is a good loss, you'll be waiting a long time. Do I wish the clock would have run out? Sure. Then I'd be happy right now, but it didn't and I don't make excuses," said Weis.

The Rundown: Notre Dame went on to win its last five regular-season games, before losing to fourth-ranked Ohio State in the Bowl Championship Series Fiesta Bowl, to end up ranked ninth by AP and 11th in the final polls at 9–3.

USC finished 12–1, losing to the University of Texas in the BCS title game at the Rose Bowl.

Statistics

Team Statistics

Category	Notre Dame	USC
First Downs	28	20
Rushing	12	6
Passing	12	11
Penalty	4	3
Rushing Attempts	52	175
Yards Gained Rushing	181	197
Yards Lost Rushing	28	22
Net Yards Rushing	153	175
Net Yards Passing	264	301
Passes Attempted	35	33
Passes Completed	19	17
Interceptions Thrown	1	2
Total Offensive Plays	87	64
Total Net Yards	417	476
Average Gain Per Play	4.8	7.4
Fumbles: Number Lost	2-1	0-0
Penalties: Number-Yards	6-62	9-98
Punts-Yards	5-199	6-275
Average Yards Per Punt	39.8	45.8
Punt Returns-Yards	4-87	3-13
Kickoff Returns-Yards	4-39	5-88
Interception Returns-Yards	2-13	1-14
Fumble Returns-Yards	0-0	0-0
Time of Possession	38:40	21:20
Third Down Conversions	10-19	5-13
Fourth Down Conversions	1-1	2-2
Sacks By-Yards	2-16	3-20

Notre Dame's Individual Statistics

Rushing: Walker 19-72, Thomas 18-52-1, Quinn 13-21-1, Grimes 2-8

Passing: Quinn 35-19-1-264-1

Receiving: Samardzija 6-99-1, Fasano 4-86, Walker 4-43, Stovall 3-30, Shelton 1-5, Schwapp 1-1

USC's Individual Statistics

Rushing: Bush 15-160-3, White 10-26-1, Leinart 6-(-11)-1

Passing: Leinart 32-17-2-301-0, Bush 1-0-0-0-0

Receiving: Jarrett 4-101, Smith 4-90, Bush 4-35, McFoy 3-19, Byrd 2-56

Notre Dame 40 • Michigan State 37
SEPTEMBER 23, 2006, AT EAST LANSING

The Irish Prevail on the Road Versus Spartans and Rain

The Run-Up: Twelfth-rated Notre Dame came in with a record of 2–1, having lost at home the previous week to 11th-ranked Michigan.

Michigan State stood at 3–0 after wins over Idaho, Eastern Michigan, and Pittsburgh.

The game marked the 40th anniversary of the famed 10–10 tie between the Spartans and Irish. Fans (third largest crowd in Spartan Stadium history) received a reprint of the 1966 game program with the 2006 version.

The Pertinent Details: The Irish were awful early (much as they had been in '98), falling behind 17–0

after the first period, 31–14 at halftime (260 yards by the home team in the first half), and 37–21 after three periods (and still with nine minutes left). That's when the Spartans began to implode, and the Irish revved it up in the pouring rain.

Quinn connected with Jeff Samardzija for a 43-yard touchdown pass. After Chinedum Ndukwe stripped the ball from Michigan State quarterback Drew Stanton at the Spartan 24, Quinn found Rhema McKnight for 14 yards and a touchdown to cut it to 37–33. Then, with 2:53 left, Terrail Lambert picked off Stanton and ran it into the end zone to give the Irish the lead. Then Lambert added another interception in

Neither a third-period rainstorm nor multiple 17-point deficits could prevent the Irish from their postgame celebration in Spartan Stadium after Notre Dame's 40–37 victory in 2006.

the final seconds to stave off the last-gasp Spartan drive. Notre Dame did it all through the air when it counted, totaling only five second-half rushing yards.

The Determining Factor: The Irish hung tough enough in the rain to put 19 points on the board in the final period, and Lambert's two interceptions in the last three minutes sealed it.

The Stars of the Show: The key player was probably Lambert, although it's hard to argue with Quinn's five touchdown passes (for a combined total of 168 yards). Lambert was named the national defensive player of the week by the Football Writers Association of America.

What the Headlines Said: "Michigan State honored the 1966 peak of its football program

Scoring Summary

Notre Dame	0	14	7	19	40
Michigan State	17	14	6	0	37

First Quarter
Michigan State: Reed 34 pass from Stanton (Swenson kick) (12:15)
Michigan State: Ringer 26 pass from Trannon (Swenson kick) (6:49)
Michigan State: Swenson 32 field goal (1:39)

Second Quarter
Notre Dame: McKnight 32 pass from Quinn (Gioia kick) (11:07)
Michigan State: Baldwin 19 interception return (Swenson kick) (9:04)
Notre Dame: Samardzija 17 pass from Quinn (Gioia kick) (6:45)
Michigan State: Reed 15 pass from Stanton (Swenson kick) (2:11)

Third Quarter
Notre Dame: Carlson 62 pass from Quinn (Gioia kick) (11:13)
Michigan State: Caulcrick 30 run (run failed) (5:50)

Fourth Quarter
Notre Dame: Samardzija 43 pass from Quinn (run failed) (8:18)
Notre Dame: McKnight 14 pass form Quinn (kick failed) (4:57)
Notre Dame: Lambert 27 interception return (Gioia kick) (2:53)
Attendance: 80,193

The tide turned in East Lansing when Terrail Lambori (No. 20) intercepted a Spartan pass and ran it in from 27 yards out to give the Irish the lead and the victory.

Saturday night at Spartan Stadium, then showed why the 40 years since have been so marked with misfortune. Add another one to MSU's long list of maddening collapses. This one belongs somewhere near the top."—*Lansing State Journal*

"Notre Dame was done. Finished. Dead. No way could the Irish come back from a 16-point fourth-quarter deficit. No way. Guess what? They did. It was the biggest fourth-quarter comeback for the Irish since their Cotton Bowl victory against Houston in 1979."—*Chicago Sun-Times*

"Stunning, unbelievable, immortal. How many other ways are there to describe Notre Dame's fourth-quarter rally Saturday night at Michigan State?"—*New York Post*

What the Players and Coaches Said: "I think at halftime the guys realized the season was starting to fall away for us. Everyone could feel the same thing. It was basically, 'Hey, fellas, what's it gonna be? Are we just going to be a bunch of also-rans or are we going to come out here and give it a chance to win the game?'" said Irish coach Weis.

"Late in the game, I made some stupid mistakes," said Stanton.

"I don't know if I've ever been through anything like that," said Irish defensive end Victor Abiamiri.

"Man, it was like being on cloud 30," said Lambert.

The Rundown: By the next morning, the game had become an ESPN *Instant Classic* selection. The Irish won seven straight games after this one, fell to number three USC to end the regular season, then fell to number four LSU in the BCS Sugar Bowl.

That left the Irish ranked 17th by the AP and 19th in the final polls.

Michigan State finished 4–8 and ultimately fired head coach John L. Smith.

Statistics

Team Statistics

Category	Notre Dame	Michigan State
First Downs	13	18
Rushing	3	12
Passing	10	6
Penalty	0	0
Rushing Attempts	17	43
Yards Gained Rushing	59	288
Yards Lost Rushing	12	40
Net Yards Rushing	47	248
Net Yards Passing	319	140
Passes Attempted	36	23
Passes Completed	20	11
Interceptions Thrown	1	2
Total Offensive Plays	53	66
Total Net Yards	366	388
Average Gain Per Play	6.9	5.9
Fumbles: Number Lost	3–1	2–1
Penalties: Number-Yards	8–58	9–75
Punts-Yards	7–303	7–328
Average Yards Per Punt	43.3	46.9
Punt Returns-Yards	1–25	1–15
Kickoff Returns-Yards	4–99	5–100
Interception Returns-Yards	2–27	1–19
Fumble Returns-Yards	0–0	0–0
Time of Possession	24:21	35:39
Third Down Conversions	1–11	3–14
Fourth Down Conversions	2–3	1–1
Sacks By-Yards	3–26	2–11

Notre Dame's Individual Statistics

Rushing: Walker 11–47, Quinn 6–0

Passing: Quinn 36–20–1–319–5

Receiving: Samardzija 7–113–2, Walker 5–15, Carlson 4–121–1, McKnight 4–70–2

Michigan State's Individual Statistics

Rushing: Caulcrick 8–111–1, Ringer 14–76, Stanton 19–53, Love 1–5, Reed 1–3

Passing: Stanton 22–10–2–114–2, Trannon 1–1–0–26–1

Receiving: Ringer 3–32–1, Reed 2–49–2, Trannon 2–23, Scott 2–16, Love 1–15, Caulcrick 1–5

9 Notre Dame 20 • UCLA 17
OCTOBER 21, 2006, AT NOTRE DAME STADIUM

Quinn to Samardzija Puts End to the Bruins' Upset Hope

The Run-Up: Notre Dame came in with a record of 5–1 and rated 10th in the AP poll.

UCLA came in 4–2 off a key win versus Oregon the week before. It marked the first Irish-Bruin meeting in 42 years.

The Pertinent Details: Pay no attention to the first 58 minutes and 58 seconds if you're a Notre Dame fan. There was nothing there you cared about.

Actually, it looked like the Irish had missed their big chance when Quinn came up short on a fourth-and-1 run attempt with the Bruins hanging on to a 17–13 advantage. But UCLA had to punt it back to Notre Dame, and the Irish took over 80 yards from the end zone with 1:02 on the clock.

First Quinn (with no timeouts left) found Samardzija in front of the Irish bench for 21 yards. Next Quinn zeroed in on David Grimes for a 14-yard gain to the UCLA 45. On the next play, Quinn rolled right, found Samardzija crossing over the middle, and Samardzija broke a handful of tackles on his way to the end zone. Irish radio play-by-play man Don Criqui's excited call of the play could be found everywhere by day's end.

The Determining Factor: Samardzija wove his way through the UCLA defense to turn a toss from Quinn into a 45-yard touchdown play to bring the Irish from behind with 27 seconds left.

The Stars of the Show: Forget the first 59 minutes. Quinn and Samardzija made the play when it counted.

What the Headlines Said: "They win, and it's the single greatest accomplishment in Karl Dorrell's four years on the UCLA job. And how good they were for nearly 59 minutes of play! But they lost...."–*Los Angeles Times*

"Brady Quinn pumped once, rolled right, and threw to his favorite receiver. In that moment, Notre Dame

Scoring Summary

Notre Dame	7	3	3	7	**20**
UCLA	0	14	0	3	**17**

First Quarter
Notre Dame: Samardzija 2 pass from Quinn (Gioia kick) (4:04)

Second Quarter
UCLA: Everett 54 pass from Cowan (Medlock kick) (13:42)
UCLA: Snead 36 pass from Cowan (Medlock kick) (7:18)
Notre Dame: Gioia 20 field goal (0:00)

Third Quarter
Notre Dame: Gioia 33 field goal (1:50)

Fourth Quarter
UCLA: Medlock 29 field goal (7:19)
Notre Dame: Samardzija 45 pass from Quinn (Gioia kick) (0:27)
Attendance: 80,795

UCLA defenders can only watch as Jeff Samardzija heads for the goal line on his game-winning 45-yard scoring reception that won it for the Irish with 27 seconds to go.

Though the Irish struggled much of the day on offense, Brady Quinn (left), offensive coordinator Michael Haywood (center), and coach Charlie Weis made all the right moves on Notre Dame's final 80-yard, three-play drive.

once again showed its flair for the dramatic."—*Observer*

"The echoes of Note Dame Stadium were silenced for an inexplicable 59 minutes of regulation. But within a matter of three plays, the UCLA football team felt the sonic eruption of all the Notre Dame pride bursting through in the fourth quarter."—*Daily Bruin*

What the Players and Coaches Said : "I moved out of the pocket, found a window to Jeff, and he did the rest," said Quinn.

"This game is for 60 minutes and it doesn't matter how we played before that," said Bruin quarterback Patrick Cowan.

"I've seen it on TV, but I've never experienced losing a game like this for myself," said Dorrell.

"Good teams make a play at the end to win games like that," said Irish coach Weis.

The Rundown: The Irish ended up with an eight-game late-season win streak before finishing 10–3 and 17th in the AP poll and 19th in the polls following a loss to LSU in the BCS Sugar Bowl.

UCLA finished up 7–6 after losing to Florida State in the Emerald Bowl.

Statistics

Team Statistics

Category	Notre Dame	UCLA
First Downs	20	12
Rushing	7	2
Passing	13	9
Penalty	0	1
Rushing Attempts	35	28
Yards Gained Rushing	79	60
Yards Lost Rushing	38	34
Net Yards Rushing	41	26
Net Yards Passing	304	217
Passes Attempted	45	32
Passes Completed	27	16
Interceptions Thrown	0	1
Total Offensive Plays	80	60
Total Net Yards	345	243
Average Gain Per Play	4.3	4.1
Fumbles: Number Lost	1-1	1-1
Penalties: Number-Yards	6-50	8-55
Punts-Yards	7-273	6-279
Average Yards Per Punt	39.0	46.5
Punt Returns-Yards	2-5	2-25
Kickoff Returns-Yards	3-53	4-81
Interception Returns-Yards	1-0	0-0
Fumble Returns-Yards	0-0	0-0
Time of Possession	34:14	25:46
Third Down Conversions	4-19	5-14
Fourth Down Conversions	4-5	0-1
Sacks By-Yards	3-26	5-33

Notre Dame's Individual Statistics

Rushing: Walker 21-53, Quinn 14-(-12)

Passing: Quinn 45-27-0-304-2

Receiving: Samardzija 8-118-2, Grimes 8-79, Carlson 4-57, Walker 4-22, McKnight 3-28

UCLA's Individual Statistics

Rushing: Markey 19-32, Bell 2-9, Moline 1-3, Cowan 6-(-18)

Passing: Cowan 32-16-1-217-2

Receiving: Everett 6-102-1, Taylor 3-39, Markey 2-8, Snead 1-36-1, Ketchum 1-13, Breazell 1-9, Moline 1-7, Baumgartner 1-3

Seven Games That Featured Amazing Individual Performances

A simple list of names is sufficient: George Gipp and Paul Hornung, Terry Hanratty and Jim Seymour, Joe Theismann and Julius Jones, and Tim Brown and Raghib Ismail.

Nary a commoner in the bunch. Rather, All-Americans all around. Two Heisman Trophy winners, two Heisman runners-up. They came from Michigan, Kentucky, Pennsylvania (two), Illinois, Texas, New Jersey, and Virginia. Their names probably require no introduction for most Notre Dame football fans. Their exploits were gaudy enough that the names say it all.

You may well not remember many of the final scores of these contests. But you probably remember where you were the night Theismann threw for all those yards in the pouring rain in the Los Angeles Coliseum.

You remember how Brown's mere presence brought you to your feet with the prospect of a big play or return—and that seemed even more magical in the night air of Notre Dame Stadium back when prime-time home games (under the Musco lights) were relatively rare. All his 1987 performance did was win him a Heisman.

And how can you forget Rocket Ismail running back not one but two kickoffs in the Big House? Not against just anyone, but against Michigan. The effort landed Ismail on the cover of *Sports Illustrated* and changed his life forever.

These were big performances (many record-setting) by big-time players in big-time settings. Check them out.

Julius Jones jumped to the top of Notre Dame's list of all-time single game rushing performances with his 262 yards at Pittsburgh in 2003.

Notre Dame 13 • Indiana 10
NOVEMBER 13, 1920, AT INDIANAPOLIS

That's Why They Called Him "the Gipper"

The Run-Up: Notre Dame came in at 6–0, including shutout wins over Kalamazoo College, Western Michigan, and Purdue, with an overall 15-game win streak on the line.

Indiana came in with a record of 4–1, with three straight wins over Mississippi State, Minnesota, and Northwestern.

The Pertinent Details: On the surface, there didn't appear to be anything remarkable about what transpired in this contest played in Indianapolis. Notre Dame won, and George Gipp contributed 52 rushing yards on 16 carries, scored one touchdown (on a one-yard run), completed three of his five passes for 26 yards, kicked one point after touchdown, and also punted nine times (then a much more important part of the field-position game) for 351 yards.

In reality, Gipp accomplished most of that despite not re-entering the contest until 10 minutes remained, with Notre Dame trailing 10–0, and while suffering from both a previously broken collarbone and a dislocated shoulder that came early in this game. After Gipp's touchdown run (ending a 60-yard, seven-play drive), he navigated his teammates down the field to the Indiana 15. Instead of dropkicking for the tie, he then hit Eddie Anderson (despite the pain in his shoulder) for 14 yards. Joe Brandy scored on the next play, with Gipp leading the blocking.

The Determining Factor: Gipp came back into the game.

The Star of the Show: Gipp, in what turned out to be his second-to-last game appearance, dazzled on the field. He already had become enough of a legendary figure that Notre Dame's appearance in Indianapolis prompted Gipp's photo to appear in store windows all over town.

What the Headlines Said: "It was, perhaps, the greatest comeback ever recorded by a football team that [Knute] Rockne's bunch pulled to save the day Saturday."–Unknown

Scoring Summary

Notre Dame	0	0	0	13	13
Indiana	0	3	7	0	10

Second Quarter
Indiana: Risley 25 field goal

Third Quarter
Indiana: Hanny 10 pass from Williams (Risley kick)

Fourth Quarter
Notre Dame: Gipp 1 run (Gipp kick)
Notre Dame: Brandy 1 run (kick failed)
Attendance: 14,000

George Gipp's gridiron exploits proved legendary all by themselves, but the circumstances of his death and the resulting "Win One for the Gipper" speech used by Irish coach Knute Rockne only added to the legend of the Notre Dame star.

What the Players and Coaches Said: One version suggests that with time on the clock dwindling, Gipp jumped off the bench and said, "I'm going in."

Irish coach Rockne replied, "Not today."

Guess who won that debate?

Another version says Notre Dame reached the one-foot mark, and Rockne sent Gipp in to get the touchdown (he got it on fourth down, with his shoulder heavily taped).

The Rundown: The Irish, in Rockne's third season as head coach, finished their second consecutive perfect 9–0 season. Only the universities of Tulsa and Alabama, with 10 victories each, won more games.

The Hoosiers ended up 5–2 following a 10–7 win over Purdue the week after this game.

Gipp contracted a strep infection and died December 14, the same day he was selected as Notre Dame's first-ever Walter Camp All-American.

Notre Dame 17 • Iowa 14
NOVEMBER 19, 1955, AT NOTRE DAME STADIUM

Hornung Does It All to Beat the Hawkeyes

The Run-Up: Notre Dame came in with a 7–1 record and rated fourth by the AP, the lone Irish loss having come on the road at number 13 Michigan State.

Iowa came in at 3–4–1, including a loss to eventual Big Ten champ Ohio State the previous week.

The Pertinent Details: Paul Hornung's signature game featured a 28-yard field goal by the junior with 2:15 on the clock in front of the largest crowd ever to come to Notre Dame Stadium (59,955). After three inches of snow fell the night before, fans saw a brutally physical game in which the Irish used only 19 players,

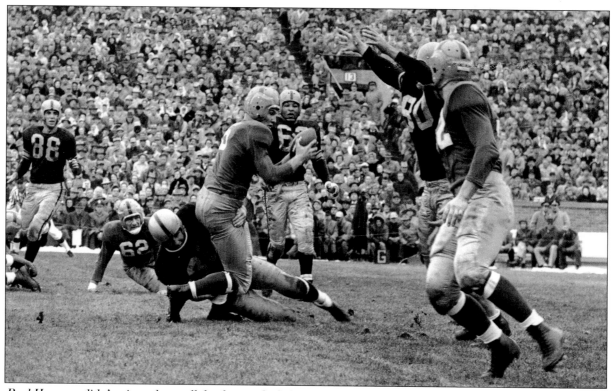

Paul Hornung didn't miss a down all day long as he helped the Irish upend Iowa.

Notre Dame stops Iowa at the goal line.

with Hornung among the four who played without relief.

The Irish scored first, but Iowa responded with touchdowns in the third and fourth periods to leave the Irish on the short end of a 14–7 count with approximately 10 minutes remaining. That's when Hornung went to work, returning the kickoff and then leading Notre Dame on a 62-yard scoring drive, with Jim Morse on the receiving end of the touchdown play in a drive that lasted all of two and a half minutes.

Notre Dame downed the kickoff on the 2, and Iowa ultimately had to punt out to its own 43. On third and 11, Hornung hit Morse, who made a huge grab at the Hawkeyes 9. The Irish ran three times and reached the 3. A Notre Dame player tossed a kicking tee onto the field and the Irish were penalized 15 yards for "coaching from the sideline," but Hornung booted the winning three-pointer anyway.

The Determining Factor: Hornung's field goal flew through the uprights.

The Stars of the Show: The game's most stellar performance came from Hornung, with Morse not far behind after catching three of Hornung's throws for 63 yards and also rushing 10 times for 26 yards.

What the Headlines Said: "Spectacular Paul Hornung and spirited Notre Dame Saturday afternoon bustled back from the brink of defeat to down Iowa's surprising sophomores, 17–14, before the largest home audience in N.D. history."—*South Bend Tribune*

"Hornung, a junior meteor on a day when seniors were supposed to sparkle in their final home appearance, was carried off the field by his teammates and a wild student throng who then tore down the goal posts for the first time in history. When his day's work had been added up in the record book, Hornung had ran for 34 yards, completed six of 10 passes for 108 more, kicked two extra points and the field goal and proved just as devastating to the fired-up Hawkeyes on defense."—*Tribune* (Hornung also punted five times for a 36.6-yard average.)

"Notre Dame, kept under pressure most of the game by Iowa's sizzling sophomore backs, today popped loose behind quarterback Paul Hornung's aerials for a touchdown and a field goal in the last 7 minutes of play for a 17–14 victory."—Associated Press

What the Players and Coaches Said: "That play was supposed to have been a screen pass to the right. Hornung had three receivers deep on the right side, but they were all covered," said Irish coach Terry Brennan of Notre Dame's second touchdown that saw Hornung nearly lose 20 yards before finding Morse alone in the end zone.

"I think after today, that anything anybody ever said about the fighting spirit of this Notre Dame team is very true. It was simply amazing the way they refused to quit time after time and held Iowa at crucial spots. This is the greatest bunch of fighters I have ever seen. They just refuse to give up. I thought Paul Hornung, Jim Mense, and Jim Morse were great factors in rallying the team in the clutch. All three played outstanding games," said Brennan.

The Rundown: The Irish fell 42–20 at the USC the following Saturday to end up 8–2 overall and rated ninth by the AP and 10th in the final polls.

This game concluded the Hawkeyes' season at 3–5–1 (2–3–1 in the Big Ten).

Statistics

Team Statistics

Category	Notre Dame	Iowa
First Downs	15	16
Net Yards Rushing	202	190
Net Yards Passing	108	99
Passes Attempted	12	20
Passes Completed	6	9
Interceptions Thrown	0	0
Fumbles: Number Lost	3	3
Penalties: Number-Yards	60	5
Punts-Yards	5	4
Average Yards Per Punt	36.6	31.5

Notre Dame's Individual Statistics

Rushing: Schaefer 10-45, Hornung 8-34, Morse 10-26, Studer 12-53, Fitzgerald 7-39, Lewis 2-5

Passing: Hornung 10-6, Morse 1-0, Studer 1-0

Receiving: Prendergast 2-28, Kapish 1-17, Morse 3-63

Iowa's Individual Statistics

Rushing: J. Reichow 4-9, Dobrino 8-26, E. Smith 4-13, Hagler 4-24, Harris 16-48, Happel 11-70

Passing: J. Reichow 13-6, Dobrino 7-3

Receiving: Gibbons 2-21, Freeman 1-8, Hatch 1-9, J. Reichow 3-36, Harris 1-23, Hagler 1-2

Scoring Summary

Notre Dame	0	7	0	10	17
Iowa	0	0	7	7	14

Second Quarter
Notre Dame: Studer 1 run (Hornung kick) (2:32)

Third Quarter
Iowa: Harris 2 run (Freeman kick)

Fourth Quarter
Iowa: Reichow 6 pass from Dobrino (Freeman kick)
Notre Dame: Morse 16 pass from Hornung (Hornung kick) (7:37)
Notre Dame: Hornung 28 field goal (2:15)
Attendance: 59,955

Notre Dame 26 • Purdue 14
SEPTEMBER 24, 1966, AT NOTRE DAME STADIUM

A Record-Setting Opening Act for "Fling and Cling" Passing Duo

The Run-Up: Notre Dame came into Ara Parseghian's third season rated sixth, after the Irish were 7–2–1 in 1965.

Eighth-ranked Purdue had beaten Ohio University 42–3 the previous Saturday to start 1–0 (the Boilermakers also had been 7–2–1 in '65).

The Pertinent Details: Hanratty and Seymour made their debuts as sophomores, with Seymour catching 13 of Hanratty's throws for 276 yards (still a record figure) as the Irish defeated eighth-rated Purdue 26–14. At the time, only one player in National Collegiate Athletic Association (NCAA) history had more receiving yards in a game than Seymour. For his part, Hanratty connected on 16 of 24 passes for 304 yards, with three touchdown passes going to Seymour worth 84, 39, and seven yards. The rest of the team accounted for three catches for 28 yards.

The game began in slam-bam fashion, with Purdue's Leroy Keyes going 94 yards with a fumble to

No Notre Dame passing-and-receiving combination ever clicked better than quarterback Terry Hanratty (No. 5) and end Jim Seymour (No. 85) in their 1966 debut.

In his very first Notre Dame varsity game, Terry Hanratty connected for 304 aerial yards.

Scoring Summary

Notre Dame	7	7	0	12	26
Purdue	7	0	0	7	14

First Quarter
Purdue: Keyes 94 fumble return (Griese kick) (5:26)
Notre Dame: Eddy 96 kickoff return (Ryan kick) (5:14)

Second Quarter
Notre Dame: Seymour 84 pass from Hanratty (Ryan kick) (5:38)

Fourth Quarter
Notre Dame: Seymour 39 pass from Hanratty (kick failed) (13:53)
Purdue: Williams 1 run (Griese kick) (11:07)
Notre Dame: Seymour 7 pass from Hanratty (pass failed) (2:46)
Attendance: 59,075

score, followed by a 96-yard kickoff return by Notre Dame's Nick Eddy.

The Determining Factor: The Hanratty-Seymour combo hooked up for two long scoring plays.

The Stars of the Show: The Irish sophomore duo lit it up in their opening act in front of the home fans. They overshadowed Purdue standout Bob Griese, who managed 14 completions in 26 attempts for 178 yards.

What the Headlines Said: "Boilers Seymour of Hanratty Than They Care To"—*Golden Glory*
"Notre Dame had the answer Saturday on what to do with Bob Griese. The Irish simply upstaged Purdue's All-America quarterback with a couple of sophomores and beat the Boilermakers 26–14. Calling Jim Seymour and Terry Hanratty 'a pair of sophomores'

was like calling Louis Armstrong 'a horn player.'"—*Chicago Sun-Times*

"Hanratty to Seymour? Never before has a teenage pass-and-catch duo hit big-time ball with a bigger splash."—*Chicago Daily News*

"In 80 years of Notre Dame football, they never saw anything to equal what Coach Ara Parseghian unveiled yesterday to an almost unbelieving crowd...."—*Chicago American*

What the Players and Coaches Said: "After looking at the films, I apologize to my pass defenders for getting mad at them. One guy defending Seymour just isn't in the cards. Our pass rush wasn't so hot. We gave Hanratty too long to unload. But the way he and Seymour were playing I don't know if we could stop them anyway," said Purdue coach Jack Mollenkopf.

"It's all just a big blur to me. I look at the moves of Paul Warfield, Gail Cogdill, and Bob Hayes whenever I can. They are the best. I wouldn't mind being like them," said Seymour.

"I was keyed up but I was relaxed at the same time," said Hanratty.

"Honest, sir. I don't know how many I caught. How many was it?" said Seymour to a reporter.

The Rundown: Notre Dame went on to finish 9-0-1, with only a tie against unbeaten Michigan State, as the Irish claimed the top spot in both final polls for their eighth consensus national title. The 14 points scored by Purdue turned out to be the most scored against Notre Dame's defense all season long.

Purdue ended up 9-2 (its only other loss to Michigan State), as a Rose Bowl win over USC left the Boilers seventh in the last AP poll.

Statistics

Team Statistics

Category	Notre Dame	Purdue
First Downs	19	17
Rushing	8	7
Passing	10	10
Penalty	1	0
Rushing Attempts	43	41
Yards Gained Rushing	158	130
Yards Lost Rushing	3	15
Net Yards Rushing	149	115
Net Yards Passing	304	178
Passes Attempted	24	26
Passes Completed	16	14
Interceptions Thrown	1	1
Total Offensive Plays	67	67
Total Net Yards	453	293
Fumbles: Number Lost	1-1	1-1
Penalties: Number-Yards	4-43	5-45
Punts-Yards	2-86	6-210
Average Yards Per Punt	43	35
Punt Returns-Yards	4-52	0-0
Kickoff Returns-Yards	2-98	6-104

Notre Dame's Individual Statistics

Rushing: Hanratty 6-6, Eddy 12-52, Bleier 8-30, Conjar 15-48, May 2-13

Passing: Hanratty 24-16-1-304-3

Receiving: Eddy 1-16, Bleier 2-12, Seymour 12-276-3

Purdue's Individual StatisticsRushing:

Griese 15-34, Sims 2-12, Williams 11-42-1, Huart 13-27

Passing: Griese 26-14-1-178

Receiving: Williams 1-2, Bierne 4-48, Griffin 1-13, Barves 1-31, Fioles 6-80, Ruble 1-4

USC 38 • Notre Dame 28
NOVEMBER 28, 1970, AT LOS ANGELES

Theismann Lights Up Soggy Coliseum with Record Night

The Run-Up: Notre Dame came in with a record of 9–0 and ranked fourth by the AP, having rated number one for one week before three-point wins over Georgia Institute of Technology and LSU the previous two Saturdays.

USC was unranked at 5–4–1, having lost three of its last four games, including 45–20 to the University of California at Los Angeles the week before.

The Pertinent Details: Joe Theismann set the Irish single-game record for passing yards by throwing for 526 in a loss at USC, but the 557 total yards and 28 first downs (198 yards and 11 first downs more than the totals for the Trojans) weren't enough for the victory.

Theismann completed 33 passes in 58 attempts, threw touchdown passes of nine yards to John Cieszkowski and 46 to Larry Parker, and also ran for two scores, from 25 yards out and one yard out (the latter on fourth down).

Down only 10 points at the half, it all went wrong to start the third period. Darryll Dewan fumbled the

No Irish quarterback has ever been more productive in a single game than Joe Theismann was in 1970 at USC.

Larry Parker catches a touchdown pass in the 1970 game against USC.

Scoring Summary

Notre Dame	7	7	7	7	28
USC	21	3	14	0	38

First Quarter
Notre Dame: Theismann 25 run (Hempel kick) (10:53)
USC: Davis 3 run (Ayala kick) (8:07)
USC: Davis 5 run (kick failed) (4:49)
USC: Dickerson 45 pass from Jones (Chandler pass from Jones) (:57)

Second Quarter
Notre Dame: Cieszkowski 9 pass from Theismann (Hempel kick) (7:24)
USC: Ayala 19 field goal (1:50)

Third Quarter
USC: Adams fumble recovery (Ayala kick) (10:35)
USC: Vella fumble recovery (Ayala kick) (9:53)
Notre Dame: Parker 46 pass from Theismann (Hempel kick) (8:22)

Fourth Quarter
Notre Dame: Theismann 1 run (Hempel kick) (13:52)
Attendance: 64,694

ball away on Notre Dame's first play from scrimmage in the half, and the Trojans went in to score, recovering their own fumble in the end zone for six points. Then Theismann lost the handle in his own end zone, and a USC recovery chalked up another six points.

The Determining Factor: USC responded to Notre Dame's initial 12-play, 80-yard drive for a 7–0 lead with successive touchdown marches of 70, 51, and 57 yards, with the touchdowns coming within an eight-minute span. USC quarterback Jimmy Jones connected on all seven of his passes in the first period.

The Star of the Show: The day's hero had to be Theismann, based on the numbers.

The Trojans nominated their defense, based on eight forced turnovers, three forced fumbles, and five sacks by linebacker Willie Hall. They also had recovered fumbles in the end zone for touchdowns by Pete Adams and John Vella within 42 seconds of each other in the third period to jump the USC lead to 38–14.

What the Headlines Said: "Irish Win Battle, Lose War"–*Glamour Game*

"U.S.C. Dashes Irish Unbeaten Hopes: Theismann Brilliant in 38–28 Loss"–*Chicago Tribune*

"Never during the 1970 season had Notre Dame made so many costly mistakes in one 60-minute span. And never had USC played such perfectly executed football."–Notre Dame *Scholastic*

"It was sort of sad the way Theismann tried to rally the troops to victory. With each incomplete pass, each interception, the camera would frame a dejected Theismann staring blankly as the season neared its destructive end."– Notre Dame *Scholastic*

What the Players and Coaches Said: "I thought we could beat them when we went in for halftime. But those two quick (third-period) TDs were too much to overcome," said Irish coach Ara Parseghian.

"Fifty years from now our seniors can sit around the fireplace and say they never lost to Notre Dame," said USC coach John McKay.

"It's as great a victory as I've ever been associated with," said USC assistant coach Marv Goux.

The Rundown: Notre Dame rebounded from the loss to knock off the unbeaten University of Texas in the Cotton Bowl, putting the Irish second according to the AP and fifth in the final polls.

The game finished USC's season at 6–4–1 (after the previous three Trojan teams had been a combined 29–2–2).

Statistics

Team Statistics

Category	Notre Dame	USC
First Downs	23	15
First Downs	28	17
Rushing	7	4
Passing	19	12
Penalty	2	1
Rushing Attempts	33	52
Yards Gained Rushing	106	156
Yards Lost Rushing	75	23
Net Yards Rushing	31	133
Net Yards Passing	526	226
Passes Attempted	58	24
Passes Completed	33	15
Interceptions Thrown	4	0
Total Offensive Plays	91	76
Total Net Yards	557	359
Average Gain Per Play	6.10	4.72
Penalties: Number-Yards	3-23	2-20
Punts-Yards	6-214	11-330
Average Yards Per Punt	35.7	30.0
Punt Returns-Yards	3-10	4-42
Kickoff Returns-Yards	4-70	4-78
Interception Returns-Yards	0-0	4-68
Fumble Returns-Yards	4-4	3-0

Notre Dame's Individual Statistics

Rushing: Dewan 7-11, Theismann 13-(-14)-2, Cieszkowski 6-17, Gulyas 3-19, Parker 3-9, Minnix 1-(-11)

Passing: Theismann 58-33-4-526-2

Receiving: Gatewood 10-128, Cieszkowski 6-70-1, Dewan 5-33, Creaney 3-37, Trapp 1-4, Parker 7-174-1, Theismann 1-7, Barz 1-7, Gulyas 1-16

USC's Individual Statistics

Rushing: Davis 33-91-2, Cunningham 2-6, Jones 5-(-9), McNeil 2-12, Evans 8-24, Harris 1-7, Berry 1-2

Passing: Jones 24-15-0-226-1

Receiving: Chandler 5-63, Davis 2-41, Dickerson 4-90-1, Evans 2-28, McNeil 1-(-9), Mullins 1-13

Notre Dame 31 • Michigan State 8
SEPTEMBER 19, 1987, AT NOTRE DAME STADIUM

Brown's Punt Returns Make Heisman His to Lose

The Run-Up: The Irish came in 1–0 and ranked ninth, having knocked off number-nine ranked University of Michigan on the road the previous Saturday.

Michigan State was rated 17th by the AP after defeating USC 27–13 the previous Saturday.

The Pertinent Details: In a prime-time matchup on ESPN, Brown returned two punts for touchdowns versus Michigan State to make him the leader in the clubhouse in the Heisman Trophy race.

Tom Schoen held the Irish single-game record for punt-return yardage with 167 (versus Pittsburgh in 1967), and Brown had 150 by halftime alone. Brown finished with 275 all-purpose yards—150 on punt returns, 57 on kickoff returns, and 72 on receptions. He did lose four yards on two rushing attempts.

The Irish actually scored before they ran a play, when the Spartans' Blake Ezor took the opening kickoff on the 1, stepped back into the end zone to down the ball, and was hit with a safety. Ted Gradel added a field goal later in the period after a 75-yard drive, then Brown brought the first punt back 71 yards at the 2:14 mark and added a 66-yarder two minutes and one second later.

For all practical purposes, the game was over. Michigan State's only points came with 66 seconds left in the game, as two interceptions and two lost fumbles thwarted Spartan offensive hopes. Lorenzo White, who later finished fourth behind Brown in the Heisman voting, managed only 51 yards on 19 carries.

The Determining Factor: Before the first period was done, Brown brought back back-to-back Spartan punts for touchdowns, making it 19–0 for the Irish before the opening quarter was concluded.

The Star of the Show: Brown, who tied an NCAA record with his two returns and became the first Notre

Scoring Summary

Notre Dame	19	5	7	0	31
Michigan State	0	0	0	8	8

First Quarter
Notre Dame: Safety, Ezor downs ball in end zone (15:00)
Notre Dame: Gradel 27 field goal (4:08)
Notre Dame: Brown 71 punt return (Gradel kick) (2:14)
Notre Dame: Brown 66 punt return (Gradel kick) (:13)

Second Quarter
Notre Dame: Safety, McAllister sacked in end zone (3:37)
Notre Dame: Gradel 37 FG (:08)

Third Quarter
Notre Dame: Johnson 3 run (Gradel kick) (10:40)

Fourth Quarter
Michigan State: Rison 57 pass from McAllister (1:06)
Attendance: 59,075

There is no Spartan defender with a chance at Tim Brown on the first of his two punt returns for touchdowns against Michigan State in 1987.

Dame player to accomplish the feat since 1926, was the undisputed champion that day. It had been 14 years since an Irish player had even returned one for a score.

What the Headlines Said: "Faster than you can say Tim Brown, Notre Dame was on the scoreboard against Michigan State. Faster than anyone else around, Brown turned a game in Notre Dame Stadium into something special."—*South Bend Tribune*

"Two for the Money"—Notre Dame *Scholastic*

"Notre Dame turned its multiple weapon, Tim Brown, loose on Michigan State Saturday night. The Spartans are still seeing stars."—*Chicago Tribune*

What the Players and Coaches Said: "He [Brown] rose to the occasion and broke our backs. Obviously he is a great athlete and the whole nation saw that," said Michigan State coach George Perles.

"They were talking about me winning the Heisman, but I thought those guys [the Irish defense] deserved it," said Brown.

The Rundown: Notre Dame went on to win eight of its first nine matchups before losing its last three, including the Cotton Bowl to 13th-ranked Texas A&M University. The Irish ended up 17th in the final AP poll.

Michigan State lost the following Saturday to Florida State University, then didn't lose again the remainder of the regular season. It also dispatched 16th-ranked USC 20–17 in the Rose Bowl. That left the Spartans 9–2–1 and ranked eighth in both final polls.

Statistics

Team Statistics

Category	Notre Dame	Michigan State
First Downs	15	13
Rushing	7	3
Passing	7	8
Penalty	1	2
Rushing Attempts	50	36
Yards Gained Rushing	168	98
Yards Lost Rushing	28	77
Net Yards Rushing	140	21
Net Yards Passing	112	208
Passes Attempted	19	18
Passes Completed	10	10
Interceptions Thrown	0	2
Total Offensive Plays	69	54
Total Net Yards	252	229
Average Gain Per Play	3.7	4.2
Fumbles: Number Lost	1–0	4–2
Penalties: Number-Yards	5–45	4–24
Punts-Yards	8–376	7–302
Average Yards Per Punt	47.0	43.1
Punt Returns-Yards	6–150	5–43
Kickoff Returns-Yards	3–55	5–58
Interception Returns-Yards	2–17	0–0
Time of Possession	33:15	26:45
Third Down Conversions	8–19	4–13
Sacks By-Yards	8–59	2–17

Notre Dame's Individual Statistics

Rushing: Green 17-46, Rice 2-28, Andrysiak 9-22, Johnson 5-13-1, Brooks 6-12, Robb 1-11, Watters 5-9, Brown 2-(-4), Jefferson 2-2, Belles 1-1

Passing: Andrysiak 17-9-0-105-0, Rice 2-1-0-7-0

Receiving: Brown 4-72, Green 3-30, Watters 2-10, Jacobs 1-0

Michigan State's Individual Statistics

Rushing: White 19-51, Wilson 1-4, Moore 1-3, Ezor 1-2, McAllister 14-(-39)

Passing: McAllister 18-10-2-208-1

Receiving: Rison 5-137-1, Bouyer 2-28, Jacobs 1-19, White 1-15, Gicewicz 1-9

6 Notre Dame 24 • Michigan 19
SEPTEMBER 16, 1989, AT ANN ARBOR

"Rocket" Returns Fully Powered for Triumph at the Big House

The Run-Up: Coming off its national title in 1988, top-rated Notre Dame was 1-0 after a 36–13 victory over the University of Virginia in the Kickoff Classic and was protecting a 13-game overall win streak.

Michigan, ranked second, was playing its season opener and coming off an 9–2–1 campaign and Rose Bowl win over USC in 1988.

This matchup between the Wolverines and the Irish marked the 25th and earliest meeting between first- and second-ranked teams in college history (based on the AP poll).

The Pertinent Details: If the college football world didn't know who sophomore Ismail was by this point, it did after this game. Ismail returned two kickoffs for touchdowns, tying an NCAA record at Michigan Stadium. His performance helped the top-ranked Irish defeat second-rated Michigan 24-19.

How impressive was the Rocket's performance? Good enough to land him on the cover of *Sports Illustrated* the next week. He did it against Wolverines special teams that hadn't given up a kickoff return for a touchdown in 32 years. No one had ever returned two against Michigan in one game.

Amazingly, Notre Dame won it against the second-ranked team in the country by running 54 rushing plays (the Irish gained 213 yards—80 by Anthony Johnson, 79 by Tony Rice) and calling two passes (one was completed and accounted for Notre Dame's first touchdown on a six-yard throw by Rice to Johnson).

The game changed when Michigan, trailing 7–6, kicked off to Ismail to start the second half on a rain-soaked artificial turf field. With Rodney Culver leading the blocking, Ismail took the ball back 89 yards for a score (one of the last potential Michigan tacklers was current Irish defensive coordinator Corwin Brown).

After Michigan quarterback Michael Taylor was injured, on came redshirt freshman Elvis Grbac (he ended up completing 17 of 21 passes), and his touchdown toss to Derrick Walker of five yards made it 17-12 for the Wolverines with just under 13 minutes remaining.

Enter Ismail, who brought the ensuing kickoff back 92 yards, again with Culver leading the convoy (the kicker suffered a broken arm during Culver's final block on him on that play).

The Determining Factor: Notre Dame ran off the final four minutes of the game, notably thanks to a fourth-and-1 conversion run by Johnson.

The Star of the Show: Rocket. This game marked the second time in his first two seasons he returned two kickoffs for touchdowns in the same game. He also did it against Rice University in 1988.

The fancy name for Notre Dame's two big-time return plays? *Middle.*

What the Headlines Said: "Bent on revenge and hiding nothing about its feelings, number-two

Michigan promised publicly that things would be different with number-one Notre Dame this time. But only the heroes changed as all the Wolverine promises were broken in half by the incredible effort of one of the days' smallest performers."–*South Bend Tribune*

"Notre Dame launched its national title defense with, naturally enough, a Rocket. Michigan saw the Rocket's afterglow as surely as they saw Raghib Ismail's heels Saturday afternoon."–*Detroit Free Press*

"They play 'Hail to the Victors' all day here on football Saturdays, the national anthem but once. From now on, however, the Michigan faithful will pay a lot more attention when they get to the part about 'The Rocket's red glare...'"–*Grand Rapids Press*

"His eighth-grade track coach nicknamed him 'the Rocket.' He has brothers named 'the Missile' and 'the Bomb.' They call his mother 'the Launching Pad.'"–*Chicago Tribune*

What the Players and Coaches Said: "He's the best I've ever seen," said Michigan's Bo Schembechler of Ismail.

"We didn't throw the ball because we didn't want to open things up and give Michigan anything they didn't earn. We were never forced to open things up," said Irish coach Lou Holtz.

"I never question anything Bo does in a game," said Holtz on the Michigan decisions to kick to Ismail.

Raghib Ismail tied an NCAA record that still stands by returning a pair of kickoffs for touchdowns in a single game.

"Once again they kicked the ball deep to Rocket and I thought to myself, 'Whoever made that decision must not be thinking that much,'" said Irish linebacker Ned Bolcar.

"I told Coach [Holtz] I wish I could find somewhere in the budget to give all the guys on the kickoff return team a game ball," said Ismail.

The Rundown: The Irish started the season 11-0 before falling to seventh-ranked University of Miami in the regular-season finale (ending a Notre Dame record 23-game win streak). The Irish defeated top-ranked University of Colorado in the Orange Bowl, finished 12-1, and ended up second (AP) and third in the final polls.

Michigan won its last 10 regular-season games, then fell 17-10 to number 12 USC in the Rose Bowl. The 10–2 Wolverines ended up seventh in the final AP poll, eighth according to the coaches.

Scoring Summary

Notre Dame	0	7	10	7	24
Michigan	0	6	0	13	19

Second Quarter
Notre Dame: Johnson 6 pass from Rice (Hentrich kick) (5:05)
Michigan: Calloway 9 pass from Taylor (kick failed) (0:25)

Third Quarter
Notre Dame: Ismail 89 kickoff return (Hentrich kick) (14:49)
Notre Dame: Hentrich 30 field goal (4:28)

Fourth Quarter
Michigan: Walker 5 pass from Grbac (failed) (12:58)
Notre Dame: Ismail 92 kickoff return (Hentrich kick) (12:46)
Michigan: McMurtry 4 pass from Grbac (Carlson kick) (4:08)
Attendance

Statistics

Team Statistics

Category	Notre Dame	Michigan
First Downs	13	15
Rushing	12	5
Passing	0	8
Penalty	1	2
Rushing Attempts	54	34
Yards Gained Rushing	220	119
Yards Lost Rushing	7	25
Net Yards Rushing	213	94
Net Yards Passing	6	178
Passes Attempted	2	28
Passes Completed	1	22
Interceptions Thrown	0	0
Total Offensive Plays	56	62
Total Net Yards	219	272
Average Gain Per Play	3.9	4.4
Fumbles: Number Lost	1-0	1-1
Penalties: Number-Yards	5-45	8-70
Punts-Yards	3-112	6-202
Average Yards Per Punt	37.3	33.8
Punt Returns-Yards	1-2	2-14
Kickoff Returns-Yards	3-192	3-86
Time of Possession	30:23	29:37

Notre Dame's Individual Statistics
Rushing: Culver 7-35, Rice 18-79, Watters 5-5, A. Johnson 20-80, Ismail 4-14
Passing: Rice 2-1-0-6-1
Receiving: A. Johnson 1-6-1

Michigan's Individual Statistics
Rushing: Taylor 6-11, Grbac 2-(-8), Howard 1-6, Bunch 5-12, Hoard 15-56, Boles 5-17
Passing: Taylor 6-5-0-44-1, Grbac 21-17-0-134-2, Hoard 1-0-0-0-0
Receiving: McMurtry 4-51-1, Calloway 7-72-1, Howard 1-17, Bunch 4-8, Hoard 3-12, Boles 1-6, D. Walker 2-12-1

Notre Dame 20 • Pittsburgh 14
OCTOBER 11, 2003, AT PITTSBURGH

Jones Takes Control of Illustrious Irish Rushing Record

The Run-Up: Notre Dame came in with a record of 1–3, having lost three straight, to number five Michigan, Michigan State, and number 22 Purdue.

Fifteenth-rated Pittsburgh came in at 3–1, fresh off a win over Texas A&M the week before.

The Pertinent Details: This game didn't mean all that much in the big picture, but it was more than a little noteworthy considering all the great efforts in the Notre Dame rushing annals.

Topping anything ever accomplished during a 60-minute period by the likes of Allen Pinkett, Reggie Brooks, Jim Stone, Vagas Ferguson, Jerome Heavens, or Phil Carter, Julius Jones set the single-game rushing record with 262 yards (24 carries) versus Pittsburgh.

It was a game in which Notre Dame's defense set the tone by simply dominating the Panthers' ground forays (Pitt finished with eight net rushing yards, compared to 352 for the Irish). After quarterback Rod Rutherford was sacked eight times, Jones turned the tables on the home team. And that's with a team rushing attack that ranked 110th in the nation coming into the game.

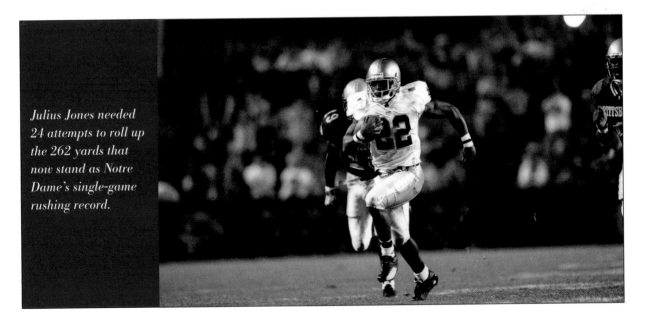

Julius Jones needed 24 attempts to roll up the 262 yards that now stand as Notre Dame's single-game rushing record.

Jones went 25 yards for the first points of the game after a Pitt fumble on a punt, then Rutherford, who led the nation in passing at the time, came back with a pair of touchdown passes to Larry Fitzgerald in fewer than two minutes. After the second of those, which came after a 71-yard punt return by Pitt's William "Tutu" Ferguson, Jones tied the score four minutes later on a 49-yard romp. The Irish held Fitzgerald without a catch in the final two periods, and Irish lineman Justin Tuck recorded 10 tackles and 3.5 sacks.

The Determining Factor: Jones sprinted 61 yards in the fourth period on the key play of a 68-yard Irish drive that took up 9:14 minutes, featured 15 running plays out of 16, and cemented the outcome—in a second half in which neither team scored a touchdown.

The Star of the Show: Jones. No running back's ever been more productive in a single game in the history of Notre Dame football. That's saying something.

Scoring runs from 25 and 49 yards out punctuated Julius Jones's record night at Heinz Field.

Scoring Summary

Notre Dame	7	10	3	0	20
Pittsburgh	7	7	0	0	14

First Quarter
Notre Dame: Jones 25 run (Setta kick) (12:08)
Pittsburgh: Fitzgerald 23 pass from Rutherford (Abdul kick) (:00)

Second Quarter
Pittsburgh: Fitzgerald 4 pass from Rutherford (Abdul kick) (13:05)
Notre Dame: Jones 49 run (Fitzpatrick kick) (8:54)
Notre Dame: Fitzpatrick 19 field goal (:33)

Third Quarter
Notre Dame: Fitzpatrick 34 field goal (7:10)
Attendance: 66,421

What the Headlines Said: "As much as tailback Julius Jones's running and a suffocating defensive performance propelled Notre Dame to its upset of Pittsburgh on Saturday night, it was the clock-draining final drive that sealed it for the Irish. Sixteen plays. Three third-down conversions. Sixty-eight yards. Nine minutes and 14 seconds gone by."–*South Bend Tribune*

"Julius Jones played the kind of game that fairy tales are made of, the type that seems usually to reside only in dreams. Only, his performance was real, played out in front of a Heinz Field capacity crowd and a national cable TV audience."–*Chicago Tribune*

"With the West Coast offense failing to produce the desired results, Notre Dame went back to basics Saturday night and simply played power football on both sides of the ball."–*Chicago Sun-Times*

What the Players and Coaches Said: "There's nothing better than having nine minutes left and just keep pounding it down the field until the game is over," said Irish tackle Jim Molinaro.

"That was unreal. I haven't seen that in a long time–the offense runs the ball at will. That was domination. That was masterful," said Irish safety Glenn Earl.

The Rundown: The Irish won three of their last four games to finish 5–7 overall.

The Panthers won their next four games, lost to Virginia in the Continental Tire Bowl, and ended up 8–5 overall (5–2 Big East).

Statistics

Team Statistics

Category	Notre Dame	Pittsburgh
First Downs	14	9
Rushing	12	2
Passing	2	6
Penalty	0	1
Rushing Attempts	56	27
Yards Gained Rushing	384	78
Yards Lost Rushing	32	70
Net Yards Rushing	352	8
Net Yards Passing	33	167
Passes Attempted	17	30
Passes Completed	5	12
Interceptions Thrown	1	0
Total Offensive Plays	73	57
Total Net Yards	385	175
Average Gain Per Play	5.3	3.1
Fumbles: Number Lost	2-0	3-2
Penalties: Number-Yards	6-50	6-40
Punts-Yards	6-224	9-391
Average Yards Per Punt	37.3	43.4
Punt Returns-Yards	5-96	3-76
Kickoff Returns-Yards	2-33	4-51
Interception Returns-Yards	0-0	1-0
Fumble Returns-Yards	0-0	0-0
Time of Possession	36:46	23:14
Third Down Conversions	7-20	2-15
Fourth Down Conversions	0-2	0-0
Sacks By-Yards	8-66	2-16

Notre Dame's Individual Statistics

Rushing: Jones 24-262-2, Grant 27-84, Powers-Neal 1-7, Wilson 1-3, Quinn 3-(-16), Clark 0-(-12)

Passing: Quinn 17-5-1-33-0

Receiving: Fasano 2-15, Jenkins 1-19, McKnight 1-6, Jones 1-7

Pittsburgh's Individual Statistics

Rushing: Walker 10-37, Polite 2-4, Team 1-(-1), Rutherford 14-(-32)

Passing: Rutherford 30-12-0-167-2

Receiving: Fitzgerald 5-79-2, Brockenbrough 3-61, Polite 2-14, Wilson 1-9, Stephens 1-4

Joe Montana, one of the most successful Notre Dame quarterbacks of all time, on the field in 1977.

Six Games That Cemented Joe Montana's Reputation as a Notre Dame Football God

Maybe it's because of all his Super Bowl success with the San Francisco 49ers. Maybe it's because his Notre Dame career had more than its share of ups and downs. Regardless, the athletics media relations office at Notre Dame never received more phone calls looking for information about any individual player than it did on Montana.

It started in South Bend, Indiana, where the Monongahela, Pennsylvania, native made a habit of bringing his Irish teams from behind to victory, often coming off the bench to do it.

Despite his success at Notre Dame, including the 1977 national title, Montana wasn't selected by the NFL until the third round by the 49ers. It didn't take long for that to become a head-shaking fact worthy of analysis. Once he hit the field in San Francisco, good things began to happen on a regular basis (translation: Super Bowl wins and MVP awards) for Bill Walsh's teams. The inquiries that began with the Bay Area media expanded to include the national journalists, as Montana and the 49ers established themselves as the professional program to beat.

After Montana positioned himself as the best quarterback in the game, writers wanted to know how it was that Montana never managed to become the regular signal-caller until his fourth season on the Notre Dame campus. They wanted to know every detail of the list of comebacks for which Montana served as architect.

By the end of Montana's college career, longtime sports information director Roger Valdiserri had created a handy-dandy single sheet that included the game-by-game numbers for those comeback efforts, with statistics looking even gaudier when listed side by side with the exact time Montana spent on the field (in a number of cases, it wasn't very much).

By 1991, the annual *Notre Dame Football Guide* contained a lengthy glossary entry (actually a full page) that detailed Montana's Irish career on a year-by-year basis. Junior varsity in 1974 as a freshman. A couple of starts and some amazing off-the-bench, game-winning rallies as a sophomore. Separated shoulder that scratched the '76 campaign. Third string at one point early in '77, only to become the starter and never a loser again that year as the Irish won the national championship. A solid all-around season in '78, capped off by the legendary comeback in the cold of the Cotton Bowl in his final college performance.

Exactly how did Montana earn the nickname "Comeback Kid"?

These six contests did the trick.

Notre Dame 21 • North Carolina 14
OCTOBER 11, 1975, AT CHAPEL HILL

Montana Needs Barely Half a Period to Dispatch the Tar Heels

Two fourth-period touchdown throws by Joe Montana (shown here in a 1976 photo) brought the Irish home from Chapel Hill with a victory.

The Run-Up: In Dan Devine's first season as head coach, the Irish came into their match with the Tar Heels at 3–1. The Irish had lost to Michigan State University the previous week in Joe Montana's first career start at quarterback.

North Carolina came in with a 2–2 record after a victory at the University of Virginia the week before.

The Pertinent Details: Down 14–0 as late as the 12-minute mark of the final period, Notre Dame somehow exploded for three touchdowns in the fourth quarter to get past the Tar Heels.

The first of those scores came on a 65-yard march led by starter Rick Slager. But after Slager threw three straight incompletions on the next possession, on came Montana. The Irish were down 14–6, with 6:04 remaining. He promptly threw 39 yards to Dan Kelleher to set up an Al Hunter touchdown run and added the two-point conversion toss. That tying drive lasted all of 46 seconds and involved 73 yards and five plays.

After Carolina missed a field goal, on came Montana again at the 1:19 mark. On the second play, Ted Burgmeier scored on a short throw that went the distance—80 yards, two plays, 16 seconds.

Carolina had grabbed the third-period lead after the Irish mishandled the snap on an attempted punt, leaving Mike Voight, who ultimately finished with 169 yards, to go 12 yards for the six points on the first play.

Carolina's Mike Voight rips off some of his 169 rushing yards, as Notre Dame's Tom Lopienski (No. 26) drags him down.

The Heels also scored on their next possession to cap a 90-yard drive.

The Determining Factor: What should have been an eight-yard gain on an audible out pattern from Montana to Burgmeier turned into an 80-yard touchdown scamper to win the football game after Burgmeier eluded a Tar Heels defensive back.

The Star of the Show: Can you guess? Montana. He was on the field all of 62 seconds, completed three of four passes for 129 yards, and produced the tying and winning touchdowns.

What the Headlines Said: "Ted Burgmeier didn't start the football game for Notre Dame Saturday. Neither did Joe Montana. But these sophomores ended it in North Carolina with an incredible 80-yard touchdown connection that gave the Irish a tremendous victory in what might have been the greatest rally in school history."—Joe Doyle in the *South Bend Tribune*

"Any time you charge $10 for a football ticket, the teams ought to put on a great show. And the 49,500—third record crowd on the road for Notre Dame this season—got their money's worth here Saturday." — *South Bend Tribune*

Scoring Summary

Notre Dame	0	0	0	21	21
North Carolina	0	0	14	0	14

Third Quarter

North Carolina: Voight 12 run (Biddle kick) (10:03)

North Carolina: Collins 39 pass from Paschall (Biddle kick) (1:34)

Fourth Quarter

Notre Dame: Hunter 2 run (pass failed) (11:27)

Notre Dame: Hunter 2 run (Buth pass from Montana) (5:18)

Notre Dame: Burgmeier 80 pass from Montana (Reeve kick) (1:03)

What the Players and Coaches Said: "I told Joe [Montana] to call a draw, but to be alert for the pass to Ted Burgmeier if the cornerback backed off. We were just trying to get the first down," said Devine.

"After I caught it, I saw the cornerback had overrun the play. I just wanted to get what I could, then get out of bounds. I gave the defender a fake toward the open field, and that neutralized him," said Burgmeier.

"That was as hard a loss as you can take, one of the biggest disappointments of my life," said North Carolina coach Bill Dooley.

"Their disappointment is only surpassed by our elation. We did everything wrong for the first three quarters. Then we did everything right," said Devine.

"I didn't think I'd be going in. But I knew there was still time," said Montana.

The Rundown: Notre Dame ended up 8–3 overall, opted not to play in a bowl game, and finished 17th in the final coaches' poll.

North Carolina lost its next four games and ended up 3–7–1.

Statistics

Team Statistics

Category	Notre Dame	North Carolina
First Downs	23	15
First Downs	18	22
Rushing	9	13
Passing	9	8
Penalty	0	1
Rushing Attempts	45	58
Net Yards Rushing	171	233
Net Yards Passing	218	161
Passes Attempted	26	22
Passes Completed	15	11
Interceptions Thrown	1	0
Total Offensive Plays	71	80
Total Net Yards	389	394
Average Gain Per Play	5.47	4.9
Fumbles: Number Lost	2–1	2–1
Penalties: Number-Yards	5–45	4–40
Punts-Yards	8	8
Average Yards Per Punt	37.8	44.4
Punt Returns-Yards	2–4	3–11
Kickoff Returns-Yards	3–84	4–61
Interception Returns-Yards	0–0	1–5

Notre Dame's Individual Statistics

Rushing: Heavens 17-109, Hunter 10-27, McLane 5-11, Eurick 1-3, Weiler 1-1, Orsini 1-6, Slager 10-14

Passing: Slager 22-12-1-106, Montana 4-3-0-129-1

Receiving: Burgmeier 3-101-1, McLane 3-36, Kelleher 2-54, MacAfee 3-36, Hunter 2-(-7), Weiler 2-(-2)

North Carolina's Individual Statistics

Rushing: Voight 36-169, Smith 11-55, Collins 3-11, C.Williams 1-5, Mills 1-2, Mabry 1-4, Tedder 3-1, Paschall 2-(-14)

Passing: Paschall 22-11-0-161-1

Receiving: Collins 4-69-1, C.Williams 3-33, B.Williams 2-27, Stanford 2-32

Notre Dame 31 • Air Force 30
OCTOBER 18, 1975, AT COLORADO SPRINGS

Second Straight Late Road Comeback Frustrates Air Force

The Run-Up: Notre Dame came into the matchup with a 4–1 record and rated 15th by the Associated Press after the Irish had come from behind to win at North Carolina the previous Saturday.

Air Force came in at 0–4–1, with a tie versus UCLA the lone bright spot.

The Pertinent Details: This time Montana came into the game just before halftime (after starter Slager had managed only one completion in seven attempts for seven yards) and played the rest of the way. Montana wasn't perfect (three interceptions), but he should get credit for getting his Irish into the end zone three times in a little more than seven minutes.

Down 30–10 in the final period, Notre Dame made great use of a 29-yard Ken MacAfee reception to the 16, then Montana bootlegged it himself from the 3. After Air Force lost a fumble at the Notre Dame 35, Montana gave it back with an interception, except the Falcons fumbled it back on the Irish 15 before that play was over. Montana hooked up with Mark McLane on a 66-yarder, then found MacAfee from seven yards out to make it 30–24. The Falcons couldn't get a first down, the Irish took over on their 45 with 4:34 left, and Hunter scooted 43 yards off right tackle to set up Jerome Heavens's short game-winning tote.

The Determining Factor: Heavens gave Notre Dame its only lead of the afternoon, with a two-yard run with 3:23 on the clock to cap off a 55-yard drive (43 of it on the one run by Hunter).

The Stars of the Show: Montana was the star that day, but with lots of company: MacAfee (three critical receptions), McLane (the 66-yard reception to set up one score), Hunter (his 43-yard run set up Heavens's final touchdown), kicker Dave Reeve (his field goal and four points after touchdown were essential), Heavens (138 yards), Jay Achterhoff (a big fumble recovery), and freshman Joe Restic (51.6 punting average).

Air Force's Jim Miller intercepted three Montana passes, but it wasn't enough.

What the Headlines Said: "Notre Dame's offense sometimes sputters but with Joe Montana, it never dies. Three times the Irish attack gave Air Force an easy touchdown shot and the aroused Falcons made the most of each shot, plus three Dave Lawson field goals. Then that same offense clicked for three fourth-period touchdowns in another fantastic victory, 31–30, with Montana again joining a list of heroes."—Joe Doyle in the *South Bend Tribune*

"Down 20 points with 13 minutes to play seems like the improbable or the impossible. But don't use those words around Notre Dame in 1975.... Last week, [Dan] Devine labeled the comeback victory at North Carolina 'my greatest ever.' But he had to revise this Saturday after the Irish cardiac kids did it again." —*South Bend Tribune*

"Did he [Devine] think that his team was ever dispirited or out of the game? 'I've been in coaching too long to ever think of giving up. We had players sitting down resting because they were exhausted. I

Scoring Summary

Notre Dame	0	3	7	21	31
Air Force	0	13	17	0	30

Second Quarter

Air Force: Lawson 45 field goal (13:56)

Air Force: Worden 16 run (Lawson kick) (7:12)

Notre Dame: Reeve 31 field goal (3:12)

Air Force: Lawson 52 field goal (:03)

Third Quarter

Notre Dame: Heavens 54 run (Reeves kick) (13:08)

Air Force: Reiner 14 run (Lawson kick) (9:54)

Air Force: Lawson 41 field goal (2:59)

Air Force: Williams 32 pass from Worden (Lawson kick) (2:43)

Fourth Quarter

Notre Dame: Montana 3 run (Reeve kick) (10:26)

Notre Dame: MacAfee 7 pass from Montana (Reeve kick) (5:29)

Notre Dame: Heavens 1 run (Reeve kick) (3:23)

Attendance: 43,204

Statistics

Team Statistics

Category	Notre Dame	Air Force
First Downs	19	19
Rushing	13	10
Passing	4	9
Penalty	2	0
Rushing Attempts	55	31
Yards Gained Rushing	343	127
Yards Lost Rushing	23	37
Net Yards Rushing	320	90
Net Yards Passing	141	251
Passes Attempted	25	34
Passes Completed	8	19
Interceptions Thrown	3	0
Total Offensive Plays	80	75
Total Net Yards	461	341
Average Gain Per Play	5.76	4.55
Fumbles: Number Lost	3-2	3-2
Penalties: Number-Yards	5-43	7-57
Punts-Yards	5-258	8-336
Average Yards Per Punt	51.6	42.0
Punt Returns-Yards	4-23	4-41
Kickoff Returns-Yards	2-49	2-27
Interception Returns-Yards	0-0	3-46

Notre Dame's Individual Statistics

Rushing: Heavens 20-138-2, Hunter 10-86, McLane 4-22, Eurick 6-44, Weiler 1-5, Montana 7-(-7)-1, Orsini 7-32

Passing: Slager 7-1-0-7-0, Montana 18-7-3-134-2

Receiving: Heavens 1-(-5), McLane 1-66, Kelleher 2-21, MacAfee 3-48-1, Burgmeier 1-11

Air Force's Individual Statistics

Rushing: Reiner 16-42, Worden 14-29, Shaw 1-4, Bushell 1-5, Mlodrgvch 1-4, Bream 1-5, Monahan 3-4

Passing: Worden 34-19-0-251-0

Receiving: Reiner 6-85, Williams 4-69, Mlodrgvch 1-4, Bream 2-6, Bushell 1-13, Covington 3-31, Monahan 1-4, Frozena 1-39

don't think this team can ever believe it would be beaten.'"– *South Bend Tribune*

What the Players and Coaches Said: "We've never tried harder and I thought we could pull it off, but that Montana was really hummin' the ball," said Air Force coach Ben Martin.

"Words can't express how proud I am of this team," said Devine.

"What's he [Montana] telling you? You know he was sounding like Knute Rockne in the huddle?" kidded Irish captain Ed Bauer.

The Rundown: Notre Dame ended up 8–3 and finished 17th in the last poll of coaches.

The Falcons won November games against Army and Tulane University to finish 2–8–1.

3 Notre Dame 31 • Purdue 24
SEPTEMBER 24, 1977, AT WEST LAFAYETTE

Montana Becomes Number-One Irish Quarterback—Finally for Good

The Run-Up: The highly regarded Irish already were in a hole after a 20–13 loss at the University of Mississippi the previous week. That made the Irish 1–1 and rated 11th by the AP coming into this one.

Purdue University was 1–1, with a loss at Michigan State University and a win over Ohio University.

The Pertinent Details: Montana came into this game (his first appearance since the end of the 1975 season) as the third-string Irish quarterback. Rusty Lisch started. When Lisch was ineffective, Coach Devine went to backup Gary Forystek. When Forystek suffered what turned out to be a career-ending neck injury and had to be carried off the field on a stretcher, the Irish went back to Lisch once more. The Irish actually led 14–10 at one point after Lisch's second touchdown pass to Terry Eurick. But when it became apparent that Lisch wasn't working out, it was Montana's turn. Mark this down—this was the last day in an Irish uniform that Joe Montana was not the starting quarterback.

Purdue's rookie sensation Mark Herrmann looked like he'd be the star of the show. He threw for 270 yards in the first half alone, and his three touchdown passes staked his Boilermakers to a 24–14 lead heading into the final period. His 51 attempts were a Purdue record.

After a Montana-led field-goal drive made it a one-touchdown deficit, Herrmann was picked off by Luther

Bradley, and the Irish were in business at the Purdue 35. Montana completed one two-yard throw to MacAfee, then went back to MacAfee for the tying touchdown.

The defense handed it back to Montana 58 yards away with a little more than three minutes to go. Completions to Kris Haines, Dave Mitchell, and MacAfee put the Irish on the Boilers 11. Heavens went for the first five, then Mitchell for the last five.

Ballgame.

Scoring Summary

Notre Dame	0	14	0	17	**31**
Purdue	10	14	0	0	**24**

First Quarter
Purdue: Sovereen 25 field goal (10:26)
Purdue: Arnold 8 pass from Herrmann (Sovereen kick) (6:28)

Second Quarter
Notre Dame: Eurick 6 pass from Lisch (Reeve kick) (13:42)
Notre Dame: Eurick 18 pass from Lisch (Reeve kick) (12:11)
Purdue: Smith 37 pass from Herrmann (Sovereen kick) (10:00)
Purdue: Pope 43 pass from Herrmann (Sovereen kick) (5:12)

Fourth Quarter
Notre Dame: Dave Reeve 24 field goal (13:18)
Notre Dame: MacAfee 13 pass from Montana (Reeve kick) (10:25)
Notre Dame: Mitchell 5 run (Reeve kick) (1:39)
Attendance: 68,966

Jerome Heavens (No. 30) led the Irish with 40 rushing yards, but it was Joe Montana's 154 passing yards off the bench that did the trick for Notre Dame in West Lafayette.

The Determining Factor: Mitchell put the finishing touches on yet another Montana-led comeback by running five yards for the game-winning points with fewer than two minutes remaining.

The Star of the Show: Once again, Montana played limited minutes but completed nine of 14 passes for 154 yards. Once again, his presence sparked another Irish comeback road triumph.

What the Headlines Said: "Miracle Man Montana Moves Mountains"—*Golden Glory*

"For so long it was simply a memory. Joe Montana had a lot to look back on in his four years at the Dome, but on this September afternoon one would swear his diary was complete. The cheers which once surrounded him were no longer heard. He was the forgotten man in the Irish attack, and why would anyone be foolish enough to think his statistics would

change within the confines of Ross-Ade Stadium?"
—Notre Dame *Scholastic*

"The bulletin board material had been loaded and fired. The freshman quarterback [Mark Herrmann] Purdue had persuaded to help write its history was in place. The Irish came forward and waited and waited for the right stage setting. Once all was in order, Notre Dame Coach Dan Devine let out quarterback Joe Montana. And the rest, my friends, is Notre Dame history."—*Golden Glory*

What the Players and Coaches Said: "I could see it in their eyes. We had them. And then it changed. They got that spark and it was like a whole new game," said Purdue's John Skibinski.

"It was one of the greatest exhibitions I've ever seen by a team. Sometimes when you back an Irishman into a corner he comes out fighting," said Devine.

"The things that worked for us in the first half just didn't go in the second half. It was our inability to move the football that made the difference," said Purdue coach Jim Young.

"When you come off the bench there is really no time for pressure. Something is going wrong anyway or you won't be coming in," said Montana.

The Rundown: The Irish never lost again, finishing 11–1 after a convincing 38–10 Cotton Bowl win over the top-ranked University of Texas. That handed the Irish the consensus national title.

Purdue won four of its next six outings to finish 5–6 (3–5 in Big Ten play).

Statistics

Team Statistics

Category	Notre Dame	Purdue
First Downs	23	23
Rushing	6	5
Passing	16	16
Penalty	1	2
Rushing Attempts	40	35
Yards Gained Rushing	134	110
Yards Lost Rushing	25	57
Net Yards Rushing	109	53
Net Yards Passing	315	351
Passes Attempted	42	51
Passes Completed	25	24
Interceptions Thrown	2	4
Total Offensive Plays	82	86
Total Net Yards	424	404
Average Gain Per Play	5.2	4.7
Fumbles: Number Lost	4-3	0-0
Penalties: Number-Yards	7-84	8-83
Punts-Yards	6-214	7-257
Average Yards Per Punt	35.7	36.7
Punt Returns-Yards	3-3	0-0
Kickoff Returns-Yards	4-54	4-60
Interception Returns-Yards	4-62	2-15
Time of Possession	29:24	30:36
Third Down Conversions	5-14	6-15

Notre Dame's Individual Statistics

Rushing: Heavens 13-40, Lisch 8-33, Mitchell 5-17-1, Fasano 1-9, Eurick 6-8, Forystek 1-4, Waymer 1-2, Orsini 1-(-1), Montana 4-(-3)

Passing: Montana 14-9-0-154-1, Lisch 25-14-2-149-2, Forystek 3-2-0-12-0

Receiving: Haines 5-120, MacAfee 9-114-1, Eurick 4-26-2, Dickerson 1-23, Waymer 3-22, Stone 1-4, Mitchell 1-4, Heavens 1-2

Purdue's Individual Statistics

Rushing: Skibinski 17-68, Brown 8-20, Leverett 2-8, Pope 3-5, Herrmann 5-(-48)

Passing: Herrmann 51-24-4-351-3

Receiving: Arnold 4-84-1, Young 7-80, Smith 4-74-1, Pope 3-64-1, Burrell 1-18

Notre Dame 26 • Pittsburgh 17
OCTOBER 14, 1978, AT NOTRE DAME STADIUM

Yet Another Magic Fourth Period Ends Well for the Irish

The Run-Up: Defending national champion Notre Dame came in at 2–2 and unranked after losing home games to the universities of Missouri and Michigan to open the season.

Ninth-ranked University of Pittsburgh came in at 4–0.

The Pertinent Details: So what else is new? Notre Dame was down 17–7 in the fourth period. That was hardly unusual for Montana and the Irish. All it took was an early fourth-quarter touchdown by Pittsburgh to jumpstart Notre Dame's offense.

First Montana headlined an 86-yard scoring march that cut the deficit to four points after a missed two-point conversion throw. After Pitt managed only a single first down and punted, Montana found Haines for 30 and Dean Masztak for 22. Montana ran it in himself for the 19–17 lead. When the Panthers

Joe Montana connected on 11 of his 15 second-half throws to fuel the Irish comeback against Pittsburgh in 1978.

Irish linebacker Steve Heimkreiter (No. 58) made 15 tackles and recovered a fumble to help Notre Dame hold off the Panthers.

fumbled the ball back at the Irish 29, Montana converted a fourth-and-2 challenge with a 13-yard toss to Dennis Grindinger. On fourth and goal from the 3, Montana rolled right and found Vagas Ferguson for the touchdown. Any chance Pitt could rebound ended when Dave Waymer intercepted for Notre Dame on the last of five Panther turnovers.

The Determining Factor: Montana cinched the verdict with his fourth-down touchdown pass from the 3 with 2:04 on the clock.

The Stars of the Show: Montana, who completed seven straight passes over one stretch of the fourth period for 110 yards and 11 of 15 passes in the second half, finished with 218 yards overall. He also ran for a score.

Scoring Summary

Notre Dame	7	0	0	19	26
Pittsburgh	0	10	0	7	17

First Quarter
Notre Dame: Heavens 1 touchdown run (Unis kick) (4:14)

Second Quarter
Pittsburgh: Trocano 3 run (Schubert kick) (4:22)
Pittsburgh: Schubert 33 field goal (2:41)

Fourth Quarter
Pittsburgh: Trocano 4 run (Schubert kick) (13:52)
Notre Dame: Haines 8 pass from Montana (pass failed) (10:59)
Notre Dame: Montana 1 run (kick failed) (7:08)
Notre Dame: Ferguson 3 pass from Montana (Unis kick) (2:04)
Attendance: 59,075

Veteran halfback Heavens, who ran 30 times for 120 yards, surpassed the great George Gipp and became Notre Dame's all-time leading rusher (Gipp held the mark at 2,341 yards).

What the Headlines Said: "Winning One for the Heavens"—Notre Dame *Scholastic*

"Jerome Heavens may have broken George Gipp's all-time rushing record here Saturday but the Irish would hardly have put this one on the win side of the ledger without one Joe Montana. It was Notre Dame 26, Pittsburgh 17 as Montana added to his long list of efforts which on so many occasions have brought the Irish back from the brink of defeat to victory."—Fort Wayne *News-Sentinel*

What the Players and Coaches Said: "I'm glad to have the record, but I'm happier with the win," said Heavens.

"We weren't worried," said Montana.

The Rundown: The Irish won five straight games after this one, fell to USC to end the regular season, then bounced back to beat ninth-ranked Houston in the Cotton Bowl. The 9–3 mark left them ranked seventh by the AP and sixth in the final polls.

Pittsburgh won four of its next five games and lost to North Carolina State in the Tangerine Bowl. The Panthers ended up 8–4 after finishing the regular season 16th in the AP poll.

Statistics

Team Statistics

Category	Notre Dame	Pittsburgh
First Downs	19	20
Rushing	6	14
Passing	11	6
Penalty	2	0
Rushing Attempts	53	57
Yards Gained Rushing	189	246
Yards Lost Rushing	15	48
Net Yards Rushing	174	198
Net Yards Passing	218	117
Passes Attempted	25	22
Passes Completed	15	10
Interceptions Thrown	0	2
Total Offensive Plays	78	79
Total Net Yards	392	315
Average Gain Per Play	5.0	4.0
Fumbles: Number Lost	3–1	4–3
Penalties: Number-Yards	6–48	4–40
Punts-Yards	7–266	5–166
Average Yards Per Punt	38.0	33.2
Punt Returns-Yards	4–(-14)	1–6
Kickoff Returns-Yards	2–42	4–66
Interception Returns-Yards	0–0	2–0
Time of Possession	28:57	31:03
Third Down Conversions	7–19	7–15
Fourth Down Conversions	-0	0–0

Notre Dame's Individual Statistics

Rushing: Heavens 30–120–1, Ferguson 10–28, Montana 10–28–1, Stone 1–(-6), Mitchell 1–3, Pallas 1–1

Passing: Montana 25–15–0–218–2

Receiving: Haines 4–70–1, Pallas 1–22, Heavens 2–28, Ferguson 2–7–1, Grindinger 3–44, Masztak 3–47

Pittsburgh's Individual Statistics

Rushing: Jacobs 19–81, Trocano 22–37–2, R. Jones 15–82, Sims 1–(-2)

Passing: Trocano 21–10–2–117–0, Sims 1–0–0–0–0

Receiving: Gaustao 3–33, G. Jones 4–58, Still 1–13, Jacobs 1–6, R. Jones 1–7

5 USC 27 • Notre Dame 25
NOVEMBER 25, 1978, AT LOS ANGELES

Montana Does It Again against Trojans—Almost

The Run-Up: Notre Dame came in 8–2 and ranked eighth by the AP, having won eight straight games.

USC came in 9–1 and ranked third (AP), the lone loss coming at Arizona State University.

The Pertinent Details: This might have gone down as Montana's greatest-ever comeback effort on a long list of those sorts of occasions, only USC refused to cooperate.

On a day in which USC rolled for 538 total yards (the most ever against a Notre Dame team), it looked like the day was done when the Trojans took a commanding 24–6 fourth-quarter lead. But when USC missed a short field goal after driving 96 yards, suddenly everything the Irish touched turned to gold. Here's what Notre Dame produced on its five second-half possessions: field goal, fumble after reaching the USC 1, touchdown, touchdown, touchdown.

Montana first threw a 57-yard touchdown pass to Haines (that capped an 80-yard possession), used a handful more of completions to Haines (four for 64) to set up a Pete Buchanan score on a 98-yard drive, then (taking over at the 1:35 mark) ended a string of 19 straight points by the Irish when he found Holohan from two yards to take the 25–24 lead with 46 seconds left.

The Determining Factor: Officials said Paul McDonald's lost football in the final minute was an incomplete pass as opposed to a fumble recovery by Jeff Weston. McDonald then threw 35 yards to Calvin Sweeney on the next play, Charles White ran for five, and Frank Jordan kicked it through from 37 yards with two seconds left to dim the memory of what Montana and his mates had done.

The Stars of the Show: Montana threw for 358 yards (20 of 41, with 17 of the completions in the second half) for the Irish.

Meanwhile, White (fourth in the Heisman vote) ran it for a career-best 205 for the Trojans.

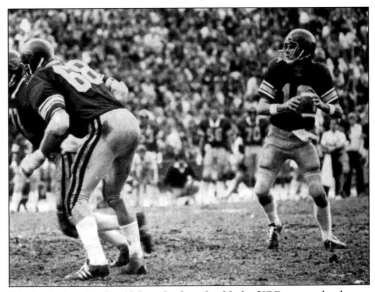

The Irish thought they'd forced a late fumble by USC quarterback Paul McDonald (No. 12), but officials ruled otherwise.

What the Headlines Said: "The Whistle of Misfortune"—Notre Dame *Scholastic*

"For ND: A Toe of Woe"—*Glamour Game*

"It's difficult to admit that one team won and the other lost in a game like this. But cold statistics must always come into play. The Irish were looking for their 600th all-time win, instead they left L.A. with their 160th all-time loss. For most, however, a loss that will stand out much more than many of the previous 599 wins."—Notre Dame *Scholastic*

"Jordan Goes Into His Two-Second Drill Again" —*Los Angeles Times*

"Sorry, Rock; Sorry, Gipper; Sorry, Pat; Sorry, Ronnie"—*Los Angeles Times*

"Move over Rod Sherman. Step aside Anthony Davis. Take your place, Johnny Baker. And while you're about it, this isn't the time to think of O.J. or Mike Garrett or Grenny Lansdell, or any of the others in a long list of Southern California heroes who have

Scoring Summary

Notre Dame	3	0	3	19	25
USC	6	11	7	3	27

First Quarter
USC: Williams 30 pass from McDonald (kick failed) (3:32)
Notre Dame: Unis 47 field goal (:43)

Second Quarter
USC: Garcia 35 pass from McDonald (Hunter pass from McDonald) (12:56)
USC: Jordan 39 field goal (3:53)

Third Quarter
Notre Dame: Unis 26 field goal (11:21)
USC: White 1 run (Jordan kick) (7:38)

Fourth Quarter
Notre Dame: Haines 57 pass from Montana (pass failed) (12:59)
Notre Dame: Buchanan 1 run (Unis kick) (2:01)
Notre Dame: Holohan 2 pass from Montana (pass failed) (:46)
SC: Jordan 37 field goal (:02)

Attendance: 84,256

Pete Buchanan runs for a touchdown in the 1978 USC game.

starred against Notre Dame. The new kid on the block is Frank Jordan and field goals are his fame."—*South Bend Tribune*

What the Players and Coaches Said: "I was praying the offense would get me in position to redeem myself," said Jordan, who missed both a field goal and point after touchdown.

"It was one of the most remarkable comebacks in the history of sport. I asked the players not to quit and they didn't. We were a different team in the second half," said Devine.

"(Paul) McDonald is the coolest quarterback I've ever been around," said USC coach John Robinson.

"I knew it was an incomplete pass," said McDonald.

"That was a crucial call. I won't be happy with it if it was a bad call," said Devine.

"It was the greatest football game I've ever seen. But maybe every USC–Notre Dame game is," said Robinson.

"I really don't think we lost," said Haines.

"It's really tough. I felt we had the game and seconds later, it's over and we lost. It's hard to believe," said Montana.

"I hit the guy and he fumbled, that's all I can say. He wasn't throwing the ball. He fumbled," said Weston.

The Rundown: The Irish beat Houston in the Cotton Bowl to finish 9–3 overall and rank seventh (AP) and sixth in the final polls.

USC defeated Michigan in the Rose Bowl to end up 12–1 and number one (UPI) and number two (AP, behind Alabama) in the final polls.

Statistics

Team Statistics

Category	Notre Dame	USC
First Downs	23	30
Rushing	6	16
Passing	15	13
Penalty	2	1
Rushing Attempts	35	57
Yards Gained Rushing	91	294
Yards Lost Rushing	38	37
Net Yards Rushing	53	257
Net Yards Passing	358	281
Passes Attempted	41	29
Passes Completed	20	17
Interceptions Thrown	1	1
Total Offensive Plays	76	86
Total Net Yards	411	538
Average Gain Per Play	5.41	6.26
Fumbles: Number Lost	2-1	2-1
Penalties: Number-Yards	4-40	8-86
Punts-Yards	5-225	5-168
Average Yards Per Punt	45.0	33.6
Punt Returns-Yards	2-4	3-13
Kickoff Returns-Yards	5-82	5-83
Interception Returns-Yards	1-19	1-9
Time of Possession	24:57	35:03
Third Down Conversions	7-16	6-14
Fourth Down Conversions	0-0	0-0

Notre Dame's Individual Statistics

Rushing: Montana 10-2, Heavens 8-23, Ferguson 11-32, Buchanan 3-4-1, Holohan 1-(-17), Pallas 2-9

Passing: Montana 41-20-1-358-2

Receiving: Heavens 2-10, Holohan 2-48-1, Haines 9-179-1, Ferguson 3-39, Mastztak 4-82

USC's Individual Statistics

Rushing: C. White 37-205-1, P. McDonald 2-(-19), Cain 11-53, Ford 6-34, Williams 1-(-16)

Passing: P. McDonald 29-17-1-281-2

Receiving: Williams 3-60-1, C. White 4-37, Cain 1-5, Ford 1-9, Sweeney 5-105, Garcia 1-35-1, Rakhshani 2-30

Notre Dame 35 • Houston 34
JANUARY 1, 1979, AT DALLAS IN THE COTTON BOWL

Chicken Broth Fuels Montana-Led Cotton Bowl Comeback in Cold

The Run-Up: Notre Dame came in with a record of 8–3 for the season and ranked 10th by the AP.

Houston came in at 9–2 and rated ninth by the AP, the only losses at the University of Memphis and Texas Tech University. The Cougars won eight straight games in the middle of the season and won the Southwest Conference title.

The Pertinent Details: Montana's final day in a Notre Dame football uniform might have been his most amazing—and his most improbable. It certainly wasn't easy because, from an early 12–0 lead, Notre Dame's defense gave up 34 straight points.

Despite suffering from hypothermia in the miserable weather (there was a minus-six degree wind chill) in Dallas, Montana engineered the greatest comeback in Irish history (as tabbed by longtime Irish athletics director Moose Krause). Notre Dame rebounded from a 34–12 deficit with seven and a half minutes remaining, throwing the game-tying touchdown pass as time expired (Joe Unis knocked the point after touchdown through for the 35–34 win).

Here's how it happened:

- With Houston punting from its own 33 with 7:37 left, freshman Tony Belden blocked it. Freshman Steve Cichy grabbed it and ran 33 yards to score. Montana followed that up with a two-point conversion throw to Ferguson to make it 34-20.

- With the ball back at his own 39 with 5:40 on the clock, Montana found Heavens for 30 yards. Montana ran for the touchdown, then hit Haines for another two-pointer, bringing the score to 34-28.

- The game appeared to be finished when Montana fumbled the ball away (the seventh Irish turnover) at the Houston 20.

Scoring Summary

Notre Dame	**12**	**0**	**0**	**23**	**35**
Houston	**7**	**13**	**14**	**0**	**34**

First Quarter
Notre Dame: Montana 3 run (kick failed) (6:55)
Notre Dame: Buchanan 1 run (pass failed) (4:40)
Houston: Adams 15 pass from Davis (Hatfield kick) (0:17)

Second Quarter
Houston: Love 1 run (Hatfield kick) (6:27)
Houston: Hatfield 21 field goal (3:00)
Houston: Hatfield 34 field goal (0:03)

Third Quarter
Houston: Davis 2 run (Hatfield kick) (6:29)
Houston: Davis 5 run (Hatfield kick) (4:40)

Fourth Quarter
Notre Dame: Cichy 33 return of blocked punt (Ferguson pass from Montana) (7:25)
Notre Dame: Montana 2 run (Haines pass from Montana) (4:15)
Notre Dame: Haines 8 pass from Montana (Unis kick) (0:00)
Attendance: 32,500

Quarterback Joe Montana looking to throw the ball against Houston in the 1979 Cotton Bowl.

- On fourth-and-1 from their own 29, the Cougars went for it, and Joe Gramke stopped Emmett King to give the ball back to the Irish with 28 seconds left.
- Montana ran right for 11 yards. He threw to Haines for 10 to the 8. He threw incomplete to Haines on the right sideline, then, as time expired, they ran the same play and hit it.

The Determining Factor: With no time left on the clock, Unis, a Dallas native, had to kick the game-winning point after touchdown not once but

Steve Cichy runs back a blocked punt for touchdown.

twice, after an illegal motion penalty against the Irish.

The Star of the Show: No contest—it was Montana, who overcame an awful first half to create a comeback win for the ages. He and many other players had bloodied knees and elbows from the salt used to attempt to melt the ice that caked the field. On top of

that, Montana's body temperature plummeted, and he remained in the locker room as the second half began, sipping chicken broth. Hard to believe you can throw four interceptions, miss significant portions of the game because of illness, fumble the ball away for an apparent game-losing turnover on a late possession, and still be the hero—but Montana accomplished that.

What the Headlines Said: "With seven minutes and 37 seconds left in the 43rd Cotton Bowl, only one unanswered question remained: Would the spring thaw reveal more victims? No one was wondering about the outcome of the game, least of all the Houston Cougars.... What happened in that final 7:37 staggers the imagination. A fiction writer wouldn't have the gall to try to peddle such a yarn."—*Dallas Times Herald*

"They call it the Cotton Bowl 'Classic,' and for the 43rd annual event which featured Notre Dame's thrilling 35–34 comeback victory over Houston, that label more than fit the bill. Cotton Bowl officials went so far as to say that the '79 Classic was the greatest in the history of the event. If not that, then it was certainly the most bizarre. How else would you describe a game in which: at one point, both teams' kicking units were lined up on the field ready to kick the ball off to each other; the Great North Wind, gusting at 30 miles per hour, deserved the defensive player-of-the-game award; 35,500 people decided not to show up for a game they had paid $12.50 each to attend; the first six scores came as the result of turnovers, and the winning point was scored with four goose eggs on the scoreboard where the time used to be displayed?"—Notre Dame *Scholastic*

"Outlined against a blue-gray January sky, people are falling on the ice like dominoes. Notre Dame students seem to be in shock, as if they expected to wake up in Tahiti and somehow found themselves in Butte, Montana."—*Dallas Morning News*

"In its 43 years of operation, the Cotton Bowl classic has never seen anything like it, but then few bowls have. Even the maybe 10,000 frostbitten souls who stayed around for the incredible finish had a difficult time believing what they had just seen. Indeed, some probably don't believe it yet, including the Houston Cougars."—*The Sporting News*

What the Players and Coaches Said: "It's just a quick out. We ran it the first time but Joe got rid of it a little too soon. He didn't give me enough time. Back in the huddle he asked me if I could beat my man again. When I said 'Yes,' Joe smiled and said, 'Let's do it,'" said Haines.

"You can quote me on this. I am all in favor of indoor football," said Houston coach Bill Yeoman.

"For these kids it was a fitting final chapter," said Devine.

"We started celebrating too soon," said King.

"I wasn't sick. I was just cold," said Montana.

"They told us Joe [Montana] was not coming back in the second half. And we thought it was over. But we've learned over the last four years that it's never over," said Irish center Dave Huffman, a Dallas native.

The Rundown: Notre Dame's final 9–3 mark put the Irish sixth and seventh in the final polls.

Houston ended up 9–3 and ranked 10th (AP) and 11th.

Statistics

Team Statistics

Category	Notre Dame	Houston
First Downs	13	16
Rushing	4	12
Passing	7	3
Penalty	2	1
Rushing Attempts	40	63
Yards Gained Rushing	144	253
Yards Lost Rushing	13	24
Net Yards Rushing	131	239
Net Yards Passing	163	60
Passes Attempted	37	13
Passes Completed	13	4
Interceptions Thrown	4	0
Total Offensive Plays	77	76
Total Net Yards	294	289
Average Gain Per Play	3.8	3.8
Fumbles: Number Lost	3–3	6–3
Penalties: Number-Yards	8–74	6–38
Punts-Yards	7–184	10–255
Average Yards Per Punt	26.3	25.5
Punt Returns-Yards	5–48	2– -2
Kickoff Returns-Yards	6–136	2–33
Interception Returns-Yards	0–0	4–43

Notre Dame's Individual Statistics

Rushing: Heavens 16–71, Montana 7–26–2, Ferguson 10–19, Pallas 4–11, Mitchell 1–3, Buchanan 2–1–1

Passing: Montana 34–13–3–163–1, Koegel 3–0–0–0–0

Receiving: Heavens 4–60, Haines 4–31–1, Masztak 3–49, Holohan 1–14, Ferguson 1–9

Houston's Individual Statistics

Rushing: Davis 19–76–2, King 21–74, Love 22–73–1, Brown 1–6

Passing: Davis 12–4–0–60–1, Brown 1–0–0–0–0

Receiving: Adams 2–35–1, Herring 2–25

Irish sophomore tailback Darius Walker scored the first touchdown of the Charlie Weis era at Notre Dame on a 51-yard screen pass from Brady Quinn to help beat Pittsburgh to start the 2005 season.

15 Other Games That Deserve Mention

This chapter is a tribute to Notre Dame's amazing track record of success over more than a century of football. Most schools have maybe only a handful of games that really qualify as legendary, or even memorable. Notre Dame has had so many remarkable seasons that there were often two or three games per year that were worth a tribute.

Take 1988. There was Reggie Ho kicking a last-minute field goal to beat ninth-ranked University of Michigan. The midseason Miami game? That one's obvious. Throw in the win at number-two ranked USC to end the regular season and the Fiesta Bowl against number three West Virginia University, and, really, where do you stop? And that's just one national championship season.

That's why this chapter took on landmark proportions. Just when you thought you'd counted up all the big upsets, all the great bowl wins, all games where the Irish seized victory from the hands of defeat at the 11th hour, and all the singular moments by individual players, you realized that there were still dozens of awesome football games left over that couldn't be left out. So we created another category just for them—the games that we decided we simply could not skip.

Here they are.

Notre Dame 11 • Michigan 3
NOVEMBER 6, 1909, AT ANN ARBOR
Notre Dame Defeats Michigan—Finally

The Run-Up: Notre Dame came in at 4–0, having shut out three opponents and outscored its four foes by a combined 141–11.

Michigan also came in 4–0, outscoring its opponents a combined 85–11.

The Pertinent Details: Notre Dame had yet to beat mighty Michigan in eight attempts, and Michigan had lost only five games in the last nine seasons combined.

Pete Vaughan scored the first Irish touchdown, apparently breaking the goalpost with his shoulder as he scored. Notre Dame outgained the home team in the first half alone by a 200–45 count in total yards.

The Determining Factor: Harry "Red" Miller blocked a potential lead-changing field-goal attempt from the 6-yard line by Michigan. Notre Dame then drove for its second touchdown, a 30-yard run by Billy Ryan.

The Star of the Show: Miller.

What the Headlines Said: "With the defeat went Michigan's chance of copping the Western Championship, for Notre Dame is now rated one of the most powerful machines in the Western Country." —*South Bend Tribune*

"All Michigan is in mourning this afternoon." —*Chicago American*

"Michigan was the stepladder by which Notre Dame today mounted the dizziest heights in its football history, the Catholics downing the Wolverines by a score of 11 to 3." —*Chicago Inter-Ocean*

Scoring Summary			
Notre Dame	5	6	11
Michigan	3	0	3

First Half

Michigan: Allerdice 22 field goal

Notre Dame: Vaughan 3 run (kick failed)

Second Half

Notre Dame: Ryan 30 run (Hamilton kick)

"Eleven fighting Irishmen wrecked the Yost machine this afternoon." —*Detroit Free Press*

"The victory of the Notre Dame football team over Michigan is a sporting event not to be lightly considered. It is the biggest victory in the field of sports which Notre Dame has achieved in many a year." —*South Bend Tribune* editorial

What the Players and Coaches Said: "It was deadly quiet. Then suddenly it was broken. 'We're going through!' someone called loudly in a hard, harsh voice I hardly recognized. It was my own," said Miller.

"They outplayed us, but we should have won," said Michigan coach Fielding Yost.

The Rundown: Notre Dame shut out Ohio's University of Miami and Wabash College at home the next two Saturdays, then tied Marquette University 0–0 in the regular-season finale. The Irish finished 7–0–1 in Frank Longman's first season as head coach (Longman played for Yost at Michigan in 1903–05).

Michigan defeated the universities of Pennsylvania and Minnesota the next two weeks to end up 6–1. Michigan called off the teams' meeting the following season in 1910, and the two schools did not meet again until 1942.

Notre Dame 13 • USC 12
DECEMBER 4, 1926, AT LOS ANGELES

Irish Find Late Victory in First-Ever Notre Dame–USC Meeting

The Run-Up: Notre Dame came into the game with an 8–1 record, having won its first eight assignments before falling 19–0 at Carnegie Institute of Technology the previous Saturday.

USC came in at 8–1, its only defeat a one-point loss against Stanford University.

Scoring Summary

Notre Dame	0	7	0	6	13
USC	0	6	0	6	12

Second Quarter
Notre Dame: Riley 16 run (O'Boyle kick)
USC: Kaer 1 run (kick failed)

Fourth Quarter
USC: Wiliams 9 run (kick failed)
Notre Dame: Niemiec 23 pass from Parisien (kick blocked)
Attendance: 74,378

Notre Dame's late-game victory at the Los Angeles Coliseum in the first meeting between the Irish and USC in 1926 should have been a hint of things to come in the rivalry with the Trojans.

The Pertinent Details: This became a landmark game simply because it was the inaugural contest in what has been the most noteworthy ongoing intersectional college football rivalry in the country. It came about based on a train conversation between Bonnie Rockne (wife of Knute) and Marion Wilson (wife of USC football graduate manager Gwynn).

The game was played evenly, with first downs even at 10 and USC holding a 289–230 edge in yards. But the Trojans hurt themselves by missing both points after touchdowns.

The Determining Factors: Rockne replaced starting quarterback Charles Riley (he scored Notre Dame's first touchdown) with Art Parisien, who threw a 23-yard touchdown pass to John Niemiec with fewer than two minutes left to bring Notre Dame from a 12–7 deficit.

The Star of the Show: The 5'7" Parisien, who had been told six weeks prior that he was out for the year because of a bruised heart, was the hero of the day. Rockne brought him to Los Angeles but apparently had no plans to play him—and didn't until the last series. Even then Parisien took part in all of three plays (he also connected with Niemiec for a 35-yard pass play earlier in the winning drive).

What the Headlines Said: "Rockne's Team Saves Game with Four Minutes to Play"—Unknown

"Parisien's Port-Sided Passes Defeat Trojans, 13-12"—*Chicago Herald and Examiner*

"Few knew his name. Few had ever heard of him. But Rockne knew his worth, knew that this was the right time to use him.... It seemed suicidal to take Riley out...'Why remove the best player you have' was the wail...out came Riley and in went Parisien, a little insignificant chap, who got down behind All-American center [Art] Boeringer and reached for the pigskin." —*Los Angeles Times*.

"Oola-la! 'Petit' Parisien, a fightin' Irishman and a slip of a boy weighing less than 150 pounds southpawed Notre Dame to a 13 to 12 football victory over University of Southern California today."—*Chicago Herald and Examiner*

"A pair of gorgeously executed forward passes in the closing minutes of a heart-breaking game enabled Notre Dame to win from U.S.C. by the margin of a single point, 13 to 12. It was a football battle that has never been excelled for brilliance, thrills and pulsating drama...."—Paul Lowry in the *Los Angeles Times*

What the Players and Coaches Said: This was "the greatest game I ever saw," said Rockne.

"I got up and took off for where I was supposed to be—and then I saw that hand come up over the crowd of players with the ball in it—that was all I saw—the hand with the ball in it. I caught the ball at the 5-yard line and stumbled over the goal," said Niemiec.

The Rundown: Notre Dame finished 9–1, with seven of its victories via the shutout route. The Irish gave up only 38 points during the season.

USC ended up 8–2, finishing second to Stanford in the Pacific Coast Conference (5–1).

Notre Dame 27 • USC 0
DECEMBER 6, 1930, AT LOS ANGELES
The Last Hurrah for Rockne

The Run-Up: Notre Dame came in at 9–0, with an 18-game win streak in what turned out to be Rockne's last season. Its most recent two wins had come on the road versus 7–0 Northwestern and 8–0–1 Army.

USC had a record of 8–1, its only loss a 7–6 decision at Washington State University, the eventual unbeaten Pacific Coast Conference champ and Rose Bowl participant. The Trojans had outscored their opponents by a combined 382–39 count.

The Pertinent Details: USC fumbled on the first play of the game, and it got worse from there for the home team. The Irish simply dismantled the Trojans, outgaining USC 433–140 in total yards (331–89 on the ground).

Who could have known that Knute Rockne's appearance on the winning sideline at the Los Angeles Coliseum in the 1930 finale would prove to be his last as a collegiate head coach?

Scoring Summary

Notre Dame	13	0	7	7	27
USC	0	0	0	0	0

First Quarter

Notre Dame: Carideo 19 pass from Schwartz (Carideo kick)

Notre Dame: O'Connor 80 run (kick failed)

Third Quarter

Notre Dame: O'Connor 7 pass from Schwartz (Carideo kick)

Fourth Quarter

Notre Dame: Lukats 14 run (Jaskwhich kick)

Attendance: 73,967

The Determining Factor: Reserve O'Connor ran 80 yards with a pitchout to give Notre Dame a 13–0 advantage after the opening period.

The Star of the Show: O'Connor, a halfback who was filling in at fullback for Savoldi, who was thrown out of school when officials found out he was married. The accomplishment was magnified with back Mullins injured and sidelined as well. When the Irish stopped in Tucson, Arizona, to practice on their way to Los Angeles, Rockne switched O'Connor's jersey to disguise his plan to put him at fullback.

What the Headlines Said: "The Irish won. And how! In an amazing game, one-sided from start to finish, punctuated by spectacular passing and scoring plays, Notre Dame vanquished Southern California 27–0, yesterday, and swept aside the last barrier to the Hoosier goal of a second successive unbeaten season."–*Los Angeles Times*

"With many saying that the 1930 team was the greatest in history, it means that Notre Dame played probably the best game of football that has ever been played. They had come to an unfavorable climate battered and weary from nine man-killing battles; they were without Joe Savoldi and Larry Mullins, their seasoned fullbacks; USC's Trojans were considered the strongest team in their history. But by some miracle, perhaps Rockne's own silent agreement with the general opinion that Notre Dame could not hope to win, his men went out to show the world what stuff heroes are made of and to crush in the worst defeat U.S.C. has had in the five years Howard Jones has coached there a great U.S.C. 11."–Notre Dame *Scholastic*

What the Players and Coaches Said: "You never saw a team so coolly and deliberate-like. Notre Dame was a machine doing things where the others were trying with their hands," said Will Rogers.

"This was the greatest Notre Dame team I've ever seen. We congratulate Notre Dame for playing football that was practically perfect," said USC coach Howard Jones.

"The boys played the greatest ballgame of the year," said Rockne.

The Rundown: Notre Dame's second straight national title came via its 10–0 record.

USC ended up 8–2, as the Pacific Coast Conference runner-up.

Four months later, on March 31, 1931, Rockne was killed in a plane crash near Bazaar, Kansas.

Notre Dame 26 • Northwestern 6
NOVEMBER 21, 1936, AT NOTRE DAME STADIUM

First Time Ever (But Not the Last) Irish Beat a Number-One Opponent

The Run-Up: Notre Dame came in at 5–2 and ranked number 11, having beaten Army at Yankee Stadium the previous Saturday.

Northwestern stood at number one in the country in the first year of the AP poll, with a 7–0 record.

The Pertinent Details: After a tough midseason stretch in which Notre Dame scored just one combined touchdown, the Irish revamped their offense to feature agile backs Bob Wilke and Bunny McCormick. Just two weeks after being shut out by Navy in Baltimore, Notre Dame rebounded on the shoulders of Wilke's 30- and 34-yard touchdown runs.

The Determining Factor: Maybe when the Associated Press chose to begin its college football ratings with this season it affected the game. That meant unbeaten Northwestern came to South Bend, Indiana, in need of a victory to wrap up its national championship. But, as became a great Notre Dame tradition, this was the first of eight wins in history by the Irish over number-one-rated (AP) opponents—and one of only three ever at Notre Dame Stadium (also Miami in '88 and Florida State in '93).

The Star of the Show: Wilke, whose two lengthy, first-half scoring excursions staked the Irish to a lead they held all day.

What the Headlines Said: "56,000 Watch Notre Dame Snap Northwestern String: Ramblers Upset Big

Scoring Summary

Northwestern	0	0	0	6	6
Notre Dame	7	6	6	7	26

First Quarter
Notre Dame: Wilke 30 run (Puplis kick)

Second Quarter
Notre Dame: Wilke 34 run (kick blocked)

Third Quarter
Notre Dame: Dandom 1 run (run failed)

Fourth Quarter
Notre Dame: Skoglund 6 pass from McCarthy (Beinor kick)
Northwestern: Geyer 2 run (kick failed)
Attendance: 52,131

Ten Champions After Seven Straight—Wilke Runs 30 and 34 Yards to Touchdowns in First Half"—*The New York Times*

"Some of his players were crying, others were throwing things around and giving vent to a wrath brought on by the loss. Many sat quietly in front of their lockers holding their heads and saying nothing. It was indeed a sad room, the kind of a scene which marks the end of every World Series and the close of a tough basketball season. How could anybody be happy when a national championship was left out on that field?"—*South Bend Tribune* description of the Northwestern postgame scene

What the Players and Coaches Said: "We shattered the Purple dream of grandeur," said Irish backfield coach Chet Grant.

"Our line was outcharged all the way. Notre Dame was more alert. The score is a very fair estimate of the relative difference of the two teams. We all hope that

Notre Dame will finish its season undefeated," said Northwestern coach Lynn Waldorf.

"My boys played the best ball they have shown all year," said Irish coach Elmer Layden.

The Rundown: Notre Dame tied USC the next week and finished 6–2–1, rated eighth in the final AP poll.

Northwestern ended up 7–1 (Big Ten champion at 6–0) and number seven in the final poll.

Notre Dame 27 • SMU 20
DECEMBER 3, 1949, AT DALLAS

Unbeaten Irish Hold Off Walker and SMU in Dallas

The Run-Up: Notre Dame came in 9–0 and ranked number one in the country, having held the top slot in seven straight polls.

Southern Methodist University stood 5–3–1 in Matty Bell's last year as head coach and finished fifth in the Southwest Conference.

The Irish had gone 38 games without a loss, and this win enabled them to finish four straight seasons without a defeat (two ties).

The Pertinent Details: With star Doak Walker sidelined by injury, SMU still gave Notre Dame all it could handle.

After the Mustangs tied it at 20, Bill Barrett's touchdown capped a 57-yard drive and turned out to be the winning points with eight minutes left in the contest. Barrett ran for 61 net yards. Larry Coutre added 55, and Sitko led with 84. In the process, Irish quarterback Bob Williams raised his single-season completion total to 74 to break Bertelli's record.

The Determining Factor: With the Irish holding a touchdown lead in the final minutes, and with SMU on the Notre Dame 4, Jerry Groom intercepted Kyle Rote's jump pass to save the day for the Irish.

The Star of the Show: In defeat, Rote, who was the Heisman runner-up a year later in 1950, ran for 115 yards, completed 10 of 24 passes for 148 yards, scored all three SMU touchdowns (two of them in the final period, the last of which tied the game at 20), and also punted for a 48-yard average.

What the Headlines Said: "Notre Dame met their match in Rote and Southern Methodist but fought back in champion style to a hard-earned victory." —*South Bend Tribune*

"Mighty Notre Dame battled against Southern Methodist for its championship life today, and, like a champion, it won."—Unknown

Scoring Summary

Notre Dame	7	6	7	7	27
SMU	0	0	7	13	20

First Quarter
Notre Dame: Wightkin 42 pass from Williams (Oracko kick)

Second Quarter
Notre Dame: Zalejski 35 pass from Williams (kick failed)

Third Quarter
SMU: Rote 3 run (Sullivan kick)
Notre Dame: Barrett 5 run (Oracko kick)

Fourth Quarter
SMU: Rote 1 run (Sullivan kick)
SMU: Rote 2 run (kick blocked)
Notre Dame: Barrett 6 run (Oracko kick)
Attendance: 75,457

"It wasn't just a football game. It was the spirit of a people—a part of these United States that has pioneered for generations in hewing a niche that fits into a pattern of achievement. Proud? We're bustin' buttons over our Southern Methodist football team! We are not in the business of 'ifs and ands.' Notre Dame beat our SMU, 27 to 20. It might have gone the other way—and it could have. But we were licked by the greatest team college football has ever known."—Dallas editorial

"The Luck o' the Irish held through 60 minutes of the wildest rock 'em, sock 'em football ever unreeled on a Southwest gridiron last Saturday."—*SMU Campus*

"Notre Dame's Fighting Irish pulled back from the shock of a thundering Southern Methodist offense that had them on the brink of defeat today to drive 57 yards for a touchdown that gave them a 27-to-20 victory for an undefeated, untied season."—Associated Press

What the Players and Coaches Said: "That's the best team we've met all season. Rote is the most underrated back in America.... This is the greatest team I've ever coached. It has guts, it has character," said Irish coach Leahy.

"I'm sorry I didn't get a chance to play against the greatest Notre Dame team of all time," said Walker in the Irish locker room.

The Rundown: The Irish claimed their third national title in four years, going 10–0 and ending up number one in the final AP poll.

SMU finished 5–4–1, ending the year with a three-game losing streak.

Notre Dame 27 • Oklahoma 21
NOVEMBER 8, 1952, AT NOTRE DAME STADIUM
Start of Notre Dame–Oklahoma Series Is a Keeper

The Run-Up: Notre Dame came in at 4–1–1 and rated 10th by the AP after beating number nine Purdue, North Carolina, and Navy the previous three Saturdays. Oklahoma was 5–0–1 (and rated number four) after a 21–21 tie with Colorado to start the season. This was the first-ever meeting between these two traditional college powers.

The Sooners boasted a 13-game unbeaten streak and averaged 42 points per game.

The Pertinent Details: This contest doesn't always rate mention with the greatest of Irish wins, but Dave Metz, a member of the Notre Dame class of 1955, felt so strongly about its noteworthiness that he recently produced an entire highlight tape about it, including interviews with the pertinent players plus a recreated audio voiceover of the game films.

Billy Vessels, the Heisman Trophy winner that year, finished with 195 rushing yards on 17 carries for the Sooners, while John Lattner, who won the Heisman the next year, had 98 yards and Neil Worden 75 for Notre Dame.

Oklahoma had only two pass completions all day, as Notre Dame recorded a 23–13 edge in first downs. There were 10 turnovers in the first half alone—with Vessels scoring on a 27-yard reception and again on a 62-yard run. He added a second-half scoring run from 44 yards out for the other Oklahoma points.

The Determining Factor: Dan Shannon made a shattering tackle on Sooners kick returner Larry Grigg on the kickoff after the Irish had tied the game late.

Grigg fumbled, and Notre Dame took over at the Oklahoma 24. Four plays later Tony Carey scored from the 1 for the 27–21 Irish triumph.

The Star of the Show: Even in defeat, it was Vessels who showed a Notre Dame Stadium crowd why he was the best player in the nation.

What the Headlines Said: "The most treasured victories in the tradition are those like Army of '28 and Oklahoma of '52 and '57 because each was by all odds

Scoring Summary

Notre Dame	0	7	7	13	27
Oklahoma	7	7	7	0	21

First Quarter
Oklahoma: Vessels 27 pass from Crowder (Leake kick)

Second Quarter
Notre Dame: Heap 16 pass from Guglielmi (Arrix kick)
Oklahoma: Vessels 62 run (Leake kick)

Third Quarter
Notre Dame: Worden 1 run (Arrix kick)
Oklahoma: Vessels 44 run (Leake kick)

Fourth Quarter
Notre Dame: Worden 3 run (Arrix kick)
Notre Dame: Carey 1 run (kick blocked)
Attendance: 57,446

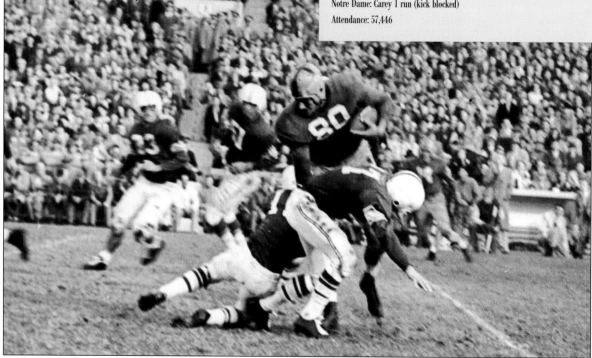

Notre Dame junior right end Art Hunter (No. 80) makes one of his three catches for 34 yards against the Sooners in 1952 at Notre Dame Stadium, helping his Irish knock off fourth-rated Oklahoma 27–21.

a game that was supposed to have been lost. They were things of the spirit, exemplification of the essence of Notre Dame."–Francis Wallace in *Notre Dame: From Rockne to Parseghian*

"A duel between a bulldog and a wolfhound."–A Cleveland sportswriter

"An inspired and courageous band of Fighting Irishmen came from behind three times on this hazy autumn afternoon to upset the splendid and heavily favored Oklahoma Sooners 27–21 in a titanic struggle that will go down as a classic in Notre Dame football lore."–Notre Dame *Scholastic*

"Larry Grigg grabbed (Menil) Mavraides' kickoff on the 6 and dashed to the 24 where he was met by one Dan Shannon in a collision that rocked the stadium and sent reverberations all the way back to the Sooner state, where the echoes will continue to haunt the Oklahomans for some time to come."–Notre Dame *Scholastic*

What the Players and Coaches Said: "Larry turned a half flip in the air and lost the ball. No back anywhere could have held onto the ball under those circumstances. Shannon was hurt, revived on the field, had to be helped to the bench, was through for the day," said Sooner coach Bud Wilkinson.

The Rundown: The Irish lost at number-one ranked Michigan State the next week, then defeated Iowa and number-two USC to finish 7–2–1 and third in both final polls.

Oklahoma defeated Missouri, Nebraska, and Oklahoma State the next three weeks to end up 8–1–1 and fourth in the final polls.

Notre Dame 28 • USC 7
OCTOBER 23, 1965, AT NOTRE DAME STADIUM
Conjar Overshadows Garrett as Irish Roll Trojans

The Run-Up: Notre Dame came in at 3–1, after a loss to number six Purdue, and rated seventh (AP).

USC came in at 4–0–1 and rated fourth, with four straight wins after a 20–20 tie with Minnesota.

The Pertinent Details: Irish students and fans hadn't forgotten the crushing defeat the year before in 1964 that ended the season and ended Notre Dame's national title hopes. In fact, the '65 game became something of an obsession.

The focus by the Irish team was so great that by halftime Notre Dame had a 226–23 lead in total yards, a 13–1 advantage in first downs, and a 21–0 lead on the scoreboard. Much of the obsession was with Trojan tailback Garrett, who came in averaging close to 170 rushing yards per game and went on to win the Heisman Trophy that year. The Irish held him to 16 carries and 43 yards (his career low), only seven in the first half; meanwhile Notre Dame halfback Larry Conjar responded with 25 carries of his own for 116 yards and all four Notre Dame touchdowns (all of them on runs of one or two yards). No one had run for four touchdowns for the Irish since Lattner did it 12 years earlier (also versus USC).

Notre Dame's defense limited the Trojans to 74 rushing yards and 10 first downs, while the Irish running game racked up 308 net yards despite only two pass completions by Ara Parseghian's unit.

The Determining Factor: Notre Dame scored touchdowns on four of its first five possessions. According to Jim Murray of the *Los Angeles Times*,

Scoring Summary

Notre Dame	14	7	7	0	**28**
USC	0	0	0	7	**7**

First Quarter
Notre Dame: Conjar 2 run (Ivan kick) (6:46)
Notre Dame: Conjar 2 run (Ivan kick) (1:55)

Second Quarter
Notre Dame: Conjar 1 run (Ivan kick) (9:13)

Third Quarter
Notre Dame: Conjar 1 run (Ivan kick) (9:24)

Fourth Quarter
USC: Thomas 9 pass from Winslow (Rossovich kick) (6:06)
Attendance: 59,235

"USC made several mistakes at the outset, not the least of which was scheduling the game in the first place. They should have seen if Yale was available."

The Star of the Show: Conjar tied a modern Notre Dame record with his four rushing scores.

What the Headlines Said: "And into the Mouth of Hell!"—*Los Angeles Times*

"Outlined against the blue-gray October sky, Notre Dame kicked the bejabbers out of USC on a leaky Saturday afternoon. The Fighting Croats did it again. The 11 Horsemen did it again. And again. The Trojans spent the day on their haircuts. Notre Dame spent it in the end zone."—Columnist Jim Murray in the *Los Angeles Times*

"Notre Dame 'remembered' and crushed old rival Southern Cal Saturday with battering ball control, the hard-hitting running of Larry Conjar and a defense that all but shut out the nation's top runner Mike Garrett. Cheered on by a student body that cried for vengeance after last year's upset in Los Angeles, the Irish stormed for a touchdown the first three times they had the ball."—*South Bend Tribune*

What the Players and Coaches Said: "Mike [Garrett] made some great runs just getting back to the line of scrimmage," said USC coach John McKay.

"There is no question the mind, the emotions, the spirit, play a very important part in this game of football," said Irish coach Parseghian.

"He was really something, wasn't he?" noted Parseghian of Conjar.

The Rundown: Notre Dame won its next three games, lost to number-one ranked Michigan State, then tied Florida's University of Miami to end up 7–2–1 and ranked eighth (UPI) and ninth (AP).

USC won three of its last four games (losing to number seven UCLA), and also ended up 7–2–1, good for ninth (UPI) and 10th (AP).

Notre Dame 51 • USC 0
NOVEMBER 26, 1966, AT LOS ANGELES
So Who's Number One? No Question Now— It's the Irish

The Run-Up: Notre Dame came in 8–0–1 and ranked number one after its epic 10–10 tie with unbeaten Michigan State the previous Saturday.

USC came in rated 10th (AP) with a 7–2 record after falling 14–7 to number eight UCLA the week before.

The Pertinent Details: The epic 10–10 tie between unbeaten teams Notre Dame and Michigan State in 1966 didn't particularly solve anything. But there proved to be one major difference in the schedule for the two powerhouses.

The 10–10 deadlock in East Lansing marked the final game of the season for Duffy Daugherty's Spartans. Unable to play in the Rose Bowl (despite claiming the Big Ten title) because they'd been there the previous year, Michigan State was finished at 9-0-1.

The Irish, meanwhile, had one opportunity remaining—an assignment the following weekend against 10th-rated USC in the Los Angeles Coliseum. And did

Senior fullback Larry Conjar (No. 32) heads for the end zone in '66 versus USC, behind the blocks of center Tim Monty (No. 55) and guard Dick Swatland (No. 59). Conjar's two-yard scoring run midway through the opening period started the scoring and marked the first of seven Irish touchdowns.

the Irish ever make the most of it, scoring a record 51 points against the Trojans.

Playing again without the likes of Terry Hanratty and Nick Eddy, Notre Dame demolished the Trojans early and often. Coley O'Brien proved spectacular in Hanratty's role, completing 21 of 31 passes and throwing for 255 yards and three touchdowns. Jim Seymour caught 11 balls for 150 yards and two of the touchdowns. The Irish defense ran back two interceptions for touchdowns and held USC to minus 12 rushing yards and only one rushing first down (188 yards overall).

If there had been any questions in the minds of the poll voters about who should be ranked number one, there were far fewer after this game.

The Determining Factor: Notre Dame took the field, rolled to a 31–0 halftime lead, and only twice saw USC pass midfield.

The Star of the Show: O'Brien. Hanratty's backup was simply superb in cinching the title for the Irish.

What the Headlines Said: "Coley O'Brien and... the National Championship."–Notre Dame *Scholastic*

"Either Notre Dame is number one in the nation or USC is far from being the West's most representative team for the Rose Bowl–or both."–*Los Angeles Times*

"Notre Dame, which has been rehearsing football since 1887, sent out a show-stopper Saturday to attract the attention of the critics who vote for the national collegiate champion."–*Los Angeles Herald-Examiner*

What the Players and Coaches Said: "I guess I've never seen a better team than Notre Dame was today. This is the best balanced offensive and defensive team

Scoring Summary					
Notre Dame	14	17	13	7	51
USC	0	0	0	0	0

First Quarter

Notre Dame: Conjar 2 run (Azzaro kick) (8:27)

Notre Dame: Schoen 40 interception return (Azzaro kick) (0:00)

Second Quarter

Notre Dame: Azzaro 45 field goal (7:17)

Notre Dame: Seymour 13 pass from O'Brien (Azzaro kick) (0:57)

Notre Dame: Seymour 39 pass from O'Brien (Azzaro kick) (0:08)

Third Quarter

Notre Dame: Harshman 23 pass from O'Brien (Azzaro kick) (12:15)

Notre Dame: Eddy 9 run (kick blocked) (2:32)

Fourth Quarter

Notre Dame: Martin 35 interception return (Azzaro kick) (2:25)

Attendance: 88,520

I've ever coached or seen," said USC coach John McKay.

Said McKay to his players: "Forget it guys, do you realize there are over 700 million Chinese who didn't even know the game was played?"

"I would say we went out to prove we are number one. And we did, didn't we?"–Irish coach Parseghian

The Rundown: With Michigan State's season concluded, Notre Dame's convincing win over Rose Bowl–bound USC handed the Irish the national title at 9–0–1.

USC lost to number-seven ranked Purdue 14–13 in Pasadena to finish 7-4.

Notre Dame 23 • USC 14
OCTOBER 27, 1973, AT NOTRE DAME STADIUM

Pennick's Sweep Left Is Tonic for Irish

The Run-Up: Notre Dame came in 5–0 and ranked eighth (AP), outscoring those five opponents 168–20.

USC came in rated sixth (AP) with a 5–0–1 mark, including a 7–7 tie with number eight Oklahoma when the Trojans were number one. The Trojans had not been beaten in their last 23 games, with the streak beginning at Notre Dame Stadium with a 28–14 win in 1971 that came after three straight USC defeats.

The Pertinent Details: In any national championship season, there generally are one or more signature victories. For Notre Dame in 1973, this marked one of them.

Victories over the vaunted Trojans had not come easily of late. In fact, since the 51–0 whitewashing of USC in '66, the Irish were 0–4–2 against the men of Troy. The '73 clash against the unbeaten USC clan would be a different story.

Eric Penick provided the Kodak moment for the afternoon. With the Irish clinging to a 13–7 lead, he took a third-period pitch on the first play from scrimmage of the half, swept around the left side, in front of the Notre Dame bench, and rumbled 85 yards for a score (with big blocks from Frank Pomarico and Gerry DiNardo).

The Irish finished with 316 rushing yards and made use of three Bob Thomas field goals to hold off John McKay's club. After scoring six touchdowns against the Irish the year before in '72 (and four more the next year in '74), Anthony Davis this time managed 55 rushing yards (and a fourth-period fumble) and a one-yard scoring run that gave the Trojans an early 7–3 advantage.

Scoring Summary

Notre Dame	3	10	10	0	**23**
USC	7	0	7	0	**14**

First Quarter
Notre Dame: Thomas 32 field goal (7:08)
USC: Davis 1 run (Limahelu kick) (2:22)

Second Quarter
Notre Dame: Thomas 33 field goal (5:26)
Notre Dame: Clements 1 run (Thomas kick) (0:30)

Third Quarter
Notre Dame: Penick 85 run (Thomas kick) (11:12)
USC: Swann 27 pass from Haden (Limahelu kick) (9:51)
Notre Dame: Thomas 32 field goal (0:22)
Attendance: 59,075

The Irish forced three final-period turnovers, with Davis fumbling at the Notre Dame 16, J.K. McKay losing the ball after a 23-yard reception (his only catch of the day), and finally Luther Bradley intercepting a Pat Haden pass (his second interception of the day).

Irish kicker Thomas connected three times for field goals after having missed eight straight attempts coming into the game.

As it turned out, Notre Dame wouldn't beat USC again until its next national title season in 1977. Still, this win was deemed noteworthy enough to prompt students and fans to pull down the north goalposts.

The Determining Factor: USC punted to the Irish 15, Penick went for 85, and the Irish had an insurmountable 20–7 lead. Others say it was the Trojans' first play from scrimmage, when Bradley knocked Lynn Swann's helmet loose with a vicious hit.

The Stars of the Show: The champions of the day were the Irish running backs, who accounted for a

316–68 edge in the running game, thanks to Penick (118 yards), Tom Clements (50), Art Best (45), Wayne Bullock (38), and Tom Parise (34). Notre Dame's ground dominance enabled the Irish to run 85 plays compared to USC's 48. The Irish held the ball for 39:36, compared to 20:24 for USC.

What the Headlines Said: "Notre Dame's football forces, roused to a fever pitch, doused Southern California's long undefeated streak and hopes for consecutive national championships Saturday in one of the storied Irish victories."—*South Bend Tribune*

"Ball control and an unrelenting defense were the keys to an Irish triumph that was as hard-fought and brilliantly-executed as any game in Ara Parseghian's 10 seasons as head coach."—*South Bend Tribune*

What the Players and Coaches Said: "I just remember breaking free. I can't remember anything else," said Penick. "I was psyched up when I went on the field and I'm still psyched up. I'll probably be psyched till the day I die."

"This isn't the Coliseum, this is South Bend—pick up your tail and get back in the huddle," Irish defender Tim Rudnick said to Davis after one early play.

USC coach John McKay met the press while humming the Notre Dame "Victory March." He said, "There's nothing else to hum. They won the game. That's it. They outplayed us which is the name of the game."

The Rundown: The Irish won their last four games in the regular season, took a number-three ranking into the Sugar Bowl against number one Alabama, and beat the Tide, 24–23. That gave Notre Dame its ninth consensus national title.

USC won its last four contests to close the regular season, then fell 42–21 to Ohio State in the Rose Bowl. The 9–2–1 Trojans ended up eighth in the final AP poll.

Notre Dame 7 • Alabama 0
NOVEMBER 15, 1980, AT BIRMINGHAM
Blanking of Tide Sends Irish to Sugar Bowl Assignment

The Run-Up: Notre Dame came in 7–0–1 and ranked sixth by AP after a 3–3 tie the previous week at unranked Georgia Tech cost the Irish their number-one ranking.

Alabama came in 8–1 and rated fifth, its loss to Mississippi State knocking the Tide off its perch after seven weeks at number one.

The game marked Notre Dame's first visit to the state of Alabama to play the Tide.

The Pertinent Details: Notre Dame's win gave the Irish a 4–0 mark against the Bear Bryant–coached 'Bama squads. And it was all defense, with Alabama never coming closer than a 37-yard field-goal attempt that hooked right, and another foray to the 37 that ended when Crable (20 tackles) stopped the Tide's Linnie Patrick on fourth-and-1. Notre Dame's next-best chance to score came when a 19-yard Harry Oliver field-goal try was blocked in the final quarter.

Phil Carter finished with 84 rushing yards, with the Irish defense holding the Tide to 10 first downs and 246 total yards. Notre Dame managed but 192 yards, with Alabama's Thomas Boyd and Tommy Wilcox each contributing 19 tackles.

Scoring Summary

Notre Dame	0	7	0	0	7
Alabama	0	0	0	0	0

Second Quarter

Notre Dame: Carter 2 run (Oliver kick) (6:02)

Attendance: 78,873

It marked only the fifth time a Bryant-coached Alabama team had been shut out—and the first time it had occurred in Birmingham since Vanderbilt University did it in a 0–0 tie in 1958.

The Determining Factor: A fumble by Tide quarterback Don Jacobs midway through the second period was recovered by Notre Dame's Scott Zettek and set up Notre Dame at the Alabama 4. Two plays later, Carter plunged over from the 2 for the only points of the afternoon.

The Star of the Show: Irish senior defensive end Zettek, who went a long way toward being named a first-team Associated Press All-American a month later, accounted for a two-yard loss on the first play from scrimmage, and that set the tone for the day. He finished with nine tackles and helped Notre Dame make it five straight games without allowing a touchdown.

What the Headlines Said: "Surviving the High Tide"—*Irish Eye*

"Alabama Coach Paul William Bryant, 67, surrounded by state police troopers, supported on each arm by an aide, walked slowly to the center of the field, his face as dark as the misty skies above. Notre Dame Coach Dan Devine already was there, sitting atop his players' shoulders, having been swept to midfield by his joyous team. That was the proper ending."—*The Washington Post*

"The large, gold buttons worn by Notre Dame's 5,000 or so supporters had a simple message for the Crimson-clad Alabama fans: 'The Tide won't roll where the River Shannon flows.' Saturday it flowed over the University of Alabama in a great, green wave of *dee-fense, dee-fense,* as the undefeated Irish rolled back the Tide, 7–0, in a game that featured more raw emotion than a tearjerker film festival."—Fort Wayne *Journal-Gazette*

What the Players and Coaches Said: "We never established anything offensively because they didn't let us. We're just not used to playing against a team that strong," said Bryant.

"I can't remember when I've ever seen a defense play better," said Devine.

"It was Alabama this and Alabama that, and Bear this and Bear that all week. This was one time when I think Notre Dame got 'out-mystiqued.' And I think it was our emotion that got us over the hump," said Zettek

The Rundown: The victory made Notre Dame's record against Alabama 4–0, with the wins coming by a combined 13 points. The win moved the Irish to number two in the polls. Notre Dame beat Air Force, lost at number 17 USC, then fell 17–10 to number one and unbeaten Georgia in the Sugar Bowl. The 9–2–1 mark left the Irish ninth in the final AP poll, 10 by UPI.

Alabama beat Auburn, then toppled number six Baylor University 30–2 in the Cotton Bowl to finish 10–2, good for the number-six slot in both final polls.

Notre Dame 31 • Pittsburgh 16
NOVEMBER 6, 1982, AT PITTSBURGH

Rookie Pinkett Keynotes Triumph over Marino and Number-One Pitt

The Run-Up: Notre Dame came in 5–1–1, ranking as high as ninth before a loss to Arizona and a tie with Oregon knocked the Irish out of the polls.

Pittsburgh was 7–0 and had been ranked number one for two weeks under first-year coach Foge Fazio (four years later he became the Irish defensive coordinator under Lou Holtz).

The Pertinent Details: Notre Dame exploded for three final-period touchdowns to dispatch the top-rated Panthers, negating Pittsburgh advantages of 25–10 in first downs, 88–48 in plays run, and 438–323 in total yards.

Notre Dame took the lead for good in the first minute of the final quarter when quarterback Blair Kiel pitched the ball to Carter on a sweep, Carter pitched it back to Kiel on the flea-flicker, and Kiel heaved it 54 yards to Joe Howard for a score—one of only six Irish pass completions all day.

The Determining Factor: Freshman Allen Pinkett dashed 76 yards for a touchdown with 8:09 remaining (one play after a John Mosley fumble recovery) to enable the Irish to break away from a tight 17–16 lead, then he scored again four minutes later to cap a 65-yard drive.

The Star of the Show: On the same field on which Dan Marino completed 26 of 42 throws for 314 yards (eight of them to Dwight Collins for 109), Pinkett stole the show with his 112 rushing yards and two late

touchdowns. It marked the first time in 20 games Marino didn't throw a touchdown pass.

What the Headlines Said: "Add One to the List" —*Irish Eye*

"They talked about mistakes, and they talked about mystiques, but more often than not, they didn't talk. They whispered. The Pitt Panthers aren't the first team in history to learn college football's number-one lesson, and as long as there is gold in the Dome, they won't be the last. You schedule Notre Dame and you take your chances."—*Chicago Tribune*

"Dreams die hard when you're young and talented and have been, oh, so close for three straight seasons. They die especially hard we you are less than 15 minutes away from winning, less than 15 minutes away from the bowl game of your choice, less than 15

Scoring Summary

Pittsburgh	3	3	7	0	16
Notre Dame	0	10	0	21	31

First Quarter
Pittsburgh: Schubert 48 field goal (4:58)

Second Quarter
Pittsburgh: Schubert 22 field goal (12:54)
Notre Dame: Johnston 38 field goal (8:53)
Notre Dame: Moriarty 4 run (Johnston kick) (3:35)

Third Quarter
Pittsburgh: Thomas 1 run (Schubert kick) (3:42)

Fourth Quarter
Notre Dame: Howard 54 pass from Kiel (Johnston kick) (14:36)
Pittsburgh: Schubert 47 field goal (12:14)
Notre Dame: Pinkett 76 run (Johnston kick) (8:09)
Notre Dame: Pinkett 7 run (Johnston kick) (4:06)
Attendance: 60,162

minutes from maintaining your number-one rating. But they die, nevertheless."—*Pittsburgh Press*

"Where else in this beer-drinking, blue-collar town but in a bar would you find the strategy for beating the number-one team in the land being unfolded? Using glasses and ashtrays for football players, Notre Dame quarterback coach Ron Hudson moved them around on top of a table like a grand master of chess on the eve of the game against Pittsburgh. With a few flicks of the wrists and apparently nothing up his sleeve, he showed how fullback Larry Moriarty would be open on a long pass over the middle and how a flea-flicker pass would burn the Panther secondary."—*South Bend Tribune*

What the Players and Coaches Said: "I don't know what to say. We moved the ball well, but we couldn't put it in the end zone," said Fazio.

"When you've got the athletes like they have and you hold Pitt under 21 points, you've done a heckuva job," said Irish linebacker Mark Zavagnin, who made 16 tackles.

"I think we got some respectability back," said Gerry Faust.

The Rundown: Notre Dame lost its final three games (including a loss to number-five Penn State and number 17 USC) to finish 6–4–1 and unranked.

Pitt beat Army and Rutgers before falling to number-five Penn State. After a 7–3 loss to number-four SMU in the Cotton Bowl, the Panthers ended up 9–3 and number nine (UPI) and number 10 (AP).

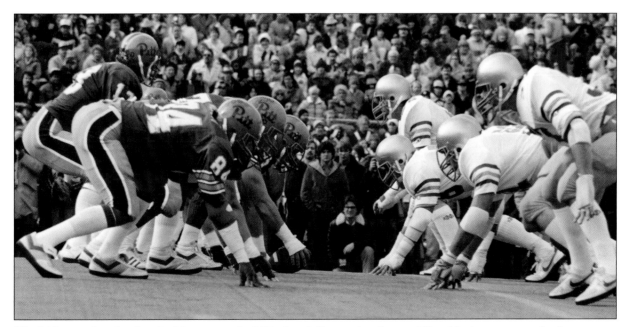

The Irish went head to head with a top-ranked Pittsburgh lineup that featured Dan Marino at quarterback.

Notre Dame 34 • Tennessee 29
NOVEMBER 10, 1990, AT KNOXVILLE

It Doesn't Get Any More Entertaining Than the Win in Knoxville

The Run-Up: Notre Dame came in number one with a 7–1 record. The Irish had ranked number one the first four weeks of the seasons before a loss to Stanford, but they regained the top slot this week after then–number one Virginia fell for the first time.

Tennessee was rated ninth by AP, with a 5–1–2 record.

The Pertinent Details: In a game in which the lead changed hands five times, this was a beauty. Tennessee, amazingly, ran 29 more plays than Notre Dame, but the Irish prevailed based on their 316 net rushing yards (Ricky Watters had 174, Rodney Culver 47, Raghib Ismail 44, Tony Brooks 41). Culver also caught a 59-yard pass from Mirer for a touchdown. Notre Dame protected its top rating despite allowing 516 yards, committing 10 penalties, losing a fumble inside the Tennessee 5, and losing an onside kick.

Notre Dame's defense had all it could do to deal with Tennessee's blue-chip pass-catching duo: Carl Pickens (13 receptions for 163) and Alvin Harper (seven for 10 and two touchdowns).

The game was played before the second-largest crowd in Neyland Stadium history (97,123).

The Determining Factor: Notre Dame's Rod Smith picked off an Andy Kelly pass on the goal line with 46 seconds to go, on a first-and-10 play from the Irish 20. That was a few minutes after a 44-yard Ismail run had given the Irish a 34–23 lead just two plays after a Donn Grimm interception. All that came after

Scoring Summary

Notre Dame	7	3	7	17	34
Tennessee	6	0	14	9	29

First Quarter
Tennessee: Burke 46 field goal (9:23)
Notre Dame: Culver 59 pass from Mirer (Hentrich kick) (7:39)
Tennessee: Burke 22 field goal (5:28)

Second Quarter
Notre Dame: Hentrich 26 field goal (7:29)

Third Quarter
Tennessee: Thompson 10 run (Burke kick) (13:36)
Notre Dame: Watters 66 run (Hentrich kick) (13:12)
Tennessee: Harper 32 pass from Kelly (Burke kick) (10:24)

Fourth Quarter
Notre Dame: Hentrich 20 field goal (14:54)
Tennessee: Burke 45 field goal (9:57)
Notre Dame: Watters 10 run (Hentrich kick) (5:30)
Notre Dame: Ismail 44 run (Hentrich kick) (3:33)
Tennessee: Harper 23 pass from Kelly (conversion failed) (1:44)
Attendance: 97,123

Kelly completed 35 of his 60 throws for 399 yards (a school record). Kelly's final touchdown came on a 23-yard throw to Harper to cap a 68-yard drive that ended with 1:44 on the clock. After an onside kick recovery, he had his Vols in full view of the Irish goal line before Smith's pick in the final minute.

The Star of the Show: This probably was the best show ever by senior Irish tailback Watters, thanks to 17 rushing carries, 174 yards, a 66-yard touchdown run in the third period that gave the Irish a 17–13 lead, and a 10-yard scoring run with 5:30 left that made it 27–23 for Notre Dame.

What the Headlines Said: "Road Warriors"—Notre Dame *Scholastic*

"True, Ricky Watters had his greatest day at tailback and Rod Smith came out of limbo to make a game-saving interception. But in the end, the difference in Notre Dame's 34–29 win over Tennessee was the Rocket—again."—*Chicago Tribune*

"If there are a couple of things a football team shouldn't be without when it travels, it's defense and discipline. Suffice it to say, Notre Dame's Fighting Irish traveled lightly this weekend. But as usual, they did pack their dependably potent one-two offensive punch to weather a Smoky Mountain of errors in a thrilling victory over Tennessee."—*South Bend Tribune*

What the Players and Coaches Said: "We deserved to win the football game. Tennessee could say the same thing. We're not pretty, but we did come into a very difficult environment and win. It was the longest day I've ever put in on the sidelines," said Holtz.

"He has the speed of Willie Gault, but with better open-field ability," said Johnny Majors of Ismail.

The Rundown: The victory ensured a trip back to the Orange Bowl for Notre Dame. The Irish lost the next week to number 18 Penn State, beat number 18 USC to end the regular season, then fell to number one Colorado in the Orange Bowl. That 9–3 record left the Irish sixth in both final polls.

Tennessee won its last three to end the regular season, then beat Virginia 23–22 in the Sugar Bowl. The 9–2–2 Vols listed seventh (UPI) and eighth (AP) in the final polls.

Tailback Rodney Culver (No. 5) opened the scoring for top-rated Notre Dame on a 59-yard touchdown reception from Rick Mirer in the epic Irish win at ninth-ranked Tennessee in 1990.

Notre Dame 34 • Florida State 24
OCTOBER 26, 2002, AT TALLAHASSEE

Victory in Tallahassee Marks Best of Times for Willingham

The Run-Up: Notre Dame, ranked at number six by the AP, came with a perfect 7–0 record after Irish wins over number-21 Maryland, number-seven Michigan, and number-18 Air Force.

Florida State came in at 5–2 and rated number 11 by the AP after losses to Louisville and Miami.

The game marked Notre Dame's first-ever appearance in Tallahassee, Florida.

The Pertinent Details: Chalk this one up as the high-water mark of the Tyrone Willingham years, the exclamation point in the "Return to Glory" season of 2002. If earlier conquests of Maryland (a 20–0 win in the Kickoff Classic) and Michigan hadn't won the country's attention, this one on the road against a prominent name like Florida State before a stadium record crowd certainly did.

In reality, this one wasn't nearly as close as the final score indicates. The Irish sent a message early when Carlyle Holiday (13 of 21 for 185 and two touchdowns) connected with Arnaz Battle on a perfectly thrown ball that turned into a 65-yard scoring play fewer than three minutes into the game. That was the first time since '85 Notre Dame scored on its first play from scrimmage. Then, from a 10–10 halftime tie, the Irish defense intercepted a pair of passes, recovered two fumbles, shut down the Seminoles running game, and harassed Florida State quarterback Chris Rix (13 of 32 passing) into such a poor performance that he lost his job.

Scoring Summary					
Notre Dame	**10**	**0**	**17**	**7**	**34**
Florida State	**3**	**7**	**0**	**14**	**24**

First Quarter
Notre Dame: Battle 65 pass from Holiday (Setta kick) (12:40)
Florida State: Beitia 24 field goal (7:05)
Notre Dame: Setta 39 field goal (1:16)

Second Quarter
Florida State: Washington 1 run (Beitia kick) (4:14)

Third Quarter
Notre Dame: Setta 35 field goal (5:26)
Notre Dame: Grant 2 run (Setta kick) (4:09)
Notre Dame: Jenkins 16 pass from Holiday (Setta kick) (3:05)

Fourth Quarter
Notre Dame: Grant 31 run (Setta kick) (10:14)
Florida State: Boldin 5 pass from McPherson (Beitia kick) (1:12)
Florida State: Maddox 29 pass from McPherson (Beitia kick) (0:12)
Attendance: 84,106

Ryan Grant's second of two touchdown runs, this one from 31 yards out with 10 minutes to go (part of his 94 yards), made it 34–10 for the Irish—more than enough to survive two late 'Nole scores.

The Determining Factor: Notre Dame forced three third-period turnovers by the Seminoles and turned them into 17 Irish points (requiring only 34 yards of offense). Courtney Watson intercepted a pass, Glenn Earl forced a Rix fumble (that Vontez Duff recovered at the two), then Carlos Pierre-Antoine forced another fumble on the next kickoff that Brandon Hoyte recovered.

The Star of the Show: It would have been easy to pick Grant or Holiday, but the Notre Dame defense held the nation's 15th-rated rushing attack to only 93 ground yards (34 by leading rusher Greg Jones), and they made life so tough for 'Noles quarterback Rix that he was lifted in the fourth period (for Adrian McPherson, who completed eight of 11 throws, threw two late touchdown passes, and took over the starting role a week later).

What the Headlines Said: "Bowden 'Bumfuzzled'" —Notre Dame *Scholastic*

"The college football season is a like a good book, and Notre Dame has become a book you can't put down."—*The New York Times*

"Admit it, Tyrone Willingham. Admit that it struck you just the slightest bit odd to be applauded in Bobby Bowden's house Saturday after having trashed the place. That it caught you off guard to see so many 'Tyrone for Pope' signs in a place where Bowden is king."—*South Bend Tribune*

"Carlyle Holiday stepped out of the tunnel, back onto the field and was immediately surrounded by reporters. The band was still playing, fans were still cheering and Holiday was still smiling. This one felt good, maybe better than all the rest."—Associated Press

"There will be no more talk of reliance on luck or magic this season, not from this particular seat. Saturday afternoon was all Notre Dame, all on its own, all in a nasty environment before a record crowd of 84,106 at Doak Campbell Stadium."—*Chicago Tribune*

What the Players and Coaches Said: "We're back. We really like that opportunity to come into someone else's house and take over," said Holiday.

The Rundown: This marked the first time in history Notre Dame had defeated ranked opponents in their home stadiums on successive Saturdays (they'd won 21–14 at 18th-ranked Air Force the week before). Notre Dame moved to number four in the AP poll with this win, but lost a week later to Boston College and eventually lost to number-17 North Carolina State in the Gator Bowl to end up 10–3 and 17th in both final polls.

Florida State won its next three games, defeated rival Florida, and lost to number-four Georgia in the Sugar Bowl to end up 9–5 and 21st (AP) and 23rd (ESPN) in the polls.

Notre Dame's quarterback-turned-receiver Arnaz Battle got the landmark 2002 win at Florida State off to a blazing start on a 65-yard scoring reception less than three minutes into the contest.

Notre Dame 42 • Pittsburgh 21
SEPTEMBER 3, 2005,
AT PITTSBURGH
Debut for Weis Era Is a Beauty

The Run-Up: Notre Dame came in unranked as it opened the Weis era on the road at Heinz Field. The Irish had been 6–6 the year before.

Pittsburgh opened the Dave Wannstedt era with a number-23 preseason AP rating. The Panthers had been 8–4 in 2004 (including a BCS Fiesta Bowl loss to Utah) before Walt Harris left to become the head coach at Stanford.

The Pertinent Details: It looked like a rerun of the past few seasons when Pittsburgh took the opening kickoff and drove 73 yards for a touchdown, scoring on a 39-yard pass play to make the score 7–0 for the Panthers. But it was all Irish from there.

It also looked like rerun of a New England Patriots game, as the Irish adapted the Pats' schemes and Brady Quinn ran them to near perfection. Notre Dame amassed 33 first downs and 502 total yards (275 rushing, 227 passing) and converted on 10 of its first 11 third-down chances.

Quinn completed 18 of 27 for 227 yards and touchdown completions to Darius Walker (51 yards on a delayed screen for the first Notre Dame points) and Jeff Samardzija. Walker ran for 100 yards, and Rashon Powers-Neal scored on three short touchdown runs.

The Irish sacked Tyler Palko five times, intercepted a pass, and recovered a fumble on a kickoff return (that led to Notre Dame's fourth touchdown).

The Determining Factor: Notre Dame scored four touchdowns in the second period, with the four scoring drives totaling 219 yards combined. That left the Irish with a convincing 35–13 halftime lead. By intermission, Notre Dame had 319 total yards, more than it managed in five complete games in 2004. The Irish built the lead to 42–13 with a third-period drive that accounted for 80 yards on 20 plays and lasted more than seven minutes.

The Star of the Show: Probably Quinn, who ran the offense the way Weis (and Irish fans) hoped in Quinn's first chance with a new system, at one point completing 11 straight passes.

What the Headlines Said: "You can see it now. You can see it clear as the ND 42, Pitt 21 on the giant scoreboard at Heinz Field. Exactly eight months and 22 days after Charlie Weis promised 'nasty,' he delivered 'nasty' in a Notre Dame win over the No. 23 Panthers Saturday that may set the tone for what this new era is all about."—*Blue and Gold Illustrated*

"The University of Pittsburgh called upon its storied past Saturday night, trotting out 10 former greats prior to kickoff, in hopes of igniting a return to glory of sorts. If only those greats could have suited up. Instead the 23rd-ranked Panthers were left searching for answers and wondering with the rest of the college football world how good Notre Dame is."—*South Bend Tribune*

"Midnight on the Monongahela left Irish guys smiling Saturday.... The coaching debut of Charlie Weis was an unfettered success."—*Chicago Sun-Times*

"Notre Dame hired Charlie Weis exactly for this. The innovative and imaginative offense. The confused looks on the faces of the opposing defense. And, yes, all those points on the scoreboard."—*Chicago Tribune*

What the Players and Coaches Said: "I'm happy for our players, I'm happy for Notre Dame and I'm happy for our fans. I think by halftime our players were starting to believe they are better than they thought they were. That's what I've been trying to tell them all along," said Weis.

"I think we came out like we had a lot to prove," said Irish safety Tom Zbikowski.

"Notre Dame is obviously a fine football team and we must have miscalculated them," said Wannstedt.

The Rundown: Notre Dame won its final five regular-season games (jumping to number five in the AP poll) before falling to fourth-ranked Ohio State in the Bowl Championship Series Fiesta Bowl. That left the Irish 9–3 and ninth (AP) and 11th (*USA Today*) in the final polls.

Pittsburgh finished 5–6.

Scoring Summary

Notre Dame	**7**	**28**	**7**	**0**	**42**
Pittsburgh	**10**	**3**	**0**	**8**	**21**

First Quarter

Pittsburgh: Lee 39 pass from Palko (Cummings kick) (10:58)

Notre Dame: Walker 51 pass from Quinn (Fitzpatrick kick) (8:19)

Pittsburgh: Cummings 49 field goal (1:40)

Second Quarter

Notre Dame: Walker 2 run (Fitzpatrick kick) (13:07)

Notre Dame: Powers-Neal 2 run (Fitzpatrick kick) (6:59)

Notre Dame: Samardzija 19 pass from Quinn (Fitzpatrick kick) (6:03)

Pittsburgh: Cummings 23 field goal (4:20)

Notre Dame: Powers-Neal 9 run (Fitzpatrick kick) (1:39)

Third Quarter

Notre Dame: Powers-Neal 4 run (Fitzpatrick kick) (7:59)

Fourth Quarter

Pittsburgh: Palko 4 run (Murphy run) (12:55)

Attendance: 66,451

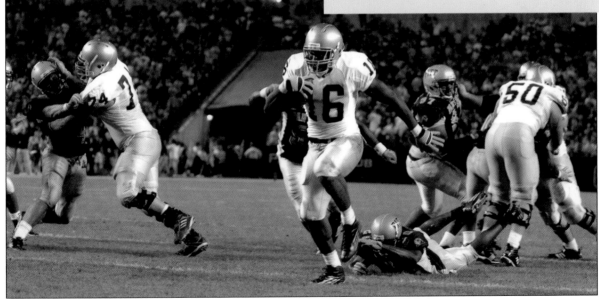

Fullback Rashon Powers-Neal enjoyed his most productive outing of his career in the 2005 opener at Pittsburgh with three scoring runs—from 2, 9, and 4 yards out.

GREATEST MOMENTS IN NOTRE DAME FOOTBALL HISTORY

Notre Dame 17 • Michigan 10
SEPTEMBER 10, 2005,
AT ANN ARBOR

Irish Defense Helps Weis Reach Rockne-esque Territory

The Run-Up: Notre Dame came in 1–0 and ranked 20th (AP) after defeating Pittsburgh the week before.

Third-ranked Michigan stood at 1–0 after a win over Northern Illinois University the previous Saturday.

Scoring Summary

Notre Dame	7	7	0	3	17
Michigan	0	3	0	7	10

First Quarter
Notre Dame: McKnight 5 pass from Quinn (Fitzpatrick kick) (12:02)

Second Quarter
Michigan: Rivas 38 field goal (14:04)
Notre Dame: Samardzija 5 pass from Quinn (Fitzpatrick kick) (4:24)

Fourth Quarter
Notre Dame: Fitzpatrick 43 field goal (14:11)
Michigan: Manningham 25 pass from Henne (Rivas kick) (3:47)
Attendance: 111,386

Notre Dame's first touchdown of the afternoon against Michigan in 2005 came on this short toss hauled in by Rhema McKnight (No. 5) from quarterback Brady Quinn.

The Pertinent Details: Notre Dame handed Michigan its first home loss after 16 straight wins and its first nonconference home defeat since 1998. Meanwhile, Weis became the first Notre Dame coach since Rockne in 1918 to go on the road in the first two games of his first season and win them both.

Quinn took the Irish 77 yards in the no-huddle, shotgun offense with an empty backfield after the opening kickoff. He found Rhema McKnight for five yards for the first points, then made it 14–3 in the second-period when his five-yarder to Samardzija capped a 72-yard drive.

Irish players found their road victory in '05 against third-rated Michigan one worth celebrating.

Weis made a friendly wager on the contest with Patriot (and former Michigan) quarterback Tom Brady, who had to wear a Notre Dame hat (he wore it backwards) to his press conference the next week.

The Determining Factor: Replay showed that a fourth-quarter, fourth-down sneak from inside the 1 by Michigan's Chad Henne actually had been fumbled and recovered for a touchback by Chinedum Ndukwe. Another replay minutes later ruled Quinn's knee was down on a play in which he fumbled. The Wolverines also drove to the Irish 5 before giving away the ball on downs, and Henne earlier threw an interception (to Zbikowski) at the Notre Dame 1.

The Star of the Show: Probably Weis, who, two games into his Notre Dame coaching tenure, had turned the Irish back into a Top-10 team.

Injuries sidelined two potential stars, as Michigan back Mike Hart went out (after four carries) in the first period after a Corey Mays hit, while Notre Dame's McKnight suffered a season-ending knee sprain in the second period.

What the Headlines Said: "Hail to the Irish Victors"—Notre Dame *Scholastic*

"Maybe the Irish defense was jealous of all the attention the offense received following Notre Dame's season-opening win over Pittsburgh. Or maybe this group is simply better than previously thought. Whatever the case, the Notre Dame defense picked a perfect time to make a name for itself."—*Elkhart Truth*

"Take the high-flying aerial acrobatics and offensive pyrotechnics and forget it. The offenses were hyped all week: Michigan's multitude of options versus the supreme game planning of Notre Dame coach Charlie Weis. Nuh-uh. Not on Saturday."—Fort Wayne *Journal-Gazette*

"A mere two games into his coaching career at Notre Dame, Charlie Weis has joined Knute Rockne in the record books—and has his team playing like the Fighting Irish of old."—Associated Press

What the Players and Coaches Said: Weis, on the Rockne comparison, said, "If I answered by dignifying that, [Bill] Parcells and [Bill] Belichick would humiliate me. I've just coached two games and they've played two games. Let's come back and revisit that in about 10 years."

The Rundown: Notre Dame ended up 9–3 and rated 17th in both final polls (the Irish had ranked as high as fifth) after a BCS Fiesta Bowl loss to number-four Ohio State.

Michigan finished 7–5 after an Alamo Bowl loss to Nebraska.

HONORABLE MENTIONS

Notre Dame 27, Army 17 (October 30, 1920)—George Gipp was never better than while amassing 357 all-purpose yards.

Notre Dame 26, Navy 2 (October 11, 1930)—The Irish dedicated their new $750,000 Notre Dame Stadium by beating Navy.

Notre Dame 60, Penn 20 (November 8, 1930)—The Irish extended their 14-game winning streak, thanks to three TDs covering 125 yards by Irish halfback Marty Brill.

Notre Dame 13, Army 12 (December 2, 1933)— With five minutes left, Wayne Millner blocked a punt and recovered in the end zone as the 2-5-1 Irish ruined Army's perfect season.

Notre Dame 28, Iowa Pre-Flight 0 (October 17, 1942)—Notre Dame intercepted six passes and recovered three fumbles in dispatching the unbeaten Seahawks.

Notre Dame 14, USC 14 (December 4, 1948)—The 9-0 Irish got an 87-yard kickoff return by Billy Gay with 2:35 left, followed by an Emil Sitko TD run to salvage the tie.

Notre Dame 9, USC 0 (November 29, 1952)—The Irish defense held USC to 149 total yards and five first downs to defeat the previously-unbeaten Trojans.

Notre Dame 23, USC 17 (November 27, 1954)—The Irish three times came from behind, the last time on a 72-yard Jim Morse run with five minutes left, as Morse finished with 179 yards.

Notre Dame 23, Army 21 (October 12, 1957)— Monty Stickles had never before attempted a field goal, but his 39-yarder with six minutes left won this game for the Irish.

Notre Dame 8, Purdue 7 (September 25, 1971)— With less than three minutes left, Clarence Ellis blocked a Boiler punt, Fred Swendsen recovered in the end zone, then Pat Steenberge threw to Mike Creaney for the winning two-point conversion.

Notre Dame 38, Georgia Tech 21 (November 18, 1978)—Vagas Ferguson had 188 rushing yards by halftime, and he finished with 255 to set the Irish single-game record.

Notre Dame 40, Miami 15 (November 24, 1979)— Vagas Ferguson rushed for 177 yards as the Irish prevailed in the Mirage Bowl at the Olympic Stadium in Tokyo, Japan.

Notre Dame 19, Boston College 18 (December 29, 1983)—Doug Flutie led the Eagles with 287 passing yards, but both Allen Pinkett and Chris Smith ran for at least 100 to win the Liberty Bowl.

Notre Dame 54, Navy 27 (November 2, 1996)—The Irish ran for 303 yards and saw Marc Edwards score three TDs to help knock off Navy at Croke Park in Dublin, Ireland.

Notre Dame 17, Georgia Tech 13 (September 6, 1997)—Autry Denson scored in the final three minutes in Bob Davie's Notre Dame debut in the dedication game for the enlarged Notre Dame Stadium.

Notre Dame 36, Michigan 20 (September 5, 1998)— Notre Dame scored 30 straight points in the second half to prevail over the defending national champions.

The Notre Dame leprechaun walks the sidelines during the closing minutes of the team's 38–0 loss to Michigan in a football game at Ann Arbor, Michigan, on September 15, 2007.

15 Agonizing Games That Still Keep Irish Fans Up at Night

Seriously now, we aren't trying to ruin your day. However, we harken back to the words of former Irish coach Ara Parseghian, who always suggested he had forgotten most of the details of many of his 95 victories at Notre Dame. But the 17 losses? Oh, he can only recite every play of those events—with an accompanying gnashing of teeth. We're assuming all of Parseghian's predecessors and successors fall into the same camp, in terms of memory.

Thus, in the interest of a balanced presentation, we offer some minimal details of some of the more head-scratching of Notre Dame defeats (and ties) through the years.

We're guessing that if you're a real dyed-in-the-wool Notre Dame fan, you haven't forgotten a bunch of these games, either.

In the spirit of sportsmanship, please keep your wailing and sobbing and your own personal gnashing of teeth to yourself.

USC 16 • Notre Dame 14
NOVEMBER 21, 1931
AT NOTRE DAME STADIUM

The Pertinent Details: It's one thing to lose a football game. It's another when that loss prompts the other team's players to have 300,000 fans show up to fete them at a ticker-tape parade in Los Angeles.

That's what happened when the University of Southern California scored in the final minute to hand Notre Dame a defeat after 26 straight Irish games without a loss (dating back to the end of the 1928 season; the loss the last time also came versus USC).

Notre Dame came into the game at 6-0-1 (a tie with Northwestern University), USC with only a loss to St. Mary's College. The Irish took a 14-0 edge into the game's final period on scoring runs by Steve Banas and Marchy Schwartz. But the Trojans made great use of pass interference penalties against Notre Dame on all three of their final-period scoring drives. Down 14-13 with four minutes left, USC drove from its own 28. On third-and-6 from the Irish 13, Johnny Baker booted the winning field goal, and Notre Dame's streak was history.

This marked Notre Dame's 43rd season of football, yet only its 49th defeat.

Great Lakes 19 • Notre Dame 14
NOVEMBER 27, 1943,
AT GREAT LAKES

The Pertinent Details: Notre Dame had been ranked number one for eight straight weeks, and the Irish had a chance for their first perfect season since Knute Rockne's final campaign in 1930.

Irish quarterback Johnny Lujack (filling in for Angelo Bertelli, who had been drafted into the Navy

but won the Heisman Trophy anyway) accounted for the only first-half points on a fourth-down sneak. Great Lakes came back to lead 12-7, the first touchdown, interestingly enough, by Emil Sitko, who attended Notre Dame the year before as a freshman and came back to star for the Irish after World War II. Notre Dame grabbed a 14-12 lead after an eight-minute drive that encompassed 20 plays and ended in a Creighton Miller run. But Great Lakes got the ball back at its own 38 with 1:08 remaining, and with 33 seconds to go out of the single wing, halfback Steve Lach found quarterback Paul Anderson all by himself for 46 yards and the win.

Notre Dame, done at 9-1, finished first in the final AP poll after leading the nation in total offense (418.0 yards per game) and rushing (313.7), with Miller individually leading the country in rushing (911 yards). Great Lakes was sixth at 10-2.

Army 59 • Notre Dame 0
NOVEMBER 11, 1944,
AT YANKEE STADIUM

The Pertinent Details: Unbeaten Army took out 13 seasons of frustration against Notre Dame in one New York afternoon. Loaded with All-Americans—including running backs Glenn Davis and Doc Blanchard, who finished second and third, respectively, in the Heisman Trophy voting that year and then won one each the following two seasons—the Cadets crushed the Irish in what remains the most one-sided Notre Dame loss in its history.

Army, on its way to the first of three straight consensus national titles, had outscored its first six opponents 360-21. Notre Dame was defending its own national crown and actually won its first five games and spent three weeks ranked number one. But the Irish were no match for the Cadets with coach Frank Leahy and many of the Notre Dame players in the service.

Davis scored three touchdowns and intercepted a pass he ran back 41 yards to set up one score (he ran it in himself on the next play). The Cadets made up for their last 12 games against the Irish (Notre Dame won 10 and tied two), with Army on the short end of a cumulative 158–37 score in those dozen outings (seven in which the Cadets didn't score, including each of the last five meetings).

Notre Dame 14 • Iowa 14
NOVEMBER 21, 1953,
AT NOTRE DAME STADIUM

The Pertinent Details: Frank Leahy's last Notre Dame team, which had been ranked number one all season long, needed 11th-hour touchdowns at the end of each half to manage a tie against an Iowa team that tied for fifth in the Big Ten yet ended up ninth in the final AP poll. Hawkeyes fans still wonder if the Irish injuries in the final seconds of both halves were legitimate.

Down a score late in the first half, it appeared the clock would run out on the Irish when quarterback Ralph Guglielmi was tackled trying to throw. But with Frank Varrichione lying on the ground, the clock stopped, giving Guglielmi time to throw 11 yards to Dan Shannon as time ran out.

The same thing happened at game's end. Down 14–7 after an Iowa score at the 2:06 mark, Heisman Trophy–winner Johnny Lattner couldn't get out of bounds at the Hawkeyes' 9-yard line as the clock wound down. This time Don Penza and Art Hunter were "injured." The clock stopped again, and

Guglielmi found Shannon again for nine yards to tie it with six seconds to go.

Despite beating 20th-rated USC and SMU easily to end the year, the Irish ended up second in the final AP poll behind a 10–0 University of Maryland team that went on to lose 7–0 to number four University of Oklahoma in the Orange Bowl.

USC 20 • Notre Dame 17
NOVEMBER 28, 1964,
AT LOS ANGELES

The Pertinent Details: As painful losses go, this one ranked right up on Parseghian's list. It came in Parseghian's first season as Irish head coach. It came after nine straight wins had elevated the Irish to the top position in the polls, and it came after the Irish had taken a 17–0 halftime lead and appeared on the verge of cinching their first season and national championship since the Leahy years (actually, 1949).

Heisman Trophy–winner-to-be John Huarte, who finished with 272 passing yards, threw to Jack Snow for one Irish touchdown, and Bill Wolski ran for the other. But USC scored twice (once on a run by the next year's Heisman winner and current Trojans athletics director Mike Garrett) to cut it to 17–13 with 5:11 remaining in the game. Then the Trojans drove from their own 40 for the winning points. Two second-half issues hurt the visitors: the Irish had fumbled once on the USC 9 and also had another scoring run called on a holding penalty.

The game produced two famous still photos. One was of Irish defensive back Tony Carey futilely on his knees as Trojan receiver Rod Sherman, who caught seven passes for 109 yards, went around him for the winning touchdown. The other was of Parseghian's arm-raised anguish after that score with 1:35 left in the game, with the Los Angeles Coliseum scoreboard in the background.

QUARTER	1	2	3	4	TOTAL
NOTRE DAME	3	14	0	0	17
U S C	0	0	7	13	20

USC BALL ON ____ YARD LINE

DOWN ____ YARDS TO GO

FIRST DOWNS USC 17 N D. 20
ATTENDANCE 83 840

The scoreboard told the sad story for Irish fans, as USC came through with 13 fourth-period points to scuttle Notre Dame's 1964 national championship hopes in the season finale.

Head coach Ara Parseghian (left) and offensive coordinator Tom Pagna (center) prepare to send quarterback John Huarte onto the field with the next play.

194

USC 55 • Notre Dame 24
NOVEMBER 30, 1974, AT LOS ANGELES

The Pertinent Details: Maybe no good Notre Dame football team in history has seen a game go so horribly wrong so amazingly quickly.

This was an Irish team that stood 9–1 and was ranked fifth in the country (AP), with only a four-point loss to Purdue preventing unbeaten status. Parseghian's squad had shown its mettle in the opening half,

breaking out to a 24–0 lead against an 8–1–1 USC team that had lost to Arkansas to start the year and later tied California.

Notre Dame had its way through the first 30 minutes, with Tom Clements throwing to Pete Demmerle for one touchdown and Wayne Bullock and Mark McLane converting short runs for scores. Only when Pat Haden connected with Anthony Davis for a USC touchdown with 10 seconds left in the first half did the home team show signs of life. As it turned out the floodgates had officially been opened.

Notre Dame defenders Greg Collins (No. 50) and Jim Stock (No. 48) made this tackle against USC in '74, but the Irish didn't make near enough of those sorts of plays while the Trojans were putting 49 second-half points on the board.

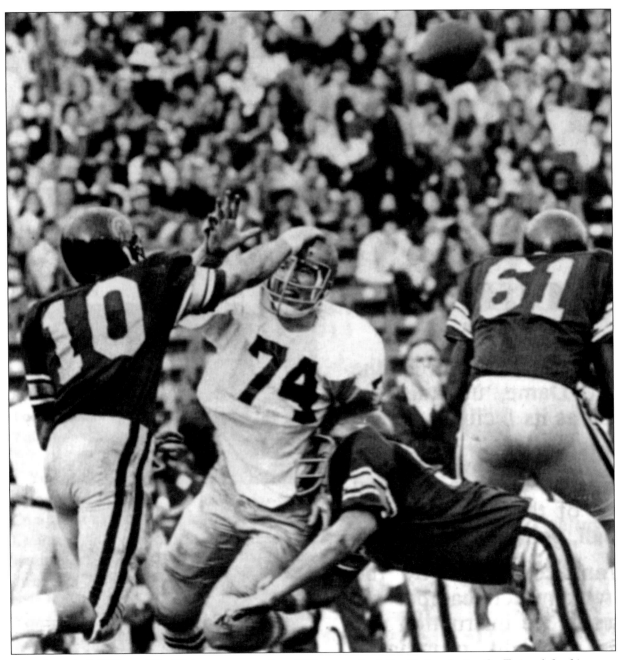

Notre Dame's Jeff Weston (No. 74) is a step away from USC quarterback Pat Haden during the Trojans' shocking comeback win in '74.

The Trojans scored 55 points in 17 minutes, 35 of them in the third period alone (Notre Dame had allowed only eight touchdowns combined in its first nine games). Davis ran the second-half kickoff back 100 yards for a score. He added scoring runs at the 11:35 and 8:37 marks of the third period, and Haden (225 passing yards, while setting a USC career touchdown pass mark with 31) threw a pair of touchdown passes to J.K. McKay. Charles Phillips intercepted his third pass of the day and ran it back 58 yards for a touchdown, and the score was 55–24 with 13:26 still left in the contest.

"We turned into madmen," said Davis.

"I still don't know what happened. I'm going to sit down tonight and have a beer and think about it," said USC coach John McKay.

It turned out to be Parseghian's last regular-season game. He resigned weeks later. It also turned out to be the most points allowed by an Irish team in 30 years (only Army with 59 in 1944 and Wisconsin with 58 in 1904 managed more). For the third straight season, the winner of this game won at least a share of the national title.

Missouri 3 • Notre Dame 0
SEPTEMBER 9, 1978,
AT NOTRE DAME STADIUM

The Pertinent Details: Notre Dame was the defending national champion, and the Irish had the star power of Montana, Heavens, Vagas Ferguson, and Bob Golic. But none of that proved enough for the Irish to manage to even score, much less win, in its 1978 opener at Notre Dame Stadium. Notre Dame found itself shut out for the first time in 132 games, dating back to 1965.

Montana struggled in the first half, fumbling twice and completing only four of 17 passes overall, with two of those intercepted. Then, twice in the third period, Notre Dame moved inside the Mizzou 15, only to come up short both times on fourth-down runs. Later, Montana threw to Kris Haines for 34 yards to the Tiger 4. But a personal foul pushed the Irish back to the 18, and a field-goal attempt went awry on a botched snap and hold on a potential 32-yarder.

Mizzou then drove from its own 14 to the Irish 16 and saw kicker Jeff Brockhaus connect from 33 yards with 13:10 left for what proved to be the only points. Notre Dame got to the Tiger 28 before falling short on a fourth-and-1 rush, later fumbled after reaching the Mizzou 28, and fumbled away a Tiger punt (the last of five Irish turnovers) with fewer than two minutes left.

Miami 58 • Notre Dame 7
NOVEMBER 30, 1985,
AT THE ORANGE BOWL

The Pertinent Details: Gerry Faust's five years as Notre Dame head coach came to an inglorious end, as unbeaten Miami scored early, late, and often in the Orange Bowl in the second-worst loss in modern Notre Dame football history (and most points by the home team in its own facility in 31 years).

It had already been a bizarre week for Irish players, who saw their current head coach resign that Tuesday, then boarded a plane to Miami on Wednesday just a few hours before Lou Holtz was named the next coach.

When Saturday came around, a national television audience watched as the 'Canes rolled up 534 yards, including 399 passing yards—the most ever allowed by a Notre Dame team (Vinny Testaverde alone hit 22 of 32 for 356). Miami never punted, scoring every time it had the football except when time ran out at the end of each half. The final Hurricane points came after they blocked an Irish punt and recovered in the end zone.

The Irish apparently were caught in the 'Canes' attempt to impress the pollsters, with one-loss Miami a slot behind a one-loss Oklahoma team that the 'Canes had beaten back in October in Norman.

The game made a villain of Miami coach Jimmy Johnson, who said, "It's a shame people were upset with the score, but what am I supposed to do?"

Stanford 37 • Notre Dame 31
OCTOBER 6, 1990,
AT NOTRE DAME STADIUM

The Pertinent Details: A 1-3 Stanford team appeared an unlikely choice to give top-rated and unbeaten Notre Dame much of a game in its own arena, particularly after the visitors needed a period and a half to muster their initial first down. But someone forgot to tell "Touchdown" Tommy Vardell.

Vardell netted only 37 yards overall, but his four one-yard scoring runs, the last with 36 seconds to go to bring the Cardinal back from an early 24–7 deficit, turned out to be the difference as the Irish saw a 19-game home win streak (dating back to 1986) end.

Notre Dame played without injured Raghib Ismail, and the Irish lost three fumbled punts. Yet, even after Stanford grabbed the late lead, the Irish drove back down the field in the final seconds, with Rick Mirer (he completed 15 of 26 for 235 and two scores, and also ran for a third touchdown) completing passes for 26 yards to Shawn Davis and 21 to Tony Brooks. Mirer's 23-yard pass into the end zone on the final play of the game fell off tight end Derek Brown's fingertips.

Irish coach Holtz called the game "the most difficult loss I have suffered in all my years of coaching."

Penn State 24 • Notre Dame 21
NOVEMBER 17, 1990,
AT NOTRE DAME STADIUM

The Pertinent Details: The number-one ranked Fighting Irish ended up on the cover of *Sports Illustrated* after this contest. Unfortunately, it was because they had been beaten.

Holtz's squad produced leads of 14–0 and 21–7 against a Penn State team that had won seven straight games after losing its first two games to Texas and USC. But the Nittany Lions turned a third-period interception into one touchdown, then picked off a second Mirer throw to set Penn State up at the Irish 20 with 59 seconds remaining. After three plays, Craig Fayak knocked through a 34-yard field goal with four seconds to go for the victory.

The loss came after a dominating first-half Notre Dame performance in which the Irish totaled 292 yards, didn't punt, converted 12 of 13 third-down attempts, played without a penalty, and held the ball for more than 20 minutes.

Mirer managed only a single second-half completion, and Ismail sat out the second half with a recurring leg injury. Penn State's Tony Sacca finished with 20 completions on 34 tries for 277 yards and three touchdowns.

Notre Dame hadn't lost at home while ranked number one since 1954, then it happened twice in one season in 1990.

Colorado 10 • Notre Dame 9
JANUARY 1, 1991,
AT THE ORANGE BOWL

The Pertinent Details: This game came down to one play—actually, a play that didn't count. With less than a minute left on the clock and top-rated Colorado nursing a one-point lead, the Buffaloes punted the ball to Notre Dame's electric kick returner Ismail, in what turned out to be the final college game for the Heisman Trophy runner-up.

The Rocket returned the ball 91 yards for what appeared to be a second straight Orange Bowl win over a number-one-ranked Colorado team. But safety Greg Davis was flagged for clipping, and the Buffs held on for the victory.

The Irish scored on a two-yard Ricky Watters run (Craig Hentrich's point after touchdown was blocked) and led 9–3 after a Hentrich field goal fewer than five minutes into the third period. Colorado scored what proved to be the winning points at the 4:26 mark of

The lone touchdown for Notre Dame in the 1991 Orange Bowl loss to top-rated Colorado came on a Ricky Watters run.

the third period after driving 40 yards following an Irish fumble, one of five Notre Dame turnovers that night.

Lombardi Award winner Chris Zorich was selected the defensive MVP after making 10 tackles and a sack in his last game.

Lou Holtz called Ismail's return that wasn't "one of the greatest individual efforts I've ever seen."

Said Colorado's Tim James, who was blocked by Davis on the ill-fated return: "Would I have tackled him? That's a tough call. This is the Rocket we're talking about."

Maybe no football game in Irish history is better remembered for a play that didn't count than was the 1991 Orange Bowl, a one-point loss to number-one Colorado after a late Raghib Ismail punt return was called back by penalty.

Tennessee 35 • Notre Dame 34
NOVEMBER 9, 1991, AT NOTRE DAME STADIUM

The Pertinent Details: All you need to know about how momentous this victory was for Tennessee is that the Vols produced an entire VHS highlight tape for their fans based on this one football game. It was titled *Miracle at South Bend.*

This one actually seemed to be decided early on. Notre Dame led the twice-beaten Volunteers 21–0 after one period and 31–7 late in the opening half—and had 233 rushing yards in the first two periods. But Tennessee regained some momentum by returning a blocked field-goal try 85 yards for a score with 35 seconds until halftime—and the second half was all orange (the Vols limited the Irish to 82 ground yards after halftime).

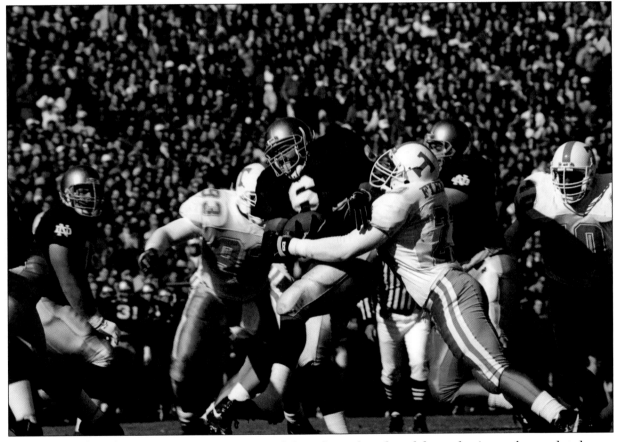

Jerome Bettis (No. 6) busted through the Tennessee defense for yards and touchdowns, but it wasn't enough to keep the Vols from posting a one-point win in 1991 at Notre Dame Stadium.

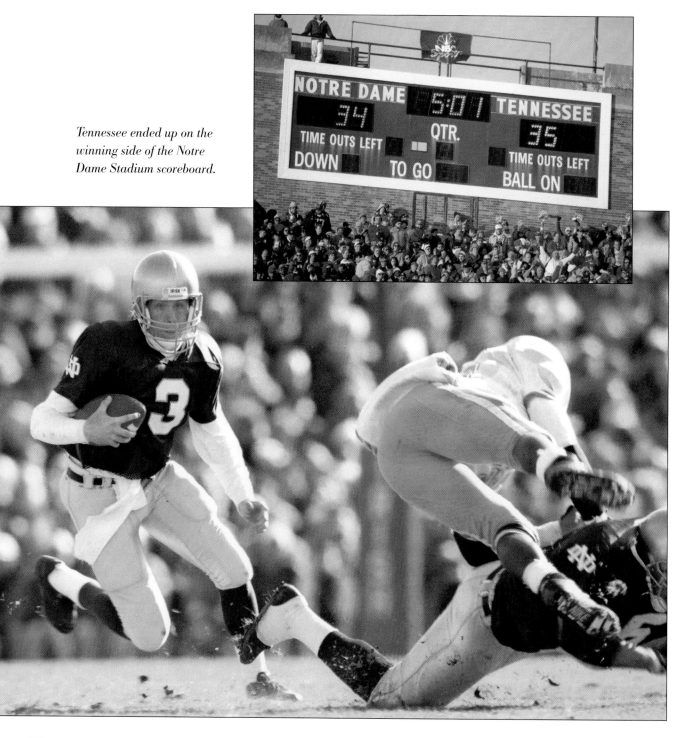

Tennessee ended up on the winning side of the Notre Dame Stadium scoreboard.

Brooks ran for 126 yards, Rodney Culver for 78, Jerome Bettis for 64, and Mirer for 47, but it wasn't enough to keep a seven-game Irish win streak from ending.

Tennessee scored the winning points with 4:03 left on a 26-yard screen pass from Andy Kelly to Aaron Hayden after a Vol interception a minute earlier.

The Irish drove deep into Tennessee territory, but with regular kicker Hentrich on the sideline with a sprained knee from an earlier blocked field-goal attempt, walk-on Rob Leonard saw his 27-yard try at the final gun blocked by Jeremy Lincoln.

Holtz said it was the "most disappointed I've ever been in my life."

Northwestern 17 • Notre Dame 15
SEPTEMBER 2, 1995,
AT NOTRE DAME STADIUM

The Pertinent Details: As it turned out, this was a Northwestern team that ended up being good enough to finish unbeaten, to win the Big Ten title, and to play in the Rose Bowl. But that was little consolation for Irish fans, who watched their team start the season with a loss for the first time since Holtz's first game as Irish coach in 1986.

Notre Dame never led, thanks to 160 rushing yards from the Wildcats' Darnell Autry and 166 yards and two touchdown passes by Steve Schnur. The Irish had a chance to tie after driving 45 yards for a touchdown with 6:16 left in the game, but on the attempted two-point conversion Notre Dame quarterback Ron Powlus had his foot stepped on by an offensive linemen (that came after the Irish missed a point after touchdown after their first touchdown). Two minutes later, after regaining the

ball, Notre Dame's Randy Kinder was stopped on a fourth-and-2 rush attempt.

It all seemed to go wrong after the Irish fumbled at midfield on their first possession, and Northwestern made the score 7–0 fewer than seven minutes into the game.

Said Wildcat coach Gary Barnett: "I told the players when we boarded the bus that I didn't want to be carried off the field when we won. I wanted them to act like we'd done this before."

The Associated Press referred to it as "one of the biggest upsets in college football history."

Michigan 26 • Notre Dame 22
SEPTEMBER 4, 1999,
AT ANN ARBOR

The Pertinent Details: This contest, which was watched by an NCAA-record crowd of 111,523, had the makings of one of the great Irish road comebacks of all time, if only Michigan had opted to cooperate.

Three times Notre Dame came from behind to take the lead. The last time, with only 4:08 left, they managed a 20-yard pass from Jarious Jackson to tight end Jabari Holloway to finish off a 65-yard drive (followed by a two-point throw from Jackson to Bobby Brown).

But the Wolverines weren't done. They went 58 yards of their own in seven plays in 2:30, with Anthony Thomas going a yard (he finished with 138) for the winning points with 1:38 on the clock. Two late penalties helped Michigan greatly: an excessive celebration call after Notre Dame's two-point conversion and a late hit violation on the Wolverines' final drive.

Even so, Jackson (he threw for 302 yards compared to 197 by Michigan's Tom Brady) drove his team to the Wolverine 12, only to see time run out with the Irish a yard short of a first down.

Boston College 14 • Notre Dame 7
NOVEMBER 2, 2002,
AT NOTRE DAME STADIUM

The Pertinent Details: Notre Dame had roared to an 8–0 start under new coach Tyrone Willingham, including the attention-grabbing win at Florida State the week before. But even green jerseys couldn't help the Irish this time. Boston College zapped the Irish on the strength of a 71-yard Josh Ott interception return of a misguided toss from backup quarterback Pat Dillingham.

The Irish defense held the Eagles to only 184 net yards, only 77 through the air, and only nine first downs. But Notre Dame's offense turned the ball over five times (seven fumbles overall) and came up empty in five scoring attempts in the red zone.

Despite a season-high 235 passing yards, Notre Dame's only points came with 2:25 left on a 20-yard Holiday-to-Maurice Stovall connection.

"Our kids took the green jerseys as a sign of respect, as if we were something to be reckoned with," said Eagles coach Tom O'Brien.

HONORABLE MENTIONS

Army 48, Notre Dame 0 (November 10, 1945)–The number-one Cadets squashed number-two Irish for the second year in a row at Yankee Stadium in the fifth worst Notre Dame loss of all time.

Purdue 28, Notre Dame 14 (October 7, 1950)–Purdue won only two games all year, but the Boilers handed the Irish their first loss since '45 and their first home loss since '42.

Nebraska 40, Notre Dame 6 (January 1, 1973 at Orange Bowl)–Heisman Trophy winner Johnny Rodgers rushed for three TDs, threw a TD pass, and caught a TD pass in Ara Parseghian's worst loss.

Mississippi 20, Notre Dame 13 (September 17, 1977)–Ole Miss took the lead for good with less than four minutes to go in the only Irish defeat of their title season.

Notre Dame 3, Georgia Tech 3 (November 8, 1980)–Top-rated Notre Dame needed a late field goal to tie a Tech team that won only one game all season.

Arizona 16, Notre Dame 13 (October 16, 1982)–Max Zendejas knocked through a 48-yard field-goal attempt into the wind as time expired to beat the 4-0 Irish.

Penn State 34, Notre Dame 30 (November 12, 1983)–The Nittany Lions scored with 19 seconds left to ruin big days by Allen Pinkett (217 rushing yards, four touchdowns) and Notre Dame (526 total yards).

Michigan 24, Notre Dame 23 (September 13, 1986)—The Irish never punted in Lou Holtz's debut, becoming the first team to move from outside the AP poll into the rankings via a defeat.

Miami 27, Notre Dame 10 (November 25, 1989)—The 'Canes put an end to Notre Dame's record 23-game win streak as they won their 32nd in a row at the Orange Bowl.

Michigan 26, Notre Dame 24 (September 10, 1994)—A Ron Powlus TD pass with 52 seconds to go gave the Irish the lead, but Remy Hamilton won it on a 42-yard field goal with two seconds to go.

Air Force 20, Notre Dame 17 in OT (October 19, 1996)—The Irish managed only 67 yards rushing, as a Notre Dame fumble on the first play of OT opened the door for the game-winning 27-yard Falcon field goal.

Michigan State 45, Notre Dame 23 (September 12, 1998)—The Spartans, coming off consecutive losses, roared to a 42-3 halftime lead and never looked back.

Stanford 40, Notre Dame 37 (November 27, 1999)—A 5–6 Notre Dame team nearly upended the Rose Bowl-bound Cardinal until Mike Biselli kicked a 22-yard field goal as time ran out to win it.

Nebraska 27, Notre Dame 23 in OT (September 9, 2000)—Julius Jones took a kickoff back 10 yards and Joey Getherall went 83 yards on a punt return, but Eric Crouch won it with a seven-yard OT run.

Michigan 38, Notre Dame 0/USC 45, Notre Dame 14/Florida State 37, Notre Dame 0 (September 13, October 18 and November 1, 2003)—Three top-five teams all posted one-sided results against the Irish, the three teams combining for a 32-7 record.

Ohio State 34, Notre Dame 20 ('06 Fiesta Bowl)/LSU 41, Notre Dame14 ('07 Sugar Bowl)—Buckeye Troy Smith threw for 342 yards and LSU's JaMarcus Russell threw for 332 as the two teams warmed up for their '08 BCS title game matchup.

Sources

Beach, Jim, and Daniel Moore. *Army vs. Notre Dame: The Big Game*. New York: Random House, 1948.

Boyles, Bob, and Paul Guido. *Fifty Years of College Football*. Sideline Communications, 2005.

Brown, Jody, and Bill Cromartie. *The Glamor Game*. Hill Press, 1989.

Chelland, Patrick. *One for the Gipper*. New York: Henry Regnery Company, 1973.

Cohen, Richard M.; Jordan A. Deutsch, and David S. Neft. *The Notre Dame Football Scrapbook*. Bobbs-Merrill, 1977.

Colletti, Ned. *Golden Glory*. Leisure Press, 1983.

Gekas, George. *The Life and Times of George Gipp*. And Books, 1987.

Gildea, William, and Christopher Jennison. *The Fighting Irish*. Prentice Hall, 1976.

Grant, Chet. *Before Rockne at Notre Dame*. Icarus Press, 1978.

Kryk, John. *Natural Enemies*. Andrews and McMeel, 1994.

MacCambridge, Michael. *ESPN College Football Encyclopedia*. ESPN Books, 2005.

Pagna, Tom, and Bob Best. *Notre Dame's Era of Ara*. Diamond Communications, 1976

Rappaport, Ken. *Wake Up the Echoes*. Strode Publishers, 1975.

Schoor, Gene. *100 Years of Notre Dame Football*. Avon Books, 1987.

Shields, Mike. *Fight to Win*. Shillelagh Books, 1982.

Steele, Michael R. *Knute Rockne: A Bio-Bibliography*. Greenwood Press, 1983.